ADCULT*USA*

ADCULT USA

THE TRIUMPH OF ADVERTISING
IN AMERICAN CULTURE

JAMES B. TWITCHELL

COLUMBIA UNIVERSITY PRESS

NEW YORK

Columbia University Press

New York   Chichester, West Sussex

Copyright © 1996 Columbia University Press

Library of Congress Cataloging-in-Publication Data

Twitchell, James B.,

    Adcult USA : the triumph of advertising in American culture /
James B. Twitchell.

      p. cm.

    Includes bibliographical references and index.

    ISBN 0–231–10324–7   PA ISBN 0–231–10325–5

    1. Advertising—United States. 2. Advertising—Social aspects—
United States.   I. Title.

HF5813.U6T87   1995

306.4—dc20   95–9339

                                             CIP

Printed in the United States of America
c 10 9 8 7 6 5 4 3 2
p 10 9

◆ FOR ART, DICK, AND JON

A thousand years ago, crucifixes were foci of fervent attention, and for centuries what men knew of the nude male form and of human agony and dignity sought expression through the crucifix carver's hands. . . . Now in our own American culture, it seems clear enough where the highest pitch of artistic energy is focused. After trying to watch the heavily hyped Winter Olympics, I have no doubt that the aesthetic marvels of our age, for intensity and lavishness of effort and subtlety of both overt and subliminal effect, are television commercials. With the fanatic care with which Irish monks once ornamented the Book of Kells, glowing images of youthful beauty and athletic prowess, of racial harmony and exalted fellowship, are herein fluidly marshaled and shuffled to persuade us that a certain beer or candy bar, or insurance company or oil-based conglomerate, is, like the crucified Christ . . . the gateway to the good life. Skills and techniques developed over nearly a century of filmmaking are here brought to a culmination of artistry that spares no expense or trouble; it has been the accomplishment of television to make every living room a cathedral, and to place within it, every six minutes or so, though it seems oftener, votive objects as luxurious and loving as a crucifixion by Grünewald or a pietà by Michelangelo. Our entire lives—our eating, our drinking, our traveling, our conviviality and courtship and family pleasures, our whole magnificent cradle-to-grave consumption, in short—are here compressed upon an ideal iconic plane; one can only marvel, and be grateful, and regret that except within narrow professional circles the artists involved, like Anglo-Saxon poets and Paleocene cave-painters, are unknown by name.

• JOHN UPDIKE, SPEECH TO NATIONAL ARTS CLUB, 1984

Advertising ministers to the spiritual side of trade. It is a great power that has been entrusted to your keeping which charges you with the high responsibility of inspiring and ennobling the commercial world. It is all part of the greater work of the regeneration and redemption of mankind.

• CALVIN COOLIDGE, SPEECH TO AMERICAN ASSOCIATION
OF ADVERTISING AGENCIES, 1926

What I would like to know is how you Americans can successfully worship God and Mammon at the same time.

• LORD REITH, FOUNDER OF THE BBC TO CBS EXECUTIVES, 1952

CONTENTS

PREFACE

I have always loved advertising. In the spirit of the oxymoronic concept of truth in advertising, I confess my lifelong love of the stuff. When I flip through magazines, I do so to skip the articles. When I channel surf, it is to miss the programs. These days I go to most movies to check out the product placements. I mention this now, because I intend to have some mildly good things to say about advertising, and who but fools, toadies, and flacks has ever risen to the defense of those who tell lies for a living?

As a teenager in the 1950s I read Vance Packard's *Hidden Persuaders*, Sloan Wilson's *Man in the Grey Flannel Suit*, and, a little later, Wilson Brian Key's *Subliminal Seduction* and John Kenneth Galbraith's *The Affluent Society*. They wrote that advertising was pretty terrible stuff and its perpetrators were wrecking American culture. Advertising was making us do all these terrible things we didn't want to do. My reaction was not to go out to the bomb shelter clutching my Davy Crockett hat and mope. Quite the contrary—these views of public relations and advertising only made me more eager to be part of it. If Madison Avenue really worked the way these authors claimed, this would be the place for me. What fun to use language and imagery that worked, that did something, that drove adults nuts. Any culture that conceived of and then sold the rear end of the 1958 Cadillac is not without a certain heroic charm.

Although these books and their melancholy paranoia made the intellectual case *for* advertising, it was movies that clinched the deal. My adolescent yearning was whetted by what I saw in the dark. I remember all the Doris Day and Rock Hudson movies, especially *Lover Come Back.* The plot is complex and took some time to sort out. Doris works for Brackett, McAlpen, & Gaines and she has moral principles. Rock works at Ramsey & Son headed by Tony Randall and has none. Doris turns Rock in to the Advertising Council for using sex to sell products. Of course Rock uses sex to sell products. Isn't that the whole point? To wreak vengeance Rock impersonates a scientist whose product, called Vip, actually makes sex inevitable by reducing all inhibition. Wearing a lab coat and thick eyeglasses Rock pretends to be a sexual stooge and convinces Doris to take him dancing, go with him to girlie shows, teach him how to kiss, and whatever. When the Advertising Council asks Rock to produce his product, he magically does and, by jove, it works! There really is such a thing as Vip. Party time. The liquor industry is distraught and gives Rock 25 percent of all its advertising if he will just suppress the product. In the next scene Doris is pregnant, and Rock marries her as she is wheeled into the delivery room. Just like that. Who wouldn't want to go into advertising after such a story? That you were paid for causing trouble, that you had to drink liquor all the time, and that sex was so simple that you never saw it made this life irresistible.

For various unimportant reasons I did not go into the advertising dodge. I opted for something suspiciously like it and became a college teacher. A few years ago I decided that teaching a course on advertising and society might give me a chance to find out what I gave up by not living on the 7:32 from New Canaan. While preparing the course, I was struck by how little had been written about advertising, aside from the jeremiads of the 1950s. What few serious studies there were either dealt with how to do it or with the economics, history, or sociology of advertising. The latter often refer to advertising as "commercial discourse." With the exception of the outraged feminists and self-satisfied Marxists, almost no one has been concerned with the culture of both the advertising business and the business partially created by advertising. In part this is because agencies have been notoriously secretive (understandable because most of what has been written about them has not been nice). And partly because advertising is so dominant, so a part of the hive we all inhabit, that—our occasional eruptions of outrage notwithstanding—we are usually unaware of its presence.

To teach the course I had to find out what really goes on in an agency, and I am grateful to the Advertising Educational Foundation for getting me into the J. Walter Thompson agency for a month. Allow me a quick story that tells a bit about the business side of advertising. When I realized I needed to see the inside of a large agency, I wrote to JWT and said essentially, "I want to observe you at work so that I can write a book." No response. I called and was directed to the public relations office of the agency and was told I could come by, but only for an hour or so. I did and listened to someone on the subject of "hot buttons" and how to push them. I got a quick tour of a few floors and was shown the door. The next year I applied to the AEF asking to study JWT as an important American institution in order to teach a course on advertising culture. I spent almost a month there and never heard a word about hot buttons. Instead, I saw what looks like a well-run university. I should mention, however, that I signed an agreement with JWT that I would not disparage either the agency or their clients. I haven't.

Of the lasting things I learned growing up with the ads of David Ogilvy was a love of lists ("How Super Shell's 9 ingredients give cars top performance," "25 facts you should know about KLM," and 22 paragraphs under the line: "At 60 miles an hour the loudest noise in this new Rolls-Royce comes from the electric clock").

Here is the first of many lists of my own. I would like to thank Burt Manning, Marty Rose, Patty Diamond, and James Patterson of J. Walter Thompson & Company, Sal Randazzo and Joe Plummer of DMB&B, Mary Alice Kennedy of Young & Rubicam, and the office staffs of Wieden & Kennedy, Chiat/Day, and Deutsch/Dworin who were kind enough to give me a tour of their various cultures. I'm also thankful to other students of advertising— Jackson Lears, Richard Zakia, "Mack" O'Barr, Ellen Gartrell, and Lyman Wood for their advice along the way. My own students also have been an enthusiastic source of support and knowledge.

• CHARLOTTE, VERMONT

ADCULTUSA

1 ✦ PLOP, PLOP, FIZZ, FIZZ

AMERICAN CULTURE AWASH
IN A SEA OF ADVERTISING

my country, 'tis of

you, land of the Cluett

Shirt Boston Garter and Spearmint

Girl With The Wrigley Eyes (of you

land of the Arrow Ide

and Earl &

Wilson

Collars) of you i

sing: land of Abraham Lincoln and Lydia E. Pinkham,

land above all of Just Add Hot Water And Serve—

from every B. V. D.

let freedom ring

amen.

• E. E. CUMMINGS, *POEM, OR BEAUTY HURTS MR. VINAL*

Papa, what is the moon supposed to Advertise?

• CARL SANDBURG, *THE PEOPLE YES*

☞ *THIS* is not a book about advertising but about culture—more specifi-
cally, about the culture created when advertising becomes not just a
central institution but *the* central institution. It attempts to explain how
"A few words from our sponsor" became a torrent.

We live in the age of advertising, and in the spirit of the endeavor I
call this new culture Adcult. I don't intend to defend it (well, maybe just
a little) but to explain how American—and, increasingly, world—culture is carried on through the boom-box noise and strobe lights of commercialism. Much of what we share, and what we know, and even what
we treasure is carried to us each second in a plasma of electrons, pixels,
and ink created by multinational agencies dedicated to attracting our
attention for entirely nonaltruistic reasons.

Once they gain our attention, they essentially rent it to other companies for the dubious purpose of selling us something we've longed for
all our lives, although we've not heard of it before. The condition of

modern selling is not so much information trading, as it was in the nineteenth century, as it is information glutting. Adcult is there when we blink, it's there when we listen, it's there when we touch, it's even there to be smelled in scented strips when we open a magazine. If we have no attention span, as academic Cassandras claim, it may be because by adolescence most of us are exhausted.

No treatment of advertising can proceed further without the familiar litany of statistics, the one usually invoked by well-meaning Commissions to Frighten Parents about how commercialism is choking Junior to death. But it may show the opposite: just how unimportant advertising has become. No matter. Here is a bit of how it goes. In 1993 companies spent more than $140 billion on advertising; in 1915 that figure was about $1 billion. The A. C. Nielsen Company reports that two- to five-year-olds average more than twenty-eight hours of television a week—forty school days a year—in front of the flickering screen.

Assuming they reach maturity with consciousness intact, the current crop of teenagers will have spent years watching commercials. No one has done the numbers on what happens if you factor in radio, magazine, newspaper advertisements, and billboards, but today's teens probably have spent the equivalent of a decade of their lives being bombarded by bits of advertising information. In 1915 a person could go entire weeks without observing an ad. The average adult today sees some three thousand every day.

Barely a space in our culture is not already carrying commercial messages. Look anywhere. Schools? Channel One. Movies? Product placement. Ads invade our urinals, telephones (while we're on hold), taxis (alphanumeric displays), fax machines, catalogs, the wall facing the StairMaster at the gym, T-shirts, doctors' offices, grocery carts, parking meters, golf tees, inner-city basketball backboards, elevators (piped-in with the Muzak) . . . ad nauseum (yes, even airline barf bags).

We have to shake magazines like a rag doll to free the pages of the "blown-in" inserts and then wrestle out those sewn in before we can begin to read. We now have to fast-forward through some five minutes of advertising on rented videotapes.

President Clinton's inaugural parade featured a Budweiser float. At the Smithsonian the Orkin Pest Control Company sponsored an exhibit on exactly what it advertises it kills: insects. Is there a blockbuster museum show not decorated with corporate logos? Public Broadcasting is littered with "underwriting announcements," which look and sound almost exactly like what PBS claims they are not. Athletes sport as many advertising decals as Indy 500 cars, which look like billboards, which themselves are looking more and more like television, eternally blinking on and off. One of the most popular games in the 1980s was called Adverteasing. To play you matched the jingle or slogan with the product's brand name. Why was it so popular? It was one of the few games the whole family could play and the kiddies would win. When

Junior goes to see "Barney and Friends" at Madison Square Garden, he passes, from streetside to seat, ninety-eight separate ads for cigarettes. The interesting question would be where is commercial speech *not* "heard."

One inescapable conclusion from such commercial saturation is that—exempting classified and supermarket ads—more than 99 percent of advertising does no "work." The martini has more effect on the schoolmarm than on the town drunk, and most of us are ad-inebriated by

Which one fits you best?

◆ When the weather is too cold for a T-shirt ad, wear a sweater ad.

adolescence. The American Association of Advertising Agencies—the "Four A's," an industry self-promotion group—estimates that of the three thousand ads we consume each day, we notice only eighty and have some sort of reaction to only twelve. Video Storyboard Tests, a company that conducts "recall testing," reports that a startling 40 percent of the twenty thousand consumers surveyed each year cannot think of a single memorable commercial.

No one knows how often provocation, or even recall, leads to a sale, but as we will see, manufacturers spend a relatively small amount of their money on advertising anyway. Believe it or not, if advertising really sold products, there would be even more. Today advertising is clearly done for many more reasons than increasing sales. In fact, no one really knows why some companies advertise in the first place. Clearly, there is a comfort value for the producer, the salespeople, and the postdecision consumer. And there is the unmentionable to consider: we like being advertised to. We like being told that "You deserve a break today," "You, you're the one," and that "You are special to us," although we may know it's not true. Not only does it make us feel important but perhaps, as Swift said, "Happiness is the possession of being perpetually well-deceived." Deception is the reality of Adcult.

The billions of dollars spent to keep us well deceived are huge, but the percentages are not. A generation ago Fairfax Cone of Foote, Cone & Belding ran the numbers to defend the industry against charges that it was adding to the costs of goods. The cost of advertising Coca-Cola, he reckoned, added about 0.006 cents per can, about a penny for each 35 cents of the cost of producing frozen foods, about 18 cents per $3,000 to the cost of a car, and so on. The economies of mass production more than offset those expenses, he contended.

Where the social cost of advertising is felt, however, is not in achieving the economies of scale but in the cultural ramifications of delivering the pitch. In giving value to objects, advertising gives value to our lives. With Fast-Moving Consumer Goods (FMCGs) especially, we consume the advertising more often than we do the goods. As Burt Manning, chief executive officer (CEO) of J. Walter Thompson, has commented apropos of the great variety of beer advertising, "People don't drink beer, they drink its advertising" (Vadehra 1993:16). This is certainly true of bottled water, which in taste tests is regularly ranked as less pleasing than New York City tap water.

Although advertising cannot create desire, it can channel it. And what is drawn down that channel, what travels with the commercial, is our culture. Adcult has its greatest power in determining what travels with the commercial. For what is carried in and with advertising is what we know, what we share, what we believe in. It is who we are. It is us.

The simple fact is that advertising is too serious not to study. There is no point pretending it does not exist and no point thinking that if we hector it with criticism it will change or go away. I mentioned to a colleague that if I were to go into a class and whistle just the first notes of the McDonald's "You Deserve a Break Today" all my students could continue the tune. But they couldn't complete what is arguably the most famous nineteenth-century sentence: "My heart leaps up when I behold . . ." To which my erstwhile departmental chairman replied, "Then you should be spending more time teaching Wordsworth." The point is well taken and speaks not only to the role of higher education but to the more general subject of teaching values in school. Most academics consider advertising valueless. Why study trash? After all, it's what we throw away.

But take a trip sometime through a college dormitory and look at what is on the walls. Adolescents decorate their walls with the aspirational images of their future. A decade ago or so they could buy poster-size reproductions of the works of great masters to thumbtack to the dorm wall. Now a company called Beyond the Wall sells students ads from Nike, Citizen Watch, Bain de Soleil, Valvoline, Sony, and the rest blown up to poster size at $10 a copy. Such posters are the mezzotints of modern life, the art of materialism. Japanese school kids have textbooks on America that are nothing more than ads. The books have proved so popular that a series of adult picture books shows General Motors ads from the 1950s. No surprise: consuming ads is how all of us have spent most of our time.

Beyond the Wall may call its jumbo ads poster art, but many of us resolutely consider such commercial speech junk. Ironically, as chapter four shows, much inspiration for modern art comes from wall posters that were regularly pasted over with newer images. Junk has its place in aesthetics; one hallmark of cultural garbage is that an item becomes a throwaway commod-

◆ Take down your
Manet, tack up
your Pepsi poster.

ity only *after* being used. Like the word *weed*, with which it shares many interesting traits, *junk* is a matter of perception. It is not a specific item or class of items per se. Rather it is what we call certain objects as we are on our way to root them out. Often the weeds become so interesting, or so indomitable, that we call them wildflower gardens instead.

Something like this is happening in academia with advertising. Since the mid-1980s we have come to appreciate the power and purpose of commercialism. Although only a few institutions of higher learning offer courses on advertising in the liberal arts curriculum (there should be more, starting in elementary school with simple lessons in persuasive techniques), and a few books have been written on the subject, academic libraries are already starting to preserve ad agency archives as if they were repositories of important history. They are. The Smithsonian has the records of N. W. Ayer; Duke University has the Benton & Bowles and J. Walter Thompson collections; for a while Northwestern had the Foote, Cone & Belding (once Lord & Thomas) papers, which have now gone to the University of Wisconsin, which also holds some of the papers of Bruce Barton (one of the *B*s in BBDO). It may well be that the study of advertising will proceed from the library to the classroom rather than the reverse. The Thompson collection at Duke, for instance, is the most-used archive at the university.[1]

A few years ago, in a tenderhearted and well-meaning way, an English professor at the University of Virginia, E. D. Hirsh, published a book called *Cultural Literacy*, with the daunting subtitle *What Every American Needs to Know*. Hirsh's thesis is compelling. If we want to get together, we first need to share a culture. We could be forgiven for guessing that a white-bred professor at a white-bread university would prescribe a cultural matrix of white bread. And in fact that's what Hirsh's prescription to the body politic is. Little wonder his book became a best-seller. Book publishing is one of the few media left that maintains the myth that Western culture is still print based. People who buy books like to be told that what they know is worth knowing and *should* be known by all.

I took a much-shortened list of what "every American needs to know" to my class of juniors and seniors at a large state-supported university. I made up the list by choosing the lower righthand entries from each page in Hirsh's appendix, cleverly entitled "What Literate Americans Know," so it is an almost random sample of the really important stuff. I asked them to briefly define or explain the following:

ampersand	Auschwitz	biochemical pathways
Bundestag	Neville Chamberlain	complex sentence
cyclotron	dog in the manger	Elysian Fields
federalism	Indira Gandhi	D. W. Griffith
Hoover Dam	installment buying	Joseph and his brothers
Leibnitz	Ferdinand Magellan	Herman Melville
National Guard	nucleotide	paradox
planets	prosecution	Reign of Terror
sacred cow	Shawnee Indians	Battle of Stalingrad
taproot	topsoil	vector
Winnie the Pooh	Richard Wright	Zurich

Of course, they are soon bored doing this. Who cares about this school stuff? they seem to say. I ask them to continue the process, only with these entries:

Just do it	Uh huh	Colonel Sanders
Morris	Feel really clean	Heartbeat of America
Mmmm mmmm good	Kills bugs dead	Mrs. Olsen

1. Adcult even has its own museum. Although a full-scale advertising museum really belongs in Manhattan, the only museum devoted solely to the cause—the American Advertising Museum—is in Portland, Oregon, that hotbed of advertising. Perhaps it is appropriate that the museum should be housed in a warehouse on the almost West Coast, because so many agencies have long deserted Madison Avenue for SoHo and Manhattan for Minneapolis.

Fahrvergnugen	Quality is job 1	Why ask why?
Two scoops!	Because I'm worth it	Tony the Tiger
Have it your way	99 44/100% pure	Master the moment
57 Varieties	Speedy	Never had it, never will
White knight	Jolly Green Giant	Mountain grown
Mr. Whipple	Do you know me?	Be all you can be
Betty Crocker	Still going	Snap, Crackle, Pop
Aunt Jemima	We try harder	That's Italian

They are so excited they are shouting entries for me to consider. Clearly they like this Adcult version, partly because it is thrilling to think that what they know has any value but also because they realize that they really share something. Blacks and whites, males and females, front row and back row do have a common culture. Professor Hirsh is correct. There is a cohesive power in the remembrance of things past. It does link us together. Let Proust have his madeleines. We have ads. Some of my students are embarrassed, of course, that cultural junk food is what they share. Perhaps they realize there is nothing behind this knowledge, no historical or cultural event, no reason to know it. Yet it is precisely the recognition of jingles and brand names, precisely what high culturists abhor, that links us as a culture. More than anything this paper-thin familiarity is what gives Adcult its incredible reach and equally incredible shallowness. It is a culture without memory and hence without depth. Ironically, concepts in advertising explain the phenomenon: the further the reach (cost per thousand) the shallower the effect (recall of individual product).

If academic culture has been slow to acknowledge the power of Adcult, its upstart rival, popular culture, has eagerly embraced it. Advertising is no longer treated with grudging respect in the press; it is front page. The national newspapers, the *New York Times* and the *Wall Street Journal*, give advertising almost daily coverage in their financial and marketplace sections. When RJR Nabisco fired an ad agency, the story made page one of the *Times*. In fact, the *Times* recently paid the ultimate high-culture tribute by referring to two BBDO copywriters as "auteurs." Advertising stories regularly appear on the first page of the *Journal*'s Marketplace section. When an occasional ad jumps loose of Adcult and perplexes popular culture, such as happened some years ago with the man-in-pajamas ad for Benson & Hedges, the press devotes tons of newsprint to explaining it.

As might be expected, the gaudy step-cousin, *USA Today*, a newspaper unabashedly dedicated to the proposition that advertising is what the Gannett chain is all about, continually runs ad stories free of any critical taint. And the line between press release and news story is often invisible. For instance, in its June 21, 1985, weekend edition, *USA Today*'s front page announced an inside story on the latest Clint Eastwood movie. What was inside? An advertising

◆ Who is the man in pajamas and what is he doing in a cigarette ad? He was on a nearby set and wandered over during the Benson & Hedges shoot. The photographer took the picture on a lark.

For people who like to smoke...

BENSON&HEDGES
because quality matters.

SURGEON GENERAL'S WARNING: Cigarette Smoke Contains Carbon Monoxide.

supplement paid for by Warner Bros. Advertisements have even started to appear on the front pages of the inside sections of *USA Today*, in the upper "ears" of the pages.

After the Super Bowl an annual feeding frenzy of the print media is to critique not the boring game but the exciting new ad campaigns. *USA Today* even wires up a select audience to test responses. For a while the paper even ran a feature called "AD-ing It Up with Elliot and Cox" in which two reporters discussed recent campaigns in a mock Siskel-Ebert debate, replacing the thumbs up or down with "play it or zap it."

Daily newspapers are not alone. Tina Brown's revived *New Yorker* dedicated almost an entire issue—including cartoons—to detailing the Stolichnaya Vodka campaign (Lubow 1994). Leslie Savan, of the raucous *Village Voice*, not only writes an occasional edgy column on advertising but almost received a Pulitzer for it. And *Advertising Age*, once a professional journal, appears on newsstands in the company of other newsweeklies, which also cover advertising.

Although television is the pure advertising-supported medium, few programs have discussed its influence. Admittedly, *Entertainment Tonight* routinely covers advertising-related show-biz stories—the celebrity commercial shoots and their new campaigns. And advertising outtakes figure prominently in the blooper genre mastered by the avuncular Ed McMahon and the ever youthful Dick Clark. Advertising parodies are the staples of *Saturday Night Live* and *In Living Color*. Occasionally PBS runs a *Nova*esque show on advertising, as it recently did (in the *Smithsonian Presents* format) of the work done by Grey Advertising for Mitsubishi's new sports car, the 3000GT. But network television offers surprisingly little coverage of advertising. It's coming: Barbara Lippert of *Adweek* expresses her opinions on *Business This Morning,* a syndicated CBS program, Bob Garfield of *Advertising Age* has taped a pilot for CNBC, and in the flurry of interest about new channels possible with fiber-optic cable an advertising-only channel is on its way.

To be sure, television shows about advertising are made difficult by copyright clearance problems. The boilerplate in performers' contracts stipulates the number of runs and the venues for which they will receive the payments known as residuals. This explains why most shows about commercials feature animated spots. Tony the Tiger and his animated colleagues have no residual rights. But television has also been slow to consider advertising as a subject for the same reason that dairy farmers drink proportionally less milk. After all, advertising is what television *is*.

What is lacking on television, and what I predict is soon to come, is a serious discussion of ads with participants from agencies, sponsors, media, and academia. The French already have a hugely popular half-hour weekly show in which intellectuals chat up the most recent ads. Each Sunday night millions of viewers watch a program called *Culture Pub*. For almost fifteen years Parisians have gathered for the annual *Nuit des Publivores* to watch nightlong screenings of as many as five hundred uninterrupted commercials. Perhaps this could be expected of a culture that produced such popcult commentators as Roland Barthes and Jean Baudrillard. Doubtless the Yale School of Advertising is even now taking shape. But not just media snobs say that the best things on television are the commercials; the ordinary viewer would agree.

The Institution of Advertising

Advertising, one of the most characteristic and most vigorous of American institutions, has been less adequately chronicled than almost any other major institution.

• DANIEL BOORSTIN, *THE AMERICANS*, 1973

So what is this inadequately chronicled but characteristic institution called advertising? Is it cultural pond scum sealing off valuable nutrients or aeration churning up new life? At its simplest it is just what it says: ad-ver-tis-ing, the drawing of attention, or, more completely, the drawing of attention to an object. As Jim Dale, CEO of W. B. Donner, has said, "What advertising does . . . is generate traffic, which is not to say it can generate the sale" (Elliot, "Subaru's Problems," 1993:D19).

But we know what generating traffic means; advertising has come to mean hawk, pitch, flog, plug, and a host of four-letter words. In the preindustrial world the object of advertising was often events, not objects, which accounts for such newspaper names as the *Daily Advertiser* and "advertising" sections that announced the arrival of ships bearing new merchandise. However, the modern world has commercialized the process. *Traffic* has changed from a noun to a verb. The business of advertising is essentially the business of trafficking in audiences. After an audience has been gathered, its attention is rented to an agent who inserts a message from a sponsor. The audience pays attention because it is traded something in return, namely, entertainment.

— Media Companies

◆ Advertising at work making new industries.

"They said father didn't keep his Life Insurance paid up!"

THE PRUDENTIAL INSURANCE COMPANY *of* AMERICA
EDWARD D. DUFFIELD, *President*   HOME OFFICE, *Newark, N.J.*

Seen from another point of view, just as the "work" you do at the self-service gas station lowers the price of gas, so consuming ads is the "work" you do that lowers the price of this entertainment. Economists call this cost externalization. It is the basis of the fast-food industry. You order. You carry your food to the table. You clean up. You pay less. In Adcult, matters are more complex. True, you are entertained for less cost, but you are also encultured in the process.

When advertising succeeds for the producer, it has the power to create new markets. Life insurance, called death insurance before advertising took it over, was an industry almost made by advertising. The face paint of prostitutes was transformed into the cosmetics of millions, thanks to advertising. The jewelry industry was transformed by the N. W. Ayer slogan, "A diamond is forever," for De Beer's. Chesterfield's "Blow some my way" introduced cigarettes to women interested in independence. Products of dubious value, such as premium gasoline, deodorants, breakfast cereal, mouthwash, cola drinks, dog food, and most modern over-the-counter nostrums (the descendants of advertising's most notorious client, patent medicines) were creations of commercial speech.

However, my concern is not with the occasional efficacy of advertising as a way to move goods through a market but with what it carries in its wake. In other words, I am not as concerned with what advertising does, or claims to do, as I am with what it does while doing it. For in that swap of entertainment for attention—the most central quid pro quo of commercial speech—resides the essence of what draws us together, what we share, what our culture is. If, as the sociobiologists tell us, the body is the genes' way of making sure they are passed into the future, modern culture may be advertising's way to ensure its survival.

Before all else we must realize that modern advertising is usually tied to things and only secondarily to services. Manufacturing both things *and* their meanings is what American culture is all about. If Greece gave the world philosophy, Britain gave drama, Austria gave music, Germany gave politics, and Italy gave art, America gave mass-produced objects. "We bring good things to life" is no offhand claim but the contribution of the last century. And the tag line "Or your money back" is the guarantee. Advertising is how we talk about these things, how we imagine them, how we know their value.

Human beings like things. We buy things. We like to exchange things. We steal things. We donate things. We live through things. We call these things *goods* as in goods and services. We do not call them *bads*. This sounds simplistic, but it is crucial to understanding the power of Adcult. Still going strong, the industrial revolution produces more and more things not because production is what machines do, and not because nasty capitalists twist their handlebar mustaches and mutter "More slop for the pigs," but because we are attracted to the world of things. Madonna was not the first material girl. Advertising supercharges some of this power.

This attraction to the inanimate happens all over the world. Berlin Walls fall because people want things, and they want the culture created by things. China opens its doors not so much because it wants to get out but because it wants to get things in. We were not suddenly transformed from customers to consumers by wily manufacturers eager to unload a surplus of crappy products. We have created a surfeit of things because we enjoy the process of getting and spending. The consumption ethic may have started in the early 1900s, but the desire is ancient. Kings and princes once thought they could solve problems by amassing things; we now join them.

The Marxist balderdash of cloistered academics aside, human beings did not suddenly become materialistic. We have always been desirous of things. We have just not had many of them until quite recently, and in a few generations we may return to having fewer and fewer. Still, while they last, we enjoy shopping for things and see both the humor and truth reflected in the aphoristic "Born to shop," "Shop 'til you drop," and "When the going gets tough, the tough go shopping." Department store windows, be they on the city street or inside a mall, did not appear magically. We enjoy looking through them to another world. It is the voyeurism of capitalists. Our love of things is the *cause* of the industrial revolution, not the consequence. Man (and woman) is not only *homo sapiens*, or *homo ludens*, or *homo faber* but also *homo emptor*.

Mid-twentieth-century American culture is often criticized for being too materialistic. But we are not too materialistic. We are not materialistic enough. If we craved objects *and* knew what they meant, there would be no need to add meaning through advertising. We would just gather, use, toss out, or hoard indiscriminately. But we don't. First, we don't know what to gather and, second, we like to trade what we have gathered. Third, we need to know how to value objects that have little practical use. What is clear is that most things in and of themselves do not mean enough. In fact, what we crave may not be objects at all but their meaning. For whatever else advertising does, one thing is certain: by adding value to material, by adding meaning to objects, by branding things, advertising performs a role historically associated with religion. The Great Chain of Being, which for centuries located value above the horizon in the World Beyond, has been reforged to settle value on the objects of the here and now.

I wax a little impatient here, because most literature on modern culture is downright supercilious about consumption. What do you expect? Most of it comes from a culture professionally hostile to materialism, albeit secretly envious. From Veblen on through Christopher Lasch runs a palpable sense of disapproval as they view the hubbub of commerce from the groves of academe. Concepts of bandwagon consumption, conspicuous consumption, keeping-up-with-the-Joneses, the culture of narcissism, and all the other barely veiled reproofs have limited our serious consideration of Adcult to such relatively minor issues as manipulation and exploitation. People surely can't want—ugh!—things. Or, if they really do want them, they must want them for all the wrong reasons. The idea that advertising creates artificial desires rests on a profound ignorance of human nature, on the hazy feeling that there existed some halcyon era of noble savages with purely natural needs, on romantic claptrap first promulgated by Rousseau and kept alive in institutions well isolated from the marketplace.

Here is a sampling of the affection extended to Adcult by the charitable souls in and around academia. Such critical comments have become so much a part of our common culture that they repeatedly appear in collections of familiar quotations.

> A considerable part of our ability, energy, time and material resources is being spent today on inducing us to find the money for buying material goods that we should never have dreamed of wanting had we been left to ourselves.
> • Arnold Toynbee

> Few people at the beginning of the nineteenth century needed an adman to tell them what they wanted. • John Kenneth Galbraith

> The modern substitute for argument; its function is to make the worse appear better. • George Santayana

> Advertising is the science of arresting the human intelligence long enough to get money from it. • Stephen Leacock

> Advertising is the rattling of a stick inside a swill bucket. • George Orwell

> Nothing's so apt to undermine your confidence in a product as knowing that the commercial selling it has been approved by the company that makes it.
> • Franklin P. Jones

> Advertising has done more to cause the social unrest of the twentieth century than any other single factor.
> • Clare Boothe Luce, also attributed to Clive Barnes

What raises the ire of these pundits is that advertising is stealing their thunder. Commercial speech, not other types of "higher conversation," is defining value for objects. At the human level novelists knew about the defining power of goods before economists did, as the works of Austen, Trollope, Dreiser, James, and Wharton attest. The novel of manners is often the novel of microeconomics. Human gesture is replaced by interaction with manufactured objects. Etiquette becomes subsumed by ownership. Even the smallest objects sometimes assume inordinate value. Many a nineteenth-century novel—especially in America, which had no elaborated history of social and class distinctions—describes at length the display of crockery, the proper machine-woven garb, the giving of a bowl, or the decor of a room. In fact, the drawing room itself was a new venue in which to display the growing collection of self-defining objects. Ralph Lauren and Martha Stewart still trade on these distinctions.

Advertising often achieves these distinctions by "branding." Branding is the central activity of creating differing values for such commonplace objects and services as flour, bottled water, cigarettes, denim jeans, razor blades, domestic beers, batteries, cola drinks, air travel, overnight couriers, and telephone carriers. Giving objects their identity, and thus a perceived value, is advertising's unique power. Think about it: would you spend $100 for a pair of sneakers, $20 for a fifth of vodka, or $30,000 for a car if your friends hadn't heard of the brand? As we will see later, religion is another such branding system—the original branding system. So are politics, education, and . . . art. To use a modern trope: if goods are hardware, meaning is software, and advertising writes most of the software.

Advertising is simply one of a number of attempts to load objects with meaning. It is not a mirror, a lamp, a magnifying glass, a distorted prism, a window, a trompe l'oeil, or a subliminal embed as much as it is an ongoing conversation within a culture about the meanings of objects. It does not follow or lead so much as it interacts. Advertising is neither chicken nor egg. Let's split the difference: it's both. It is language not just about objects to be consumed but about the consumers of objects. It is threads of a web linking us to objects and to each other.

The real work of Madison Avenue is not to manipulate the doltish public but to find out how people already live, not to force consumers to accept material against their better judgment but to get in the path of their judgment, not to make myth but to make your product part of an already existing code. Advertisers are not interested in what we claim to want, or what scientists claim we should want, but in determining what indeed we do want as tracked by what, and how, we purchase. (Sometimes such "observational research" becomes absurd. Nissan once sent a researcher to Costa Mesa, California, supposedly to observe young Americans "in their natural habitat." The researcher rented a room from a couple and accompanied them on all their shopping excursions, taking copious notes but never divulging his purpose. Once the couple realized what he was doing, they sued. Nissan, denying the charges, settled out of court. Cultural anthropology is not without risks.) Nonetheless, a simple product like bread is laden with emotion. We squeeze it, we smell it, and we look at it. Then we buy it. We even do the same with such products as wine, drugs, and cosmetics with which our senses can't possibly assist us.

Wise advertisers will always attempt to find out first what it is that we are after and then fashion a campaign with which to position their product. Only a fool, soon to be bankrupt, attempts to change our patterns of desire. Still, many otherwise intelligent people believe that is exactly what advertising does. Advertising agencies themselves, especially when they are pitching new accounts, have often invoked the hypodermic theory of injecting helpless consumers with expensive desire. Claude Hopkins, copy chief at Lord and Thomas, boasted to fellow businessmen in 1909 that "there is scarcely a home, in city or hamlet, where some human being is not doing what we demand. The good advertising man comes pretty close to being an absolute czar" (Lears 1984:359). When N. W. Ayer was down on its luck some years ago, the agency considered replacing its grand old motto, Keeping Everlastingly at It, with We Create Your Wants, We Create Your Desires. And more recently, Chiat/Day tacitly allowed a book to be written about that agency with the daunting title *Inventing Desire.*

Alas, in truth it is the advertising, not the audience, that is manipulated. This is what Marshall McLuhan meant when he claimed that the audience works in the consumption of the image. For advertising does not invent or satisfy desire. It expresses desire with the hope of exploiting it. Over and over and over. It is, as economist Marshall Sahlins says, updating Wordsworth's definition of the poet, "man speaking to men through the world of things" (Leiss, Kline, Jhally 1990:319).

What Is Advertising?

And now I have discovered the most exciting, the most arduous literary form of all, the most difficult to master, the most pregnant in curious possibilities. I mean the advertisement. . . . Advertisement writers may not be lyrical, or obscure, or in any way esoteric. They must be universally intelligible. A good advertisement has this in common with drama and oratory, that it must be immediately comprehensible and directly moving. But at the same time it must possess all the succinctness of epigram. . . . The advertisement is one of the most interesting and difficult of modern literary forms. Its potentialities are not yet half explored. Already the most interesting and, in some cases, the only readable part of most American periodicals is the advertisement section.

• ALDOUS HUXLEY, "ADVERTISEMENT," 1968

The purest form of advertising is harmless enough and is the goal of all commercial speech: word of mouth. A good comment about a product supposedly reaches five to ten people, so its geometric power is potentially explosive.

In the nonadvertising world we know this verbal contagion as *buzz* in Hollywood, *tip* on Wall Street, and *spin* in Washington. That each of these centers of American culture should have manufacturers (or "doctors") on hand to incubate the word-of-mouth organism and send it forth to the body politic is a tribute to its virulence. In the early days of television many ads showed housewives whispering accolades about a product. Although the exchange of sound waves between friends hardly qualifies in Adcult as a selling technique (it is now more likely the domain of advertising's cousin, public relations), it needs to be mentioned because the motive is in the aspiration. Gossip generates traffic.

Sometimes Adcult experiments with word of mouth. A small New York agency recently hired personable actors to go into swanky watering holes like the Royalton, Cafe Tabac, and Bloom and ask for a martini made with Hennessy cognac rather than the usual gin or vodka. When the barkeep said that he had never heard of such a drink, the actors would explain in loud detail exactly what brands to use. Meanwhile Hennessy was running ads in such magazines as *New York* and sponsoring tastings at concerts and parties. Shades of the days when J&B Scotch would hire beautiful women to walk into bars, order J&B, and grandly turn on their heel if there wasn't any. This was all done the day before the J&B jobber came to call.

Word of mouth may not be at the center of how we order martinis, but it is still the basis from which most of us choose to use certain professionals, such as doctors and lawyers. Word of mouth is how certain colleges and prep

◆ Word of mouth in action: what Chemical Bank considers "referred by a source," Basic knows is just gossip.

schools get "hot," how Broadway shows survive, how restaurants attract customers (echoed in Zagat surveys), how Club Med gets its business (about 60 percent of its trade is generated from customers' conversations with others), and how movies find an audience (*Chariots of Fire* was shown to forty Boy Scout troops around the New York metropolitan area before general release). For a long time the popularity of Coors beer was almost totally the result of conversations between friends. Book clubs can make or break the sales of mass-market books. On computer services like CompuServe and Prodigy, as well as on the Internet, word of mouth—or, better yet, word of electron—accounts for the sales of many software programs. Some concerns like the Body Shop, which sells only environmentally correct products, take a public stand against advertising, having instead an "anthropology department" to promulgate their righteousness. Companies like Tupperware and Amway do a twist on word of mouth by placing the mouth and the products inside your house, Fuller Brush–style.

Noncommercial airwaves are notoriously hard to control, as the force of gossip attests. Bad word of mouth can cause presidents to fail, stock markets to crash, movies to flop. And as Procter & Gamble learned with its supposedly satanic logo, McDonald's with the allegations of worms in the Big Mac, and Pepsi Cola with claims of razor blades in cans, it can cause entire companies to go into spasm. When it works, it can make a company like Ben & Jerry's, the Body Shop, or Starbucks. Still, most advertising has to earn its audience the old-fashioned way, by renting it from the producer of a medium. The history of modern culture is essentially the history of new advertising-supported media, as chapter two shows, but we can abstract some characteristics. Here are a few: advertising is *ubiquitous, anonymous, syncretic, symbiotic, profane,* and, especially, *magical.* layers upon itself

First, it's *ubiquitous.* Advertising has soaked into everything—and I really mean everything. It cannot *not* be found. The most common complaint about advertising from clients, consumers, and even agencies is clutter. When the agencies complain about the overabundance of advertising, they are rather like the doctor who pumps a patient full of adrenalin and then instructs the poor soul to calm down. Is there a wall, either real or metaphoric, not posted with handbills? Is there a part of the electromagnetic spectrum not filled with messages? Companies have taken to buying "roadblock" ads on all the major networks at the same time in hopes of combating clutter. Techniques like advertorials (multipage inserts in magazines from several advertisers eager to be associated with the subject of the articlelike copy they surround) and infomercials (program-length commercials dressed up to look like regular programming) are testaments to the depth of clutter. You can even see this in print ads as they attempt to camouflage themselves as part of the editorial matter.

Since the 1980s commercial speech has crossed over into hitherto protected space. Product placements are all through the movies and television

◆ How to fight advertising clutter: pretend that advertising is text.

shows. Whereas ads once preceded the feature film and occurred in pods around television programs, they have infiltrated the entertainment. Brand-name products are prominently displayed in exchange for cash if it is a film or "production subventions" (free products) if it is a television show. This free-for-all has produced such hybrids as "ambush ads" in which companies battle to display their sponsorship. So Visa sponsors the Olympics, but American Express sponsors the telecast, while Mastercard supports the individual sporting team.

The world may have been "charged with the grandeur of God" for earlier generations, but for us it is chock-full of paid messages. Some advertising executives have seriously suggested that ads appear on stamps. After all, what was good enough for Elvis should be good enough for General Motors. And what of the currency? Why not replace that anachronistic eyeball atop the pyramid on the dollar bill with the golden arches? This franchising of public space is not so farfetched; the state of Iowa has already sold space in the state income tax booklet for $38,225 per page with a guaranteed circulation of 1.3 million motivated readers. Already Pepsi and Coors have attached their names to athletic arenas. Why not sponsor highways, airports, and court-houses? Chapter two shows how the most predictive element of a medium's success is its ability to sustain advertising and deliver the goods. Suffice it to say now that, unless there is plenty of billboard space on the off-ramps, the information superhighway will be only a back road.

Next, advertising is _anonymous_. This is most distressing for academic types who need an author-text-audience paradigm in order to do their work. The very absence of acknowledged authorship explains why pop artists were so entranced, and deconstructionists so intrigued, by advertising. The authors are there all right, but we'll never find them. Who knows whose hand first penned "Where's the beef?" "Just do it," "Look, Mom, no cavities," "Does she . . . or doesn't she?" "Mmmm mmmm good," "Try it, you'll like it," "Snap! Crackle! Pop!" "The closer he gets, the better you look," "It's the real thing," "Fahrvergnugen," "When it rains, it pours," "Ninety-nine and forty-four one hundredths percent pure," "I'd rather fight than switch," "Finger-lickin' good," and countless other phrases we know by heart. Leo Burnett, father of the agency that created the Jolly Green Giant, the Pillsbury Doughboy, Tony the Tiger, and the most recognized character in the world—the Marlboro Man—prided himself on not being recognized: "We have absolutely no pride of authorship here. Nobody knows for sure who produced our ads" (Fox 1984:223).

Although Burnett could sustain anonymity with grace (after all, his name was over the door), we may sometimes feel sorry for the immortalizers of the slogans known to all. As Martin Mayer wrote in his early account of agency life, _Madison Avenue, U.S.A._:

> The advertising man in the typical case needs the challenge and the thrill of the numbers game as much as he needs his salary. Advertising is selling, and the

great satisfaction of selling is closing the sale. The advertising man never can close a sale; in fact, he can never be certain that it was his effort which made the sale possible. Worst of all, he works in black anonymity. Everybody in America may know his ad, but not one citizen in a thousand will know so much as the name of the agency which prepared the ad, and within the agency only a handful of people will know that this individual advertising man had anything to do with the ad. • (1958:31)

The éminence grise of all ad execs and the first great copywriter, Claude Hopkins, addressed the Sphinx Club in Manhattan in 1909, confessing, "Perhaps you, as I, have longed to be a Jack London. It is a happy position where one may contribute to the amusement of mankind. Such men are known and applauded. They are welcomed and wanted, for they lift the clouds of care. But those who know us, know us only as searchers after others' dollars" (Fox 1984:56). To be sure, it may be asking too much to expect kudos for the coiners of "Ring around the collar," "Take it all off," "You've come a long way, baby," "How do you spell relief?" "It don't get no better than this," and "Winston tastes good like a cigarette should"; in fact, anonymity may have a purpose. Still, ask the infamous man on the street to name any copywriter and he will be stymied. Sooner ask, "Who wrote the Lord's Prayer or the Nicene Creed?"

Modern advertising is also *symbiotic*. By this I mean that Adcult shares the energy of other social organisms. The something with which it lives is on the surface entertainment and below the surface the deep concerns of the specific culture. Generations ago advertising depended on the "gratitude factor," on the belief that if you sponsored a radio show, for instance, the mere mention of your sponsorship would generate a goodwill that could be merchandised. Hence the attaching of the client's name to the backs of the musicians: the Browning-King Orchestra (a clothing store), Goodrich Silvertown Orchestra, Cliquot Club Eskimos, Gold Dust Twins, Ipana Troubadours, A&P Gypsies, and Kodak Chorus. But such indirect advertising was short lived. The gift was a fraud.

However, as chapter four shows, the phenomenon still exists in the high-culture world of art sponsorship and accounts for the blockbuster museum shows brought to you by Philip Morris, IBM, and AT&T. The sympathy sell will not usually work in the world of the ever present remote control, ceaselessly zapping, zooming, zipping across channels. A few stalwarts like Hallmark Cards and Cadillac still give it a go—and the fact that they are not interrupting the *Hallmark Hall of Fame* or the Masters Golf Tournament is a major part of their pitch.

Not only must the ad be surrounded by attractive entertainment but now, in a cluttered environment, the ad itself must satisfy. So in a sense the cycle has come full circle. In the 1930s you might have patronized the sponsor because you got ad-free entertainment. Today you might patronize a sponsor whose ads you like. As Sid Hecker, copy research director at Young & Rubicam, has said, "You've got to entertain and reward viewers. . . . In some cases the advertising is the product. Consumers are buying the advertising more than the product" (Rowe 1987:14). One look at the Benetton, Nike, Camel, and McDonald's campaigns shows how enticing this modern Scheherazade can be. Alas, the most likable ads often do not sell much more than themselves. Seven package-goods brands in the top twenty-five consumer products had ads that tested among the most popular of 1993; five had flat or declining sales. Shaquille O'Neal, the Energizer Bunny, and the young coffee lovers, Tony and Sharon, were delightful to have around but did not sell much in the way of Pepsi, batteries, or Taster's Choice (Bird 1994:B1).

It is literally possible to hear the symbiotic linking of advertising and new trends as commercial messages glom onto whatever new music teenagers are listening to. Music has always been a most dependable trigger of attention. From the Plain song of the church, to the realization in the nineteenth century that certain music, such as Beethoven's "Ode to Joy," had the power to generate emotions irrespective of age or culture, to Hitler's discovery that amplifying martial music with loudspeakers was crucial for motivating crowds, to the application of music to film, our emotions have been keyed to sound. Little wonder Ronald Reagan wanted to use Bruce Springsteen's "Born in the U.S.A." in his campaign. He wanted only the opening title, preferring to overlook the first line ("Born down in a dead man's town/ First kick I took was when I hit the ground") and the fact that the protagonist goes to prison for torching an oil refinery—hardly "Morning in America" material. Reagan's handlers knew why musical eruptions are important in Adcult. They are our Gregorian chants.

Advertising has become a fungus, attaching itself to sounds. Alternative rock, punk, post-punk, grunge, the Seattle Sound—call it what you will—innovative sounds are the metonomy of cool, and Adcult is nothing if not cool. Of course, cool has the half-life of a neutrino, a built-in self-destructive mechanism that renders it passé almost as soon as it becomes familiar. But until then cool has the attraction of a magnetron. For all its claims of being ad-proof Generation X is right there in the checkout line of K-mart, loading up on combat boots, nose rings, and machine-faded flannel. When the grunge rocker group Nirvana had a hit, "Smells Like Teen Spirit," that referred in passing to Mennen deodorant as a symbol of commercialization, what did McCann-Erickson do? The agency immediately produced a new TV commercial that boldly proclaimed "Smells like teen spirit" as an endorsement. Since Jovan sponsored the 1981 Rolling Stones' U.S. tour, insisting that its name be printed on every ticket, every "concert" (even the Gen X'ers' own Lollapalooza was coproduced by the William Morris Agency and underwritten by Warner Bros. and Sony, which record most of the headliner bands) is an extension of corporate advertising. But as Pepsi found out with Michael Jackson, it is not always wise to hitch your commercial wagon to a pop star.

More controllable are popular songs slid into the commercial as accompaniment. Title catalogs are traded like precious commodities because who can tell which songs will resonate with an audience years hence? Who today knows that the provenance of McDonald's "It's MacTonight" traces through Ray Charles to Bobby Darren to versions of "Mack the Knife" by Louis Armstrong and Lotte Lenya to the 1933 Broadway rendition of *The Threepenny Opera*, which itself was based on a song by Bertoldt Brecht and Kurt Weill, "Moriat," a recreation of a Weimar cabaret tune?

Although some high-culture music enters Adcult as acoustic bombast (Puccini's "O Mio Babbino Caro" for Tott's Champagne and his "Nessun Dorma" for Delta Airlines, and Tchaikovsky's finale to the *1812 Overture* for Quaker Oats, come to mind), the more usual leakage is from popular culture. "I Heard It Through the Grapevine" is adapted for the California Raisins; "I'm Gonna Wash That [Grey] Right Outta My Hair" and "I Can See Clearly Now the [Pain] Has Gone" are variations on songs we all know for the appropriate products ("I Can See Clearly Now" is also used by Windex). "Mustang Sally" enlivens Miller beer, the Beach Boys' "Good Vibrations" sells Sunkist soda pop, and Steppenwolf's "Born to Be Wild" is domesticated by Ford. Certainly most distressing to those of us growing up in the 1960s is the co-opting of Bob Dylan's "The Times They Are a-Changin'" by an accounting company. The unspeakable: Nike's plundering of the Beatles' "Revolution." Sometimes the sellout occurs in months. Right Said Fred's "I'm Too Sexy" and Technotronic's "Shake That Body" are adapted at almost the speed of sound to sell Revlon products. Let a musical sensation loose and it is soon absorbed by the Adcult sponge. Even the Pillsbury Doughboy raps.

Occasionally, the process works in reverse, surely every advertiser's dream come true. The commercial jingle and tune create an audience for the elaborated music. "Friendship Is for Keeps" moved from Bell Telephone to popular culture, as did "I'd Like to Teach the World to Sing" from Coca-Cola. Sometimes the jingle becomes a smash: "We've Only Just Begun" from Crocker Bank, Coke's "First Time," and the Volkswagen song by Clannad moved to the top of the pop charts.

The cross-fertilization of popular culture and Adcult reaches its loamy ? best on MTV where visuals and music interact twenty-four hours a day nonstop around the globe. Of course, what is MTV but Adcult in its purest form? What are the videos but ads for the audio recordings? Like the infomercial and the advertorial, MTV videos show how the colonizing power of commercial speech can quickly consume discrete forms and make them one. A character like Michael Jackson, for instance, can move back and forth between advertising and entertainment so often that the demarcation is effaced. "Is he live or is he Memorex?" is recast as "Is this a commercial, or is this performance?" Neil Young, a Canadian pop star with a history of iconoclasm, even recorded a video for his song "This Note's for You" that included these lines:

"Ain't singing' for Pepsi/Ain't singin' for Coke/I don't sing for nobody/Makes me look like a joke." MTV, well aware of who butters its commercial bread, refused to run the video.

The symbiosis of advertising is what consigns so many slogans to the ash heap. Once the target dies, so does its advertising campaign. Coke supposedly has stayed away from its marvelous line "The pause that refreshes" because its target teenage audience wants refreshment on the run. GM dropped "See the U.S.A. in your Chevrolet" because families were no longer using the car for sightseeing. And poor Burger King has eaten up more than thirteen slogans since 1974 because every time it has hopped on a bandwagon, it was headed in the wrong direction. Likewise, 7-Up retired and resurrected "the Uncola" four times, thinking that the times were right for crystal clarity. Miller Brewing has been equally off balance, thinking that "Tastes great, less filling" could be changed to "It's it and that's that" and finding out otherwise. Slim stayed in.

Although commercial speech seems to spend most of its energy just shouting for attention, it is instead filled with shifting nuance. American culture lives in ever-reverberating commercial slogans. Thus a powerful but sexist line like Packard's "Ask the man who owns one" can return as Suzuki's "Ask anyone who owns one." But there can be no return for Aunt Jemima's "I'se in town, honey," American Tobacco's "Reach for a Lucky instead of a sweet," and Yardley's "The gay-hearted fragrance."

Ads are also culture specific. The worldwide conglomeration of advertising agencies in the 1970s was predicated on the belief that globalization of brands was inevitable. The rallying cry was one campaign for one world. So when Eastern Europe opened up to capitalism in the 1990s, the first colonizers to appear were the multinational advertising agencies, all set to peddle the wares of the West. Alas, the communists had used advertising only when they had to disgorge a surplus of poor quality goods, so the populace associated commercial speech with shoddy goods. Furthermore, aside from a few washed-up politicos, they had no stable of celebrity endorsers. Other cultures have also proved impervious to global campaigns. The British, for instance, like ads that have the temerity to assume some knowledge of history. The French love language, especially puns. The Germans are controlled, and the Japanese often outrageous, whereas the Spanish have an exquisite sense of class distinctions. Worse still, in a cluttered environment ads often rely on humor, and humor depends on a shared culture and language. Not all is lost: the ineffectiveness of advertising that attempts to cross cultural boundaries is what gives logos such power. The eye decodes what stymies the mind, hence the golden arches, the Pillsbury Doughboy, Apple Computer's apple, the Budweiser Clydesdales, the red of Coca-Cola, the Marlboro tattoo, and the ever present logos of Nike, Visa, Cadillac, and Toyota, among others.

Advertising is *syncretic*. In addition to living with other cultures (symbiosis) Adcult layers itself on top of other cultures (syncretism). Just as Christianity joined its ceremonies to the earlier rituals of the host culture, so Adcult

◆ Can you name the company or brand by these symbols? If you can't, millions of dollars have been wasted.

ceaselessly covers the patterns and rhythms of yesterday with today's commercialism. The process whereby dominant cultures absorb indigenous traits is hardly new. Take, for instance, Halloween, which started as a Druid ceremony expressing the concerns of dying light and the onset of winter. It was co-opted by Christianity and reformatted as All Hallows Eve, which was in turn taken over by the candy companies to become Halloween, a night of harvesting sweets. Although UNICEF tried for a while to make trick-or-treating an act of feel-good generosity, it was not successful. However, even as you read this, Halloween is being commandeered by the brewers, who ardently wish that this night would belong to Michelob, Coors, and the usual suspects. Chapter three looks in detail at Christmas as well as Super Bowl Sunday, Mother's Day, St. Patrick's Day, and the stillborn Professional Secretary's Day®, which are in the process of being locked into the commercial calendar of Adcult.

One of the most interesting aspects of Adcult is that it has become so much our lingua franca that we cannot understand it without having consumed it. Like the hermetic world of high art, where artists capture attention for their work by consciously (or, if we believe Harold Bloom, unconsciously) rewriting the works of their predecessors, so much of modern advertising depends on the audience's already knowing what has come before. So, for instance, the world of movies provides an almost endless memory bank for images that can be reformatted to sell products. A Toyota commercial adopts a motif modeled after *Total Recall's* memory implant, a Burger King spot uses two diapered babies chatting as in *Look Who's Talking*, and a Minolta camera advertisement pays visual homage to *Field of Dreams.* This transposition of imagery makes perfectly logical sense once you realize that movies are the literature we now share and that the same people who directed the action playing on the big screen down at the Cinema 16 are also making pin money by freelancing for ad agencies. Although critics may insist on a hierarchy of forms, the audience doesn't care.

What is truly remarkable is that ads have become so much the vocabulary of our times that they are layered over other ads like so much alluvial sediment. So the Pepsi ad in which Shaquille O'Neal walks over to a youngster drinking a Pepsi, only to have the kid refuse the star's request for a swallow, is built over a Mean Joe Green Coke ad in which the same interaction occurred, only this time the kid shared. Clearly, the point is that Pepsi is more valuable than Coke. The only way to know this is to have consumed not the drinks but the ads. Take a motif like the ball bearing rolling down the perfectly formed hood of the Lexus automobile to show the precision engineering. Now we have a plethora of things put on cars to show how stable they are. Chevrolet has even dumped what appears to be a railroad car full of bearings on its truck to show how well made it is. Nor are there hard feelings in Adcult when it comes to stealing: Lexus then borrowed the superslow-motion dropping of a pin in the Sprint ad and put it inside one of its sedans to show how quiet the car is. When the Energizer Bunny walks across the literal turf of other ads, only those who know the other ads can appreciate the trek. To understand the *Entertainment Weekly* ad, we need to know McDonald's advertising. To appreciate the Nickelodeon ad, we need to know the antidrug ads: "This is your brain. This is your brain on drugs." The Grundig ad depends on our knowing the United Colors of Benetton campaign. And Howard Gossage's Rover ad is an homage to David Ogilvy's famous Rolls Royce ad. What was it that T. S. Eliot said? "Artists borrow, amateurs steal." But there is a more profound epistemological point here: ads are what we know.

Like religious ceremonies, advertising continually recycles itself in a never ending self-referential loop. Doubtless in the years ahead some graduate student will write a thesis about how tortured generations of copywriters struggled to throw off the oppression of the previous generation and make a language fresh and their own. "I want my Maypo," said Mickey Mantle with tears in his eyes. Fifteen years later Mick Jagger said, "I want my MTV." But advertising will layer itself over just about anything that captures attention. Anything is fodder: old television and movie footage, stock footage documentaries, industrial and training films, cartoons, and travel sequences (especially in black and white because, as advertisers know, when you shoot it as a commercial it looks like one). In fact, one of the profit centers of the BBC is the selling of old film stock to advertisers around the world. The BBC subsidiary, appropriately in Adcult called Library Sales, refers to these sequences as *retro* and reports that one of the most popular background clips is of a lizard trudging across the desert. Viewers cannot seem to stop watching him, regardless of

what print is superimposed on the foreground. Best yet, lizards have no agents and demand no residuals.

Advertising is *profane*. Although I will later argue that advertising has co-opted the language of salvation to move the surplus goods of this world, it must be recognized that the sale is always made here in the dirt of earth. To

ACURA INTEGRA. THE SECOND MOST FUN CAR ON THE ROAD.

DIVIDED COLORS OF GRUNDIG.

TV Color con Scanner System.
GRUNDIG
made for you

The Rolls-Royce Silver Cloud—$13,995

"At 60 miles an hour the loudest noise in this new Rolls-Royce comes from the electric clock"

What makes Rolls-Royce the best car in the world? "There is really no magic about it—it is merely patient attention to detail," says an eminent Rolls-Royce engineer.

"At 60 miles an hour the loudest noise in this new Land-Rover comes from the roar of the engine"

What makes Land-Rover the most conspicuous car in the world? "There is really no secret," says an eminent Land-Rover enthusiast.

get the attention of earthlings, advertising must always be probing the para-
meters of sensation as well as of propriety. It often shocks because it must. In
a recent *New Yorker* cartoon, ad execs marvel at the hyped copy: "The truly
amazing thing about our new and improved product is that it's seventy-three
per cent more effective than our previous product, which, in turn, was eighty-
five per cent more effective than our original product, which, it must be
admitted, wasn't really effective at all." If advertising is a mirror, written in the
mirror is "Objects appear larger in the ad than in real life." Magnify or Be Forgotten is the motto of advertising speech.

Or maybe it's Excite or Get Lost. The copywriters' audience has a finite
number of eye blinks (estimated at five thousand a day) and to get their share
ads need to literally get in your face. To get in between those blinks, television
advertising has become nothing short of frantic. Thanks to digital film editing, sound compression, and a generation of kids raised on Nintendo and
MTV, we have ads that the rest of us could understand only by using superslow
motion on the VCR. The Coca-Cola bottle-cap ad that has sixteen hundred
cuts in sixty seconds, the Pepsi ad showing a young boy growing up in a real
hurry, and the Nike 1993 Super Bowl ad in which Michael Jordan and Bugs
Bunny battle Marvin the Martian and his flock of giant green chickens are
clearly targeted to an audience that enjoys sensory overload.

Were we any different? Not likely. Who now would be shocked by Bill
Bernbach's setting "You don't have to be Jewish to love Levy's" in 80-point
type, Mary Wells's having Braniff paint its planes to look as if they belonged
in the hangar of the Museum of Modern Art, Avis's bragging that it was the
perennial number two to Hertz, or Alka-Seltzer's showing us all those vulgar
stomachs bumping, burping, and churning?

The more mundane the object, the more likely the possibility of interchangeable products, the more desperate the need for brand separation, and
the more intense the verbal or visual hype. Nothing is more profane than
human skin. We can't keep our blinks off it. The sights of parts of it are shocking, which is why Calvin Klein insists on showing youngsters dressed only in
sepia doing things together, why Timberland sells outdoor wear by showing a
man dressed only in socks, and why Benetton enjoys nothing more than
exposing body parts in taboo ways. Certain products like blue jeans for
women have taken edginess so far that the only spot left is utter nonsense.
Hence the line for Joop! jeans, "In the uterus of love, we are all blind cave-
fish," and Diesel ads of kinetic confusion. When profanity takes hold, the
campaign is called break-through, which means that it is sufficiently disrup-
tive to translate shock into product recognition. Such campaigns are usually
created by small agencies for which risk is a survival strategy and then stolen
by large firms for which imitation is a survival strategy.

Advertising is repetitious. Profanity is partly created by repetition. Put
the *Mona Lisa* on too many washcloths or hear the *William Tell Overture* too

often, and they will leave Upper Aesthetica and become part of Lower Vulgaria. Rosser Reeves, the master of old-time, never-say-die advertising of the 1950s, wagered that, "given identical products, identical budgets, and identical sales forces, I will let you have a brilliant campaign every six months, provided you change it every six months—and I'll take a less-than-brilliant campaign and beat your tail off with it because I'll run it ten years." An executive of Minute Maid once complained about Reeves's refusal to fiddle with the orange juice advertising, saying, "You have 47 people working on my brands, and you haven't changed the campaign in 12 years. What are they doing?" To which Reeves retorted, "They're keeping your people from changing your ad" (Fox 1984:20). Reeves was hardly alone in the "tell 'em what ya gonna tell 'em, tell 'em, tell 'em what ya told 'em, and then do it again" school. The patrician Bruce Barton was simply more concise: "Reputation is repetition." To the old-style, hard-sell school this credo from 1885 is mantralike in its inevitability:

> The first time a man looks at an advertisement, he does not see it.
> The second time he does not notice it.
> The third time he is conscious of its existence.
> The fourth time he faintly remembers having seen it before.
> The fifth time he reads it.
> The sixth time he turns up his nose at it.
> The seventh time he reads it through and says, "Oh brother!"
> The eighth time he says, "Here's that confounded thing again!"
> The ninth time he wonders if it amounts to anything.
> The tenth time he thinks he will ask his neighbor if he has tried it.
> The eleventh time he wonders how the advertiser makes it pay.
> The twelfth time he thinks perhaps it may be worth something.
> The thirteenth time he thinks it must be a good thing.

The fourteenth time he remembers that he has wanted such a thing for a long
time.

The fifteenth time he is tantalized because he cannot afford to buy it.

The sixteenth time he thinks he will buy it some day.

The seventeenth time he makes a memorandum of it.

The eighteenth time he swears at his poverty.

The nineteenth time he counts his money carefully.

The twentieth time he sees it, he buys the article, or instructs his wife to do so.

• ("Repetition and Reputation," 1885, quoted in Vinikas 1992:97)

Let us be thankful that such repetition is no longer efficacious or affordable. The brutal jack-hammering of Reeves's Anacin ads of the 1950s—which
promised Anacin works "fast, Fast, FAST!"—will no longer be tolerated in
such a cluttered environment with so much viewer control. Let that harpy
whine about "Ring around the collar," and millions of itchy fingers punch the
remote. The rule of thumb is that after an ad gains about one thousand gross
rating points (the total sum of all the ratings that a commercial gets based on
the programs in which it appears), it loses half its effectiveness. For a typical
commercial this would be about ten weeks and $4 million in ad spending.

In truth, most ads nowadays are usually taken off the air because the
sponsor gets tired of them or the agency wants to try something new, not
because the audience refuses to respond. But the key is to build a context
around the message so the concept stays fresh while the execution varies. The
Energizer Bunny has more than thirty versions, Absolut keeps freshening up
the campaign by putting the bottle in bizarre places, Joe Camel is still weirdly
appealing whether at a drag race or playing pool with the guys, and chapters
are being added to the soap-serial of
the Tasters' Choice couple.

Of all the characteristics of
advertising, none is more important
than *magic*, however. In addressing
his colleagues at a convention of
advertising agencies in 1955, Leo Burnett explained the obvious:

> After all the meetings are over, the
> phones have stopped ringing and
> the vocalizing has died down,
> somebody finally has to get out an
> ad, often after hours. Somebody
> has to stare at a blank piece of
> paper. This is probably the very
> height of lonesomeness. Out of the
> recesses of his mind must come

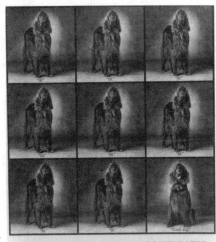

**SOME MESSAGES HAVE TO BE REPEATED
A FEW TIMES BEFORE THEY SINK IN.**

When times are hard, your audience may be harder than ever to persuade. Finding the
right advertising message and repeating it often have never been more important.

• The consumer as
seen by advertis-
ers: "Sit. Sit. Sit.
Good dog." From
the *Wall Street
Journal* campaign.

words which interest, words which persuade, words which inspire, words which sell. Magic words. I regard him as the man of the hour in our business today.   • (quoted in Simpson 1964:83)

Adcult is a magical culture. In a strictly formal sense, if objects carried intrinsic value, we would not need much in the way of language. To paraphrase Archibald MacLeish, things would mean, not be. Clearly, however, objects around us don't have such value. They have attributed value, and that process of attribution is continually shifting. It is magical.

The hoary comparison of advertising with religion is as felicitous as it may be trite. I am hardly the first to recognize that advertising is the gospel of redemption in the fallen world of capitalism, that advertising has become the vulgate of the secular belief in the redemption of commerce. In a most profound sense advertising and religion are part of the same meaning-making process: they occur at the margin of human concern about the world around, and each attempts to breach the gap between us and objects by providing a systematic understanding. Whereas the Great Chain of Being organized the world of our ancestors, the marketplace of objects does it for us. They both promise redemption: one through faith, the other through purchase.

But how are order and salvation effected? By magical thinking, pure and simple. The greatest power of magic is that it is so resolutely denied as the major organizer of meaning. We acknowledge all manner of nefarious magic and have special names for it: black magic, sorcery, voodoo, witchcraft, and necromancy. What we overlook is that until modern times our ancestors also believed in their ability to convince a beneficent power to do or not do something. They called this theurgy, or white magic. The ability to coax beneficent spirits from their habitations was very much a part of classical beliefs. These spirits, be they gods, dryads, nymphs, or mythic personages with names like Zeus, Hera, Jupiter, and Ajax, became the saints, cherubs, and seraphim of the Christian heavens. The Jolly Green Giant, the Michelin Man, the Man from Glad, Mother Nature, Aunt Jemima, Speedy Alka-Seltzer, the White Knight, and all their otherworldly kin are descendants of the earlier gods. What separates them is that they now reside in manufactured products and that, although earlier gods were invoked by fasting, prayer, rituals, and penance, the promise of purchase calls forth their modern ilk.

The magi were the ancient Zoroastrian theurgists whose actions animated the universe. They were the ones who knew the buried codes. Little wonder, then, that it was members of this caste who traveled to Jerusalem to bear witness to one of their own—the Christ child, the new and improved magus. And little wonder that the modern magi are in advertising around the globe, adding "value" to interchangeable objects. They make disposable goods into long-lasting charms. It is ad execs who produce Budweiser beer trucks in the middle of the desert, transform monsters into gentlemen hulks with a spray of Right Guard, activate those cute scrubbing brushes for Dow Cleanser, put the smile on the pitcher of Kool Aid, change a deep-swimming shark into a Chevrolet Baretta, and make millions of pimples disappear in the mirror . . . like magic. When the harried housewife tells Madge the manicurist that soaking her hands in Palmolive has made them feel so great that "It's black magic," Madge corrects her. Madge says, "It's real magic." And she is right. Only in a magical world could the phrases "Nationally advertised" and "As seen on TV" be transformed into a recommendation.

How do we think things work if not through the powers of magic? Why should we think that ours is an age of reason, an age of scientific observation, an age devoid of wishful thinking? The days of the Inquisition, Ponzi schemes, rain dances, the South Sea Bubble, witchcraft, and Dutch tulip mania are hardly over. In their place we have the stock market, state-supported gambling, chain letters, abstract expressionism, credit cards, national debt, filter tips, premium gas, anorexia, vitamin supplements, Amway, Lourdes, horoscopes, social security, trickle-down economics, leveraged buyouts, long-range weather forecasting, higher education, installment buying, the rhythm method, UFOs, hedge funds, eat-more-but-lose-weight diets, the value of diamonds, astrology, prayer, language, and, of course, almost all advertising. Economists like John Kenneth Galbraith make careers by pointing out how American economic culture is based on various pipe dreams, but they often forget that without the magic of these dream worlds we would not have "reality." They also forget that their specialty, economics, is one of the most magical of all human organizing systems. Consider the magical thinking that gives paper money its value. Even better, consider gold. But then again it is an irony worth noting that modern science, now the vastest repository of magical thinking, has given magic such a bad name.

In one of the best books ever on advertising, *The Golden Bough* (1922), anthropologist James Frazer outlines the two kinds of magic that make up our reality: theoretical and practical. The theoretical has to do with heavens, weather, tides, and cycles of planets and is the province of religion. It governs our far-off concerns, such as what we see when we look up or how we feel when we think about death. The practical kind of magic is when we cast our eyes downward and contemplate ourselves and the objects around us. Frazer divides the practical, or nearby, magic into the contagious and the imitative. The contagious is the basis of all testimonial advertising—the explanation of the importance of celebrity endorsement—and has its religious counterparts in such matters as the relics of Christ. If you use this product, if you touch this stone, if you go to this holy place, if you repeat this word, you will be empowered because the product, stone, place, word . . . has been used by one more powerful than you. Imitative magic, on the other hand, is a variation of circular thinking. Because the product is made of something, you will be likewise, if you consume it. So Africans use the powder of rhino horns, the Japanese crave certain mollusks, and we deodorize our bodies and then apply musk (from the Sanskrit for *testicle*) perfume. Then all over the world we get into a car with an animal name (yet more imitative magic) and go on the prowl for mates. Magic is such second nature that even when advertising sticks it in front of our noses, we are not stupefied. We expect it. Have a look at the ads for Pepsodent, Madame Dean's corsets, Xerox, General Foods International Coffees, Baileys, Tanqueray, Glenfiddich, Cunard, Dr. Scholl's, Nestlé, and the Big Red Boat.

Traveling with the totemic is the taboo. The magical power concocted to transform objects into salvation is the same power that can exile them. Where did such widespread afflictions as body odor, halitosis, iron poor blood, gray hair, water spots, vaginal odor, dishpan hands, various small glands and muscles, and split ends come from? Where were they a generation ago? Clearly, magical thinking is at work, or we would expose this charade for the protection racket that it is. To observe the push-pull of magic, the conflict between totem and taboo, a trip to the perfume counter will suffice. How to explain such names as Tabu, Forbidden Fruit, Vampire, Scandale, Obsession, My Sin, Shocking, Poison, Voodoo, Sorcery, Love Potion, Black Magic . . . , other than as a kind of unrequited tension between the desired and the forbidden? Because the tension was magically created, it is magically resolved.

In this context is it naïve to complain that advertising is suffused with sexual innuendo? Of course it is. Naturally enough, the advertising directed at the adolescent is invariably the most drenched in libidinous magic oil. Look at any magazine from *Details* to *Rolling Stone*, and you will see more adolescent hands in other people's pockets and down their trouser fronts, more faux intercourse with motorcycles, automobiles, and cigarettes, and more simply lewd positioning of the human form than in any R-rated movie. What do we expect? In adolescence we lather our bodies in unguents, slither into the most uncomfortable clothing, perform ritualistic dances that often include slamming into immovable objects, drive hunks of pig iron at breakneck speed, and ingest poisons, until finally we exchange amulets, repeat mystical vows, and at last get on with it. All the time we are quite unaware of the authority of such behavior, and later when our children start to consume the same magical mumbo-jumbo, we say, "My, my, isn't this advertising dreadful? It's making Missy and Buck behave so badly."

Once we realize that magical thinking is at the heart of both religion and advertising, why magical symbolism and language have become such a productive approach becomes clear. Once we realize that the consumption of an object often has more to do with meaning than with use, we will appreciate the vast power of the amulets, icons, images, statues, relics, and all the assorted stuff of organized systems of transcendental barter. Advertising fetishizes objects in exactly the same manner that religion does: it "charms" objects, giving them an aura of added value. An archbishop of Canterbury supposedly said, "I do not read advertisements—I would spend all my time wanting things," quite forgetting that indeed he does "read" advertisements and that he does spend much time "wanting things" as well as exchanging them. His ads just appear in different texts.

It is no happenstance that the advertising executives, or "attention engineers," who helped bring about the rise of consumer culture were steeped in the Christian tradition. They understood both the nature of yearning and how to franchise it. They knew the language of sincerity. They knew the power of promise, large promise. They knew how to make the sale and close the deal. Advertising was a white upper-middle class *Christian* endeavor, in part because most of the educated population was Protestant and in part because the procedure for selling manufactured resolution to life's problems was so similar to what religion had developed to sell future redemption.

Look at the early apostles of advertising. Among the most important ministers of commerce with deep evangelical roots were

- Artemas Ward, son of an Episcopal minister, whose slogans for Sapolio soap were almost as well known as the Songs of Solomon
- John Wanamaker, a staunch Presbyterian who considered the ministry and whose marketing genius helped make both the modern department store and such holidays as Mothers' Day that give us time to use it
- Claude C. Hopkins, who came from a long line of impoverished preachers, preached at seventeen, and translated his talent into copywriting for beer, carpet sweepers, lard, and canned meats
- James Webb Young, who sold Bibles door-to-door as a true believer until he went to work at J. Walter Thompson, where he did much the same job
- Helen Lansdowne, the daughter of a Presbyterian minister who studied three years at Princeton Theological Seminary before applying her talents to selling all manner of products to women
- Theodore MacManus, one of the few devout Catholics in early advertising, who held honorary degrees from three Catholic colleges and was the master of the "soft sell" until he quit, disgusted with advertising, especially its huckstering of cigarettes as health foods
- Rosser Reeves, son of a Methodist minister, who mastered the "hard sell" and left as his legacy the Anacin ads with all the hammers pounding their anvils
- Marion Harper Jr., the president of his Methodist Sunday school class, who went on to manage McCann-Erickson
- F. W. Ayer, a devout Baptist and Sunday school superintendent, who gave his own agency his father's name, N. W. Ayer & Son, because it sounded more established, and then coined the motto Keeping Everlastingly at It to make sure the point was made

◆ Magical thinking is the reality of Adcult.

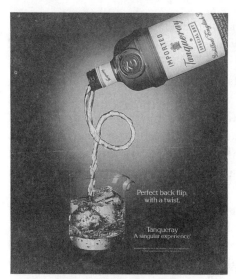

These are only a few of the anonymous priesthood of advertising, but the list shows that the vast majority of early advertisers came by their theological zeal honestly.

Of all the evangelical con artists none was more influential in translating magical thinking to sectarian matters than Bruce Barton. And none was more typical. As did so many of his colleagues, he came from the heartland (Oak Park, Illinois), moved East for a blue-ribbon education (at Amherst), had no intention of going into advertising (he did graduate work at the University of Wisconsin), and spent time writing and editing (at *Every Week* magazine, a Sunday supplement).

Quite by happenstance Barton met someone equally at loose ends (Roy Durstine), and they decided, rather in the manner that musical comedies are staged, to go into advertising. Barton had two other attributes common to early advertising executives. His father was a powerful Baptist minister and the younger Barton was subject to spells of nervous exhaustion, or nervous prostration, as it was called. When you read about the first and second generation of advertising impresarios, this configuration occurs with such startling regularity that it is hard to believe that the combination was haphazard. Almost as if they had to shove aside the old father in order to get to the new text, the junior copywriters proceeded to apply what they had been taught about ecclesiastical study to create a new parochial gospel of salvation. The transition was not easily made, hence the neurasthenic crisis.

Moving the merchandise of Mammon was not without compensation, however. Batten, Barton, Durstine & Osborne soon became a powerhouse of advertising, doing the selling for such American institutions as General Motors and General Electric. The agency's name—which Fred Allen quipped sounded like "a trunk falling downstairs"—became synonymous with the aspirational advertising of the 1920s. While building BBDO into acronymic success (it would become the fourth largest agency by the 1920s, later consumed by Omnicom, the agency holding company), Barton felt it was time to pay back his debt and perhaps relieve a guilty conscience. He did this in a characteristically American Protestant way. He wrote a book of instruction about the path to success. In the context of literary history Barton's book, *The Man Nobody Knows* (1926), fits into a robust genre of "What if Jesus were alive today: how would He act?" Best-selling books like C. M. Sheldon's *In His Steps: What Would Jesus Do?* (1897), which encourages us to imagine what life would be like if we were to respond to day-to-day problems by consulting the Lord, were as popular with our grandparents as "how to be your own best friend" books are today. Barton's Jesus was an advertising executive busy at "my father's business," selling redemption by the newly named but ancient devices of advertising. Here is a dapper Jesus at a cocktail party or a ballgame with the rest of us, a man among men who knows well what his people need and struggles to explain how to get it. So what if his explanation sounds a little like BBDO advertising copy?

In *The Man Nobody Knows* Jesus and his little band of eleven entrepreneurs are shown carrying the word to the modern world. He is no "lamb of God" but a full-fledged salesman out on the hustings. The omniscient narrator, the voice of advertising, often glosses the text with up-to-date information, but essentially the chapters represent a Christological musing on American business. Here's a bit of how it reads:

> Let us begin by asking why he was so successful in mastering public attention and why, in contrast, his churches are less so? The answer is twofold. In the first place he recognized the basic principle that all good advertising is news. He was never trite or commonplace; he had no routine. . . . [In the second place] he was advertised by his service, not by his sermons. Nowhere in the Gospels do you find it announced that:
>
> > Jesus of Nazareth Will Denounce
> > The Scribes and Pharisees in the
> > Central Synagogue
> > Tonight at Eight O'Clock
> > Special Music
>
> . . . If he were to live again, in these modern days he would find a way to make his works known—to be advertised by his service, not merely by his sermons. One thing is certain: he would not neglect the market-place. . . . Jesus would be a national advertiser today. I am sure, as he was the great advertiser of his own day. • (126, 136, 138, 140)

Jesus was a businessman; advertising is a business. Jesus spoke in parables; advertising speaks in parables. Christianity is a product; advertising sells products. Jesus did miracles; advertising works magic. The similarities are too powerful to overlook. As Barton once said to a meeting of advertising agencies, "If advertising speaks to a thousand in order to influence one, so does the church" (quoted in Simpson 1964:81). However much Barton's Babbittry in the cause of faith may seem philistine, it cannot be denied that he made the connection between the two merchandising systems.

Barton's charm, as well as his slightly unnerving danger, was that he was absolutely sincere. "Without sincerity," he remarked, "an advertisement is no more contagious than a sprained ankle." Communicating that sincerity by offering access to the supernatural worlds or to a used car out in the lot was Barton's stock-in-trade. He was a fearless Republican who never forgave Franklin Delano Roosevelt for the New Deal and who represented the silk-stocking district of Manhattan in Congress for a number of terms. Perhaps of more lasting importance, in 1952 he helped Rosser Reeves develop the first coherent advertising campaign for a presidential candidate. Dwight D. Eisenhower claimed that this was a "hell of a way to get elected," but for Barton religion and politics and refrigerators were part of the same culture, a culture based on providential realism in which the powers of advertising could only spread the "good word" and reenchant the world.

The powerful allure of religion and advertising is the same: we will be rescued. This act of rescue, be it effected by the Man from Glad or the Man from Galilee, transports us to the promised land of resolution. We will find the peace that passeth understanding. We will find the garbage bag certified by the American Association of Sanitary Engineers. The stigmata will be removed. Ring around the collar will disappear. Sin, guilt, redemption: problem, anxiety, resolution—the process of transformation is clear. The more powerful the redemption-resolution, the more otherworldly becomes the final site of salvation.

If you wish to see the similarities between religious and advertising pitches, turn on your television set. The television commercial is an almost perfect mimic of a religious parable. It is a a morality play for our time. We sit meditatively before the electronic altar, absorbing sermons from corporations on how to get "the most out of" your detergent, your cold, your floor wax, your family, your love life. In the television commercials we all know by heart, someone, a young female (if the sponsor is a household product) or a middle-aged male (if it is a cold remedy) is in distress. This Everyperson is middle class and white. She or he needs rescue and consults some other figure who promises relief. This other person testifies, gives witness; the product somehow appears, is tried, and poof! resolution. From on high the disembodied voice of the male announcer makes the parable unambiguous by reiterating the curative powers of the product. Our Everyperson is well on the way to Valhalla.

Along the way to this Happy Valley runs a parallel universe peopled with emissaries from the eternal beyond. In the Christian scheme this is the world of the apostolic church, consisting of pope, bishops, priests, nuns, and functionaries inside holy orders, all variously tied to the other world. In addition, slightly above the Church Triumphant is a mythic world of all those who have migrated between "here" and "there"—the various seraphim, cherubim, archangels, and saints. Below the world is yet another hierarchy, this time of maleficent spirits surrounding Satan, fallen angels like Mammon, Beelzebub, Mephistopheles, and all manner of demons, fiends, succubi, ghouls, vampires, and ogres who reverse the force fields of supernatural powers. Perhaps Christianity was built on the classical template because these chains of command resemble the Greco-Roman orders, descending from Zeus to the likes of Jupiter, Apollo, Hermes, then to the levels of Poseidon and Neptune, and then to the netherworld. Between are all manner of dryads, nymphs, sprites, gnomes, and the host of natural spirits.

Although we may have lost the superhuman beings and regions of classical and Christian mythologies, we have not lost our desire to link with this parallel world. It is, after all, a source of abiding comfort to think we are not alone. Just on the far side of the membrane are others who care about us. We are not alone. Also it is a powerful belief that we, by the powers of prayer and devotion, can encourage the intercession of these forces beyond our ken to enter our world. Once invoked, they do more than give aid and succor. They give it meaning and purpose.

What characterizes Adcult is that our parallel world, our utopian other-land, what cultural critic Richard Simon has called "adtopia," has been populated by new beneficent spirits. The spirits magically reside not in nature, holy books, magical signs, or chants but in objects as mundane as automobile tires, rolled-up tobacco leaves, meat patties, green beans, and sugar water. The Man with a Thousand Faces simply has a few more, and he spends most of his time inside containers on shelves down at the A&P.

Here we have all manner of creatures vying for our companionship. We have characters from

- Greek mythology: Hermes carrying flowers for FTD, Ajax the white knight with that magical lance, and Pegasus at the Mobil Station
- Folklore: the Keebler elves living in the Hollow Tree; Snap, Crackle, and Pop residing in Rice Krispies; and the Jolly Green Giant inhabiting Happy Valley
- Toontown: Elsie the Cow, Mr. Bubble, Bibindendum (or Mr. Bib, the Michelin tire man), Poppin' Fresh (the Pillsbury Doughboy), E.B. (the Energizer Bunny), Reddy Kilowatt, Tony the Tiger, Cracker Jack, and the Underwood devil
- Cross-over land, characters from the world of half-human–half-cartoon: Mr. Peanut, Ronald McDonald, Johnnie Walker, the Quaker Oats' Quaker, the Smith Brothers. and Mr. Clean
- The human world: the Philip Morris bellhop, the Morton Salt Girl, the Marlboro Man, Aunt Jemima, Betty Crocker, Mrs. Olsen, Mr. Whipple, Little Miss Coppertone, Little Debbie, Madge the Manicurist, and Josephine the Plumber
- The animal world: Nipper the dog, White Owl, and the John Deere leaping deer
- The world of bizarre mutations: Joe Camel, who was a dromedary on the cigarette pack and is now in the cartoon world as Smokin' Joe, super cool musician

Starting decades ago with Sunny Jim for Force Food, the bent-over washerwoman for Dutch Cleanser, and the Campbell kids, the creation of imaginative characters and the lining-up of these characters with commodities has shown that we have not lost the deep desire to animate the world around us with the stuff of meaning. Just as we create gods to give us creation, so in Adcult we externalize the magic in order to give meaning to the profoundly unmagical world of packaged goods. The process is so powerful that it even

extends to graphic forms, such as the golden arches, checkerboard square, the Coca-Cola signature, and the Heinz keystone. In a bizarre kind of parthenogenesis we can even witness megacorporations creating fantastic new entities to disguise the very nature of production. So Gallo creates the illusion that two good ol' boys who call themselves Frank Bartles and Ed Jaymes are vintners, Philip Morris would have us believe that a person named Dave actually makes Dave's Cigarettes, and Coca-Cola pretends that Fruitopia is a Snapple-like beverage, not a marketing ploy from Atlanta.

It is as simplistic to say, "Here are the nasty advertisers capturing our imaginations and manipulating them for their own profit" as it is to say "Here are the nasty churchmen capturing our imaginations and manipulating them for their own aggrandizement." These transformations are not imposed on us any more than Zeus really terrorized the ancients. We need the gods more than the gods need us. That our gods are now in the hands of commercial manipulators, that folklore has become fakelore and folklure, that holy grails have become spot removers, and that the magic of the Eucharist has been stolen by liquor campaigns are possible only because the yearnings of humans, and the power of institutions to direct those yearnings, remain. However much we may feel comforted by thinking "They are doing this to us," in truth we are doing it to ourselves.

So we find advertising loaded down with the rhetoric of religious thanksgiving: "Thank you, Paine-Webber," "Thank you, Tasty-Cakes," "I love what you do for me," "Thanks, Delco," "Thanks, Crest." Conversely, the sense of self-worth and salvation is also apparent: "I'm worth it," "Master the moment," "Be all you can be," "I found it!" "Looking good makes us feel good," "You deserve a break today," "You, you're the one," "You've come a long way, baby." In Adcult, companies are patiently beneficent in their concern for us: "Ford wants to be your car company," "You asked for it, you got it—Toyota," "Have it your way," "Something to believe in," "We bring good things to life," "It's the right thing." With the product you have a constant friend: "You're in good hands." Jesus has entered your life. It's "Me and my R.C.," "Me and my Arrow." Advertising does not create these relationships; they were established long before Christianity. Advertising exploits them.

ADVERTISING AS A CULTURE

The multi-billion dollar, nation-wide educational programs of the ad-men (dwarfing the out-lay on formal education) provide a world of symbols, witticisms, and behavior patterns which may or may not be a fatal solvent for the basic political traditions of America, but which certainly do comprise a common experience and a common language for a country whose sectional differences and technological specialisms might easily develop into anarchy.

• MARSHALL MCLUHAN, "AMERICAN ADVERTISING," 1947

Advertising is the educational program of capitalism, the sponsored art of capitalism, the language of capitalism, the pornography of capitalism. Most of all, for all the high-sounding phrases, advertising is the culture developed to expedite the central problem of capitalism: the distribution of surplus goods. The industrial revolution is usually studied from the point of view of the producer, how machines made things. But the real revolution was in how things were distributed, how advertising made things worth buying. Adcult is so much our culture, so much the value-application program of capitalism, that we might appreciate it more if we examine the cultures it has displaced or colonized. What follows is a thumbnail listing of the divisions that used to be made between and among our various cultures. I put forward this hierarchy not because it is new but because it shows how completely advertising has triumphed. These cultures are, in descending order, high, modern, popular, and folk.

The term *high culture* is synonymous with *art culture* or the *fine arts*. In advertising jargon these terms "own" the concept of the "best that has been thought and said." Yet as we are reminded daily, what is in high culture is what a particular class of self-styled elite gatekeepers says is in high culture. The claim of these gatekeepers since the eighteenth century is that this stuff has intrinsic value. Supposedly, art both encapsulates truth and is eternal. The creators of such objects are individuals, called artists, who have a special trait, called genius. The evaluators are called critics and until recently were thought to be a cut below artists but with analogous duties. Art can only be appreciated with study. We go to school to be close to the critics. Not coincidentally, art culture has flourished along with the two institutions that sustain and depend on it: higher education and museums.

Folk art, the opposite of high art, continued meanwhile to produce objects as in days of old. In folk art authorship was communal, acceptance was by audience acclamation, and the criterion was not uniqueness but the pleasure of participation. The creators were called artisans, and the measure of their success was the degree of use. No critics need apply. This culture was initially agrarian, but with urbanization it moved from field to street. So from field songs to rap, from pictographs to graffiti, from basket making, weaving, and pottery to all the myriad stuff made at home and sold on sidewalks throughout the world, folk art has persevered but—thanks to machinery— hardly flourished.

As high art evolved into modern art, folk art expanded into popular art or, keeping the terms straight, *popular culture*. Popular culture is a modern development in the sense that it is the management of folk entertainments for profit. Just as the gatekeepers get between the audience and the works of art, so in popular culture a class of merchandiser organizes a folk entertainment and charges admission. The success of popular culture is judged by the length of the line and the amount of the take at the end of the day—the criterion of profit and loss. The gatekeeper is the box office, the Nielsen ratings, and the best-seller list. Mass culture comes from popular culture via the machine. It is manufactured by vast production industries, distributed simultaneously to thousands, and quickly consumed into oblivion, so that more of it is almost immediately needed. To high culture this is the creation of trash. To low culture this is just for fun. From newsprint to radio transmissions to television programming, mass culture has been the dominant culture of the twentieth century and, especially since the 1960s, has crossed all lines of genre, nationality, media, and taste.

The great conglomerated empires of Sony, Time Warner, Paramount (now Viacom), News Corp., Matsushita, Bertelsmann, and Advance Publications are well on their way to merging such disparate devices as the telephone, film, magazine, radio, television, shopping mall, and mail into a new electronic hybrid: the so-called information superhighway.

Now clearly these four cultures are not as separate as I have made them. They continually leak into each other or, in the obtuse term of modern academia, they are *heteroglossic*. A painting such as, say, the *Mona Lisa* will start in high culture, be reconfigured by Duchamp in modernism, and then appear on neckties in mass culture. Ditto in reverse when a folk song is expropriated by a high-culture composer only to be reconfigured later as a way to sell hamburger patties. "Mack the Knife" cuts many ways. The collapsing hierarchies are so complete that we think nothing amiss when reading a middlebrow book like John Grisham's *The Client* and find that the descriptive nouns and adjectives of storytelling have been replaced by brand names. The world of this novel is literally suspended, as is everything else in Adcult, in the logos of commercialism, to wit: Dr. Pepper, Sprite, Diet Coke, Nike, Camel, Mazda RX-7, Snickers, Nikon, Virginia Slims, Grolsch, Domino's, Holiday Inn, Wal-Mart, Cadillac, GI Joe dolls, *Esquire*, Liquid Paper Corrector, Triumph Spitfire, the Yellow Pages. . . .

So, recognizing that these are divisions more important for heuristic than actual distinction, I put them forward only to withdraw them. For the thesis of this book is that Adcult is overpowering *all* these cultures. Modern advertising's overwhelming mandate to attract attention has made it invade provinces hitherto off-limits to commercialism. In so doing Adcult has collapsed these often contentious cultures into a monolithic, worldwide order immediately recognized by the House of Windsor and the tribe of Zulu. From high culture to folk, from high brow to low, from Aesthetica to Vulgaria, commercial speech is not so much shouting down competing voices as enlisting them to sing the same tune. If ever there is to be a global village, it will be because the town crier works in advertising.

Let me briefly illustrate what the rest of this book will explain. I contend that high culture, the enclave of canonical works once created by the likes of John Ruskin and Matthew Arnold, collected by the robber barons of capitalism like J. P. Morgan and Solomon Guggenheim, and now enshrined in universities is at risk not because of any multiculturalism or diversity nonsense but rather because the myth of truth residing in art has been replaced by the myth of value residing in objects. In chapter four I argue that the world of art objects is rapidly becoming another province of adtopia, a concocted world in which objets d'art are presented with a commercial product in order to elevate the product. Nothing difficult here—just value by association, what in advertising is called borrowed interest. Today works of art are better communicated by commercial interests than by academic ones, because their commercial value is greater than their supposed social value. Putting jeans on Michelangelo's *David* is a typical example, so unexceptional that its cross-pollinating power is simply taken for granted. Yet from an art history view, it is simply outrageous.

Not only is the objet d'art expropriated in the specific to give value to a product, entire collections are assembled and schlepped around the world to give value to the sponsoring corporation, now called an underwriter. The interpenetra-

♦ An improvement, to be sure, but no matter what he's wearing the arms still look too big.

tion of art value and commercial value is complete. Name an art exhibition since the 1960s, especially one of the so-called blockbuster shows, that is not done under the promotional aegis of Philip Morris, IBM, General Motors, or some other multinational corporation. Artworks in our time are more sustainable as extensions of commercial interests than as aesthetic culture. The minister of cultural affairs is not in Washington or at Yale but on the twenty-fifth floor of the Philip Morris Building in Manhattan, trying to figure out if a Matisse show will outdraw Magritte. Thomas Hoving first realized this, and his intellectual heir, Thomas Krens at the Guggenheim, has made it a modus operandi. Museums are essentially franchising their holdings to commercial interests in the same way that Hollywood studios used to rent the endorsements of their celebrities.

One of the more interesting developments in modern times is that the artists understood the power of Adcult long before the rest of us. As abundantly illustrated in the Museum of Modern Art's curiously self-conscious show entitled "High & Low: Modern Art and Popular Culture," the clear beneficiary of this interchange is high culture. The avant-garde of mid-century modernism, the so-called pop artists, reveled in this irony. What was Andy Warhol but first and foremost an advertising man? He started his creative career arranging window displays, graduated to designing record covers, book jackets, stationery, and Christmas cards but found fame creating shoe ads for Bonwit Teller. "Who's art?" he supposedly asked. "I don't believe I've met the man." The mass production of his objects, the naming of his studio The Factory, his never ending attempts to get bigger and bigger commissions, and longer and longer production runs made his statement, "The highest form of art is making money," a sincere paean to Adcult.

At the other end of the spectrum folk and popular cultures have essentially been subsumed into advertising culture without a whimper. Folk culture has almost totally disappeared. The vernacular of the street, really all that is left of once vibrant folkcult, is constantly being plundered for resonate language. Words like *gotta, yo, gonna, hey* and *uh-huh* are becoming as important an aural ingredient to catch the unsuspecting ear as the winking and blinking of special effects are to catch the eye. As contrasted with Wordsworth, who claimed he was going to write in the "language really used by men," Adcult resolutely trafficks in the language of the street. Of course, advertising has never rigidly adhered to the King's English, as "Winston tastes good like a cigarette should" and "Us Tarreyton smokers would rather fight than switch" demonstrated in the 1960s. If a product called New Stayfree Ultra Plus seems to be pushing language into nonsense, or that Dimetapp Cough Elixir "works as good as it tastes" seems to be idiotic, does anyone expect anything different?

Far more important than bad grammar is the colonizing of aphorisms. A brief example: one central force in folk culture is the passing on of maxims—called momisms in contemporary urban anthropology—like "A stitch in time saves nine" or "Look before you leap." These momisms are rapidly being replaced by commercial slogans. So "Just do it" has replaced "He who hesitates is lost"; "You deserve a break today" replaces "Don't be so hard on yourself"; "Just say no" is "Don't be a follower." In an interesting play on how advertising has co-opted the parental role of advice giver a Xerox spot has M. C. Hammer, the rap artist, repeating, "Listen to your mother," as color Xerox copies of mommy cutouts from the 1950s flash on the screen. Printed clichés such as "Be in by 9:00" appear in cartoon bubbles next to the mommy mouths. These phrases include such doozies as, "Don't pick your nose" and "You'll go blind." Hammer's voice is used cleverly, so that he keeps repeating "your mother" in variations until we hear the "Yo mama" beneath. If the language of the street develops a punch, it will soon become the language of advertising and vice versa. What is startling is that this is all done to sell a machine few in the audience can afford.

There is a danger here. The lingo of Adcult is not tied to folk traditions or wisdom. It is tied to a product. Without a second thought, we immediately recognize such phrases as the "Teflon president," "McPaper," "Velveeta-voiced," "Mr. Clean politician," "doc in the box," "Maalox moment," "Pepto Bismol pink," and even "the Edsel of . . . " because the codes of communication have been resettled on advertising claims. Think only of the hundreds of times you've heard turns on "I can't believe I ate the whole thing," "You deserve a break today," "When E. F. Hutton talks," and "Where the rubber meets the road," and you will realize that, like jazz riffs, we play with the language of Adcult because we know that the tune is already familiar. When in their first debate Michael Dukakis said George Bush "may be the Joe Isuzu of American politics," we needed no explanation. The whole country immediately connected the zinger with the car maker's "liar" campaign. So too when Walter Mondale asked, "Where's the beef?" We speak in brand names because we now think in them.

If folk culture has contracted, popular culture has exploded. Take sports. Is there a sporting event not saturated with advertising? We might expect that automobile racing, a natural outgrowth of commercial culture, would become a moving billboard. And perhaps we might expect the outfield walls and scoreboards of baseball and football to become prime sites of commercial messages for a captive audience. But the real influence of Adcult on sports is not on the field, as it were, but in the transmission. After all, most of us don't go to the game but participate through an interlocutor, the announcer. The Europeans may be able to watch sports with the audio off, but we don't. We need to be told what we see. Radio started this transformation. In the early days of baseball Mel Allen would refer to a "White Owl Wallop" or a "Ballentine Blast" at Yankees' games. "Miller time" came from old-time baseball, the beer break when the pitcher went to the bullpen. Take a typical broadcast today and you'll hear, as on a recent telecast for an Atlanta Braves game, references to the "Pepsi Starting Lineup," the "Aflac Trivia Quiz," the "Rolling Rock Braves Report," the "MCI Seventh Inning Stretch," the "Holiday Inn Player of the Game," the "Rolaids Relief Pitcher," the "Delco Play of the Day," and the "Irish Spring Fielding Leaders."

Sporting events are commercial parades. (Ditto parades themselves, for that matter.) Is there a golf tournament without a named commercial sponsor? Even the late Bing Crosby clambake succumbed to the AT&T Pebble Beach tournament. The Masters is a heroic holdout. Is there a football bowl game not co-opted? My favorite is the Poulan/Weedeater Bowl. Are we surprised when Andre Agassi, under contract to a sunglasses manufacturer, wears his dark glasses for a few games on overcast days? As chapter three shows, the granddaddy of amateur sport, the Olympics, is as well the granddaddy of commercial intrusion. The Olympics has become a veritable Olympian display of advertising competition, in which sponsors of the event compete with sponsors of the transmission, which compete with sponsors of the individual teams which, in turn, compete with sponsors of the specific amateur athletes.

Adcult: How It Works

A good ad should be like a good sermon: it must not only comfort the afflicted—it also must afflict the comfortable.

• BERNICE FITZ-GIBBON, *MACY'S, GIMBELS AND ME,* 1967

Clearly, these high and low cultures have been shaken up and reconfigured because of the power of the modern upstart—Adcult. Mass culture is the conduit of Adcult and vice versa; they are joined at the hip. Given that advertising supports more than 60 percent of magazine and newspaper production and almost 100 percent of the electronic media, what could we have expected? But how does it operate? Figure 1.1 is a schematic of that process as it has developed in the twentieth century. The paradigm is hardly definitive and, as we shall see, is still in flux.

At the center is the advertisement. It sits inside a medium that is usually, but not always, consumed for entertainment value. The object advertised is commonly known by a brand name, which is how it is separated from other like objects, and is the result of the agency's attempt to position the object in a constellation of similar things. If the system is working properly, you don't buy beer, you buy "Bud."

Above the advertisement is the agency. Since the mid-1970s the producers of ads have conglomerated, as have the producers of products and media, into massive worldwide entities, except that ad agencies have a strange bias toward the British. While it would be nice to think this is related to a relatively more sophisticated use of language and image, it is instead the result of advantageous tax laws. These international agencies, with weird sci-fi names like WPP, Interpublic, True North Communications, Cordiant Omnicom,

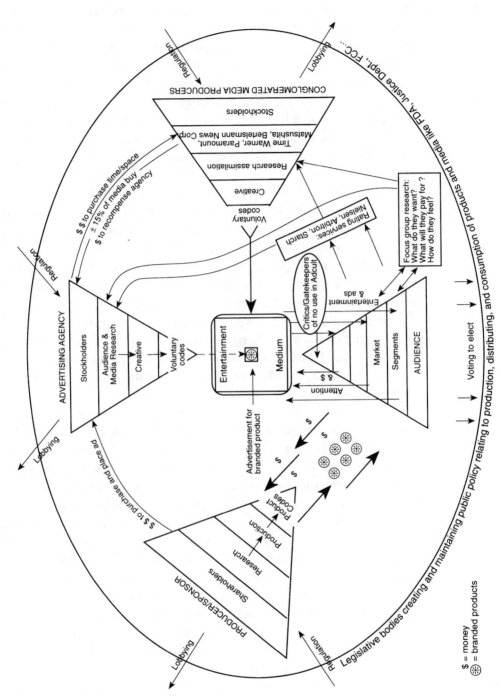

◆ Modern Advertising Made Simple.

Dentsu, and Euro RSCG are often collections of established agencies linked together to provide "full service" to the client. So, for instance, WPP (which started making wire products like shopping carts) owns J. Walter Thompson and Ogilvy & Mather, Interpublic controls Lintas and McCann-Erickson, Omnicom is made up of BBDO, DDB Needham and TBWA.

Although most large multinational agencies are publicly owned, a few, most notably Young & Rubicam, N. W. Ayer, and Leo Burnett, are still in private hands. These holding companies and their subsidiaries then own bits and pieces of regional agencies to give them local outlets. There are a number of reasons for having autonomous units with different names, the most important being that clients don't want to have their agency work with a competitor because this might lead to a leakage of competitive information. The umbrella holding company gives the client the necessary illusion of proprietary service while giving the mega agency the economies of scale. So a Colgate toothpaste might be a client of BBDO and a Lever Brothers' toothpaste a client of DDB Needham, whereas the overarching company, Omnicom, would be free of any conflict of interest. Occasionally, this reaches the level of a Gilbert and Sullivan operetta, with a mini agency being created with an established agency owned by a holding company in order to maintain the illusion of client-centered control. The process is rather like the imprints of publishing companies that give the named editors and their authors the sense of being at a company that really cares about their welfare.

The modern agency does not just create the text. It also buys media into which to put the ad, tests and researches what can be done to improve it (as well as the product), and advises the client about marketing decisions to make it more effective. Advertising agencies started as ways to buy space in print media efficiently, and this is still a primary purpose. In fact, space buying is often far more creative than writing copy. The ability to buy space at advantageous rates is still how many large agencies survive. After all, if you could go to NBC and promise to purchase 20 percent of its fall schedule, you would expect to be given advantageous rates. You then resell that space to your clients. What conglomerated the agencies in the 1970s and 1980s was the promise of more competitive pricing, but alas this hasn't always worked. The unbundling of services may prove the way of the 1990s. Boutique agencies, which provide only creative ideas and execution, can go to suppliers of research as well as buyers of media space and therefore not have to carry the expenses of unused departments.

What frightens Madison Avenue more than threats from Washington (that the IRS might remove the deductibility of advertising expenses) or from the courts (that they might remove the First Amendment protection for certain products like tobacco and liquor) is the threat from Hollywood. The Hollywood dream factory could easily retool and sell its services to corporations. The fact that Coca-Cola bypassed McCann-Erickson, the agency for its flagship brand, for Creative Artists Agency (CAA), a Hollywood talent agency, portends a profound realignment of client-agency relationships. CAA's campaign, with those happy-eyed lumbering polar bears kicking back a Coke, looks to many along Madison Avenue like the grizzly bears stealing the plumpest clients.

No matter how the agency is organized, it is usually recompensed in a most peculiar manner. The agency buys space, or rather rents audience attention, in a medium provided by some supplier of plasma, be it print, electrons, or pixels. Until recently, the agency was paid a flat percentage of that buy as its primary income. This is called an open contract and was pioneered by the N. W. Ayer Company of Philadelphia. So if the agency bought $1 million-worth of space for Ford, it would be paid a percentage, historically about 15 percent, or $150,000, for its work. Now everything is up for negotiation, but the general process remains. The agency buys space wholesale, then skims off a percentage as it presents the retail bill to the client. On the face of this you can see why the client would balk. First, for historical reasons the agency is really in the service of the media, for the more space it sells the greater its recompense. And second, and more relevant, if advertising worked as advertised, the compensation would be tied to the increase in sales (or attitude change) attributable to the ads. It is not.

The space providers—say, Time Warner, the New York Times Company, or CBS—attempt to guarantee that their entertainment medium will be consumed by a certain number of people who are divided by demographic sections. So the agency essentially buys or—better yet—rents, the attention of, say, two hundred thousand 18- to 24-year-olds for a certain period of time at a certain cost per thousand, or CPM. For the temporary use of those retinas they pay wholesale and are repaid retail. Most media suppliers are also publicly owned, so they are trying to maximize their earnings by supplying not what they think is entertainment or news but what is most demanded by those audiences that might be attracted to the sponsor's products. The process is resolutely (and often refreshingly) amoral. It returns us to the carnival. Carnies do not care what is behind the tent. They care only about the length of the line out front.

There are still more ironies, not the least of which is that both the supplier of the ad and the provider of the media are telling each other and the sponsor that they are cutting costs as close as possible. At the same time they are saying to the shareholders that they are maximizing profits. This irony was not lost in the marketplace when private agencies went public and then conglomerated at exorbitant prices. The jig was up once the sponsors saw the once-hidden agency profits. Madison Avenue is still reverberating from this trauma of the 1970s, which to some degree has created the current free-for-all in the billing system. "The clients don't trust us anymore . . . we used to be partners, now we're just suppliers" is the oft-heard plaint of the agency today. The wonder is that the trust-us compensation system lasted so long.

Far more profound than the changes in agency life, however, has been the transformation of advertising-driven media. The history of American media is the history of a Darwinian struggle for attention, not just any kind of attention but the attention of certain audiences. Any number of services provide data on viewers and/or readers and are used by both agencies and media providers. The company best known is Nielsen, and its service, which is far more complex than a radio and television rating, really attempts to gauge audience attention at every point from ad to purchase and even thereafter. These services are important because no one knows how ads work—if they really do. Lord Leverhume (of Lever Brothers) and Joseph Wanamaker (of the Philadelphia department store) are both credited with the quip that each knew half his advertising budget was wasted but that he couldn't figure out which half. There is no meter, no dial, no needle that can be placed on an individual ad. Advertising is like grass: You never see it grow, but every once in a while you have to get out the lawn mower. It is possible to judge where the magazine or television show is going, who is seeing it, and even how much concentration is being exerted in the act of consumption. But a good ad is one that produces increased sales. And, with some exceptions, that is very difficult to calculate. The Volkswagen ads of the late 1950s by Bill Bernbach are always considered the great campaign of "the golden age of advertising." In a sense they were. But Volkswagen sales increased almost at the same rates in cultures like Latin America where there were no Doyle Dane Bernbach ads.

To the left of the agency is the producer-sponsor. In adspeak producer-sponsor is called *the client* and his advertising business is referred to as *the account*. Because it is so hard to know if his account is being handled well (advertising increasing his sales), the client is tempted to treat the agency as he treats any supplier, with short-term enthusiasm and long-term suspicion. This attraction-repulsion is a recent development and is partly the result of the buyout fever of the 1970s and 1980s, when it became clear exactly how much chicanery was occurring between what the agency said its services were worth and how the markets evaluated their take-over value. As well, the loss of faith in the branding process itself, thanks to clutter and such merchandising methods as couponing and discounting, have added to the malaise. When generic cigarettes, or generic gasoline, or soft drinks, or breakfast cereals, or cosmetics, or any number of a host of nonbranded products increase proportionally, as they do in recessionary times, Philip Morris, General Motors, and Procter & Gamble must wonder why they have spent so much money branding their objects. It must be a relief when they are reminded what a small percentage advertising takes from their production costs. Besides, which would you rather do: buy advertising or pay taxes? Still, rather like universities, when money is scarce the producers cut first where the squeals are least heard. Library budgets get axed, ad agencies get fired.

At the bottom of the graph is the object of everyone's attention, the consuming audience. It is a mistake, however, to ever consider the audience as separate from the process, as this schematic implies. The audience is never "over there," just out of sight. Rather, as in all lasting institutions, it actively anticipates and creates its own interactions. As James Joyce perceptively commented in a postmodern moment, "Are my consumers not also my producers?" (Not by happenstance is Leopold Bloom, his modern Ulysses-Everyman, employed selling advertising space for a Dublin throwaway sheet.) Although it is comforting to contend that *they* are doing this to *us*, such is almost never the case.

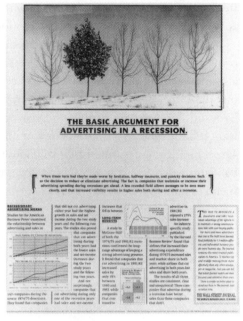

THE BASIC ARGUMENT FOR ADVERTISING IN A RECESSION.

♦ The first expense to be cut when recession hits is advertising. What do companies know that their ad agencies want to deny?

You may not like what is happening when you go to church, or watch television, or read the newspaper, or even are hauled into court, but each of these media is trying to cater to specific demands of specific audiences. People choose denominations as they change channels to find what they want. Although the institution may pretend to receive their programming decisions from on high (God's word, All the News That's Fit to Print, the Constitution . . .), in truth they are listening first to their audience (no matter that they don't always understand what the audience is saying or the audience isn't sure of what it wants). If history shows us anything, it is that the most successful institutions are those that claim to lead by following some abstract code but in truth are the most sensitive to audience concerns. The most powerful institutions over time are those that give the impression of being impermeable but are the most porous.

So too with advertising. In a sense we create our own advertising as we create our own news, religion, politics, law, or entertainment . . . or art. Reader-response theories, which argue that meaning in, say, a poem or a painting is the result of an ongoing interaction between the text and the reader (to hell with the artist's intention and critical voodoo), offer the appropriate approach to understanding the power of commercial speech. What makes advertising unique and provocative in this regard is that the process is opened up for minute inspection. Advertising research is usually ridiculously thorough and sometimes just ridiculous. Focus group after focus group, elaborate questioning and teasing out, charts, graphs, computer models—you name it, if there is a technique to explore the human condition, advertising will try it. This obsession with the audience, with the consumer, is not because advertising intends to invent desire, although it is strangely comforting to think so, but because no one knows how to direct human desire. Advertising is thus cultural anthropology in slow motion.

It is abhorrent to most of us to consider that not only do we create our own advertising (in the sense that we create our own literature or politics) but also that we then proceed to buy not the product but the advertising. If we buy the sizzle, not the steak, is there any possibility that it is the sizzle that we want? For which do we thirst—Evian advertising or the water? Clearly, we want it both ways. We want the joys of materialism with no attendant guilt. The conundrum of puritanism is still powerfully unresolved and gives Adcult its vigor: work, work, work, to save for a rainy day but then spend, spend, spend as if there were no tomorrow.

2 ✦ WE BUILD EXCITEMENT

THE DELIVERY OF ADCULT

The Hatter in the Strand of London, instead of making better felt-hats than another,
mounts a huge lath-and-plaster Hat, seven feet high, upon wheels; sends a man to drive it
through the streets; hoping to be saved *thereby*. He has not attempted to *make* better hats, as
he was appointed by the Universe to do, and as with this ingenuity of his he could very
probably have done, but his whole industry is turned to *persuade* us that he has made such!
He too knows that the Quack has become God.

• THOMAS CARLYLE, *PAST AND PRESENT*, 1843

 THOMAS CARLYLE just didn't get it. The Hatter in the Strand of London was not in the business of making hats to make better hats. He made hats to make money. The Victorians may have commanded the manufacturer to make the best of what he set out to do, but the culture of capitalism does not care so much about what he makes as about what he can sell. Hence the "best" hat becomes the most profitable hat. Ironically, perhaps he cannot make hats profitably unless he can market what he makes efficiently. The selling determines the making. And once he makes those best hats, especially if he has a machine to help him, heaven help him if he makes too many. If he has to spend some of his productive time acting like a nut in order to sell those hats, so be it.

The ingredients necessary to concoct an Adcult are not complex. The Hatter in the Strand of London is crucial. Because the Hatter probably has enough hats for his own use, he makes something that has exchange value. Assuming that he can control the retail price, the more he manufactures, the more he takes advantage of the economies of mass production and the greater the profit. To control that retail price, however, he needs some method to differentiate his hat or he will produce more than he can sell. After all, because the product is partially machine made, it is essentially interchangeable with a competitor's product made with the same machinery.

The process of differentiation, called branding, is the key ingredient in all advertising. Make all the machine-made felt hats, biscuits, shoes, cigarettes, automobiles, or computer chips you want, but you cannot sell effectively until you can call it a Fedora, a Ritz, a Nike, a Marlboro, a Chevrolet, or an Intel 386. If everybody's biscuits are in the same barrel, and if they look pretty much the same, urging people to buy biscuits probably won't do the trick. Chances are, they won't buy your biscuit. As Thomas J. Barratt said at almost the same time that Carlyle was having at the Hatter, "Any fool can make soap. It takes a clever man to sell it" (Turner 1953:110). Barratt was a clever man. He made a fortune by the end of the century by calling his soap Pears' Soap and making sure everyone knew about it by defacing miles of Anglo-American wall and newsprint space with "Have you had your Pears' today?" In many ways modern culture has been a battle between Carlyle and Barratt. If you aren't sure who won, look around you.

Adcult also requires purchasers with sufficient disposable income to buy your product. And it doesn't hurt if your audience members have enough curiosity to listen to you tell them your biscuits are different when they know all biscuits are the same. But watch out: this process is not without risk. When money is tight, brands take flight. For reasons no one can understand, from time to time markets fall apart, advertising loses its grip, and the charade has to be reenacted. Procter & Gamble spent billions building its soap brands, Philip Morris did the same with premium cigarettes, as did IBM with the personal computer, only to have the demand for their brands suddenly plummet. Generics appear to eat up what advertising created. Brands can suddenly become just commodities again. The Hatter in the Strand soon responds by dropping his prices and by making a still larger lath-and-plaster hat.

With those ingredients in the pot all an Adcult still needs is a plasma, or conduit, between producer and consumer within which producers can, in the jargon of modern criticism, *inscribe* their message. The ever bigger lath-and-plaster hat is soon subject to diminishing returns. The brand may appear *on* his hat, but its name recognition is created *in* a medium. So along with his sign the Hatter may even decide to hire someone to advertise his product by voice. In the nineteenth century consumers still heard the cries of the coster-monger (the coster is a kind of English apple) or other traders announcing their wares:

> One-a-penny, two-a-penny, hot cross buns!
> One-a-penny, two for tup'ence, hot cross buns!
>
> Dust, O! Dust O! Bring it out today.
> Bring it out today! I shan't be here tomorrow!

THE DELIVERY OF ADCULT

◆ The billboard on wheels: earth-bound blimps and eyesores.

I sweep your Chimnies clean, O!
I sweep your Chimney clean, O!

Buy my Diddle Dumplings, hot! hot!
Diddle, Diddle, Diddle, Dumplings, hot!

Maids, I mend old Pans or Kettles,
Mend old Pans or Kettles, O!

Muffins, O! Crumpets! Muffins to-day!
Crumpets, O! Muffins, O! Fresh to-day!

Street cries and moving hats "set upon wheels" are no longer major conduits in modern Adcult. True, the urban bus has become a billboard. And the billboard plastered on a truck is making a comeback in cluttered cities (the sides of such rolling billboards are lit fluorescently and can change panels every ten minutes), and the human voice can still be heard on street corners.[1] But they are no match for ink and electrons.

With the advent of print and paste, signs moved to walls. From the late seventeenth century to the middle of the nineteenth the great cities of western Europe were nightly plastered over—sometimes twice a night—with what

---

1. In a sense, of course, advertising in various media is ancient. Commercial speech starts with the snake's spiel in the Garden of Eden, is heard in the cries of vendors in ancient Persia, is seen on walls of Pompeii as the marks listing prices of various prostitutes, is carried in our surnames (as with Smith, Weaver, Miller, Taylor, Baker . . .), and remains in the coats of arms over European hostelries with names like the Red Crown, the Gold Fox, and the Three Stars as well as in the symbolic images of the barber's pole or the golden balls of a pawn shop.

became known as posters. Seventeenth-century London streets were so thick with signs that Charles II proclaimed that "no sign shall be hung across the streets shutting out the air and light of the heavens." Although it was against the law, even Fleet Street Prison was posted. As the "post no bills" regulations took hold, posters became free-standing billboards. The "boards" grew so thick in America that people could barely seen Niagara Falls through the forest of Coca-Cola and Mennen's Toilet Powder signs. N. W. Ayer Company executives bragged that if all the boards they had erected for Nabisco were painted on a fence, the fence would enclose the Panama Canal on either side, from sea to shining sea.

What distinguishes modern advertising is that it has jumped from the human voice and printed posters to anything that can carry it. Almost every physical object now carries advertising, almost every human environment is suffused with advertising, almost every moment of time is calibrated by advertising.

Start the day with breakfast. What's on the cereal box but the Ninja Turtles, Batman, or the Addams Family? Characters real or imagined once sold cereal; now they *are* the cereal. Once Wild Bill Hickock, Bob Mathias, Huckleberry Hound, and Yogi Bear touted Sugar Pops or Wheaties. Now the sugar gobs reappear every six months, renamed to cross-promote some event. When the most recent Robin Hood movie was released, a Prince of Thieves Cereal appeared on grocery shelves. Alas, the movie did not show Mr. Hood starting the day with his own brand. But Kellogg has tried for this brass ring of promotion anyway. It has marketed cereals with Jerry Seinfeld and Jay Leno on the boxes and then gone on to buy commercial time on their network, NBC. It is of some comfort that while cereals sporting Barbie and Donkey Kong have gone stale on the shelves, the redoubtable Fred Flintstone and his Flintstones cereal survive.

Go to school. The classroom is the Valhalla of place-based media. Better than the doctor's office, the shopping mall, the health club, the hospital, and the airport, here you have the ideal—a captive audience with more disposable income than discretion. Advertising material is all over the place. For home economics classes Chef Boyardee supplies worksheets on how to use pasta; Prego counters with the Prego Science Challenge complete with an "instructional kit" to test the thickness of various spaghetti sauces. General Mills sends out samples of its candy along with a pamphlet, "Gushers: Wonders of the Earth," which encourages the kids to learn about geysers by biting the "fruit snack." Monsanto donates a video suggesting that the world cannot be fed without using pesticides; Union Carbide does the same, saying chemicals "add comfort to your lives." Exxon has an energy awareness game in which nonrenewable natural resources are not losers. K-Swiss sneakers provides shoes for participants in a video creation of an ad for . . . you guessed it. And Kodak, McDonald's, and Coca-Cola plaster a national essay contest about why kids should stay in school with corporate logos and concern. Clearly, one reason to stay in school is to consume more advertising.

The logical extension of such education is Christopher Whittle's (now Henry Kravis's) Channel One, which puts the video monitor in the classroom to extol the value of M&MS and Big Macs in exchange for a little information about world events. The prize for advertising in higher education should go to the Harvard professor who recently paid $600 to have a banner flown above Cambridge during class registration: SCI-A-17 NOON MWF SCIENCE CENTER HALL D—TRY IT. This noble attempt proved feckless. Only 110 students showed up for "The Astronomical Perspective," about 50 fewer than the previous year. No quid pro quo. Had he only promised to exchange something worthwhile, he might have succeeded. Perhaps substituting NO GRADE LOWER THAN A for TRY IT might have worked, even for Generation X.

Go shopping. The war, as they say, is in the store. Food shoppers make almost two-thirds of their buying decisions when they set foot in the aisle. Capitalizing on these last-minute decisions is why grocers don't alphabetize soup sections, why all the raisin bran cereals are not bunched together, and why high-profit toothbrushes are both nestled with toothpastes and stacked almost at random throughout the store. With more than fifteen hundred new items introduced to supermarkets each month, the need to inform and convince the querulous shopper of the new product is intense. The experience of food buying has become an advertising adventure.

A company called Ad-Tiles puts its ads on the floors in Pathmark stores, charging what amounts to 50 cents per thousand impressions. Flashing coupon dispensers are omnipresent, except near the upright freezers and open dairy case, because shoppers do not like to open doors to compare prices—too cold. They won't even open the door for coupons. The latest hot places for advertising are the checkout line and the shopping cart. The shopping cart, which revolutionized food shopping

• Back-scratching in action: the cozy relationship between sponsor and media.

In September, our new serials swept the ratings.

NBC's new shows #1

This fall, our favorite cereals sweep the country.

After getting off to a great start with our new series premieres, awareness of our returning shows gets a huge boost from our incredible Kellogg promotion. With 125 million NBC boxes on grocery shelves nationwide, it's easier than ever for viewers with great taste to dig into shows like *Seinfeld, Blossom, Saved by the Bell, Wings, The Fresh Prince of Bel-Air* and *The Tonight Show with Jay Leno*.

🦚 **NBC** *Marketing*

◆ Ideas better than the real thing: Checkout Channel and VideOcart. But why watch the ad channel after you've made your purchases?

as much as self-service, because it determined the amount of food a shopper could buy, has come alive. VideOcart is here, almost. This shopping cart has a six-by-nine-inch screen affixed to what used to be the kiddie rumble seat, and infrared censors on the ceiling cause it to flash ads, messages, and recipes as you pass various products. The same technology that scans the Universal Product Code on your can of beans now scans the shopper. You are the can.

Both resident geniuses of place-based media—Ted Turner and Chris Whittle—have experimented with "checkout channels," eye-level monitors that broadcast a continuous loop of tabloid news and commercials. Four thousand to five thousand supermarkets on one channel mean demographics better than *The Cosby Show*'s. Only a few crucial problems: the store personnel keep turning off the sound (a problem also faced by Whittle with Channel One), and—even more horrendous—the checkout line is where you go *after* you have made those hundreds of decisions. Turner lost about $30 million finding this out. NBC may have the successful system. Its Shoppers' Video monitors are scattered throughout the store and are soundless. A less expensive method would be to put advertising on the conveyor belt that carries groceries to the cash register.

Turn on your computer. Surely here is an ad-free environment, just you and your screen. Not quite. You can buy screen-saver programs in which the Energizer Bunny hops across your dormant screen or a pair of Nike shoes eternally treads through the pixels. And the minute you plug your telephone line into the modem, you're asking for it. The three commercial information networks—Prodigy, owned by IBM and Sears; America Online, owned by Apple Computer and others; and CompuServe, owned by H&R Block—are slowly opening their chips to advertising. Originally designed to be supported by line charges, the on-line services are begging for a little advertiser "support."

The users of these services have one thing in common: they buy computer gear. When users want to read news from *Time* magazine on America Online, they have to click past a window that announces, "Sponsored by Compaq." So what is Coors Light doing sponsoring the Coors Light Fan Pick Poll on Prodigy, a football poll of sixty-five sportswriters and broadcasters in which you can participate with a few strokes on the keyboard? Computer nerds also drink beer. Once you enter the poll, the Coors logos start scrolling down the screen. The only problem: an advertiser cannot *knowingly* sell beer to minors. Easy to solve: because Prodigy knows the ages of its users, all those younger than twenty-one see a public service announcement about the dangers of underage drinking.

The next network to fall to commercialization will be the Internet. A vast computer world, with roughly thirty million users from universities, businesses, and labs all over the world, Internet was once supported solely by federal funds. As the government cuts funds from the "high-speed data backbone," the support structure will increasingly be commercial. The signs along the superhighway already point to Adcult. Rupert Murdoch (a man with an almost unerring ability to predict new advertising media—he started the Fox network and satellite-beamed Sky TV) bought Delphi Internet Services, an on-line service that taps into Internet. A computer "magazine" called *Global Network Navigator and Marketplace* is already taking paid advertising. A few brave souls, lawyers by trade, have broken the unarticulated code of "netiquette" by soliciting business. Internet users, "residents of cyberspace" as they call themselves, have struck back. In an activity called flaming, they not only attack those who have been caught using the network to sell but also hector and sabotage the 800 numbers that are often used for replies and direct reams of blank paper through the offender's fax machine. But if Internet behaves like other media, the residents of cyberspace will find themselves being elbowed aside, especially if advertising can find a way to make the service easier or less expensive to use.

Go to a sporting event. It's football season. Let's go to a bowl game. Which one? Or which product? The Orange Bowl has become the Federal Express Orange Bowl, the Cotton Bowl has become the Mobil Cotton Bowl, the Sugar Bowl has become the USF&G Sugar Bowl, and the Sun Bowl has become the John Hancock Bowl. Not to mention the Sunkist Fiesta Bowl (now the IBM OS/2 Fiesta Bowl), the Mazda Gator Bowl (now the Outback Steakhouse Gator Bowl), the Sea World Holiday Bowl, the Domino's Pizza Copper Bowl, the California Raisin Bowl, and everyone's favorite, the Poulan/Weed Eater Independence

Bowl. For a while even the Heisman Memorial Trophy was up for grabs. Merrill Lynch paid $1.5 million for promotional rights but not for a name change. Not yet. No matter: Merrill Lynch already has a golf tournament.

What about college basketball? Coaches have been paid as much as $200,000 to insist their players all wear the same kind of sneaker. Athletes have become living billboards. Michael Jordan earned nine times his $3.9 million salary off court. Professional tennis players look like NASCAR drivers. Monica Seles earned $500,000 on a hair contract with Matrix shampoo, Perrier paid her $300,000 to wear a patch on her shoulder for a few years, and for $3 million she used Fila shoes, clothing, and a Yonex racket. When a lunatic stabbed her, the joke went, her sponsors screamed. Corporations spend almost $2.3 billion on sporting events; surely they ought to be able to dress the participants.

In the National Hockey League, referees are instructed to call penalties on players using equipment that displays the names of companies that have not paid the league for the privilege of advertising. Everyone knows about major league baseball stadiums, especially the ads that appear on the electronic scoreboards. But have you looked at a Little League ballpark recently? At least in baseball stadiums such as the Houston Astrodome, a black plastic sheet now covers the omnipresent Marlboro sign, and in Dodger Stadium and in Fenway Park cigarette ads have been totally banned from the scoreboards. The Little League doesn't have the Chevrolet Player of the Day, the Delco Play of the Game, and the Everready Relief Pitcher. Yet. Is there a sporting event not commercially sponsored? Just try to find it. The North American Croquet Association is sponsored by Rolex. The prize for the nastiest sponsorship surely was the Virginia Slims tennis tournament. It might have been better named the Emphysema Slims. Second prize: the Kool Jazz Festival. A celebration of respiratory prowess by the product that destroys it.

Take a trip. Get away from Adcult. Weren't we told in the famous Cunard advertisement that getting there is half the fun? Hop in a taxi. Some urban cabs have alphanumeric signs that scroll ten ads per minute across a panel on the back of the front seat. Gannett, the billboard-and-newspaper conglomerate, has been experimenting with installing these "electronic gutters" in subway cars and has contracted with the Transit Authority of New York to put them in six thousand cars. Nothing revolutionary here, just the electrifying of the advertising card, which has been a staple of public transportation since the first trolley. The company has also introduced what it calls the brand train and the brand bus in which a sponsor can buy all the ad space on a particular vehicle that runs a specific route. So Donna Karan's DKNY line has taken over an entire ten-car train that runs under Lexington Avenue on Manhattan's East Side, endlessly running beneath DKNY's superstore in Bloomingdale's. Gannett also installed radio equipment in bus shelters around midtown Manhattan for a news and business station. The New York

City Department of Transportation ordered Gannett to pull the plug—too much noise.

At the airport Turner Broadcasting will show you "free TV" on its Airport Channel, just as it attempted to do at the A&P with the Checkout Channel. Need money for the trip? Try the ATM machine. It will soon have ads in the space where it now proclaims, "Your transaction is being processed." Why waste space? Once on the plane *USA Today*, the newspaper published by the billboard company—Gannett—has Sky Radio. Your plane picks up a live audio signal from Gannett headquarters in Virginia, complete with eight 30- or 60-second ads per hour. Gannett's motto, The Business Traveler's Only Live Connection to the World Below, is really, The Advertiser's Only Live Connection to the Business Traveler. Like the in-flight magazine, this radio signal is for a captive audience coveted by hotel chains, car rental companies, computer makers, and vacation destinations. Many airlines now have a video presentation of the safety spiel that used to be done by a live flight attendant. Ads precede and follow the canned video spiel. When you pick up your luggage from the airport carousel, an operation called Revolving Media has contracted with airports to install CarroSell, an eighty-by-five-foot advertising screen mounted over the maw that spews your suitcase.

Is there an ad-free vacation destination? Hardly. An enterprising firm in Miami Beach has sold space on the wings and fuselage of a junked 727 jetliner sunk eighty feet off the coast to be used by sport divers. You can post your message for $9,000 a wing, $1,000 for a three-by-five-foot space, or $35,000 for the entire craft. Ads are on ski lift towers, on menus, beamed to clouds over San Francisco by laser, all over national parks like Yellowstone and Yosemite, and all over privately owned parks like Disney World and Six Flags. In fact, such parks are gigantic ads for the products of Disney and Time Warner.

Ads are all over the streets of New York, literally. Called "trashvertising" and usually pimping dial-a-porn or escort services, these ads are made to look like money or like American Express cards. Tourists pick them up from where they are scattered on the street. Locals fall for a variation involving the ad made to look like a parking ticket placed under the windshield wiper. Ads appear on the walls of buildings, not as posters but as graffiti called aerosol advertising. It is applied by the very same artists denied their subway cars. *Wild posting*, or *sniping*, refers to pasting ads on boarded-up construction sites. It's perfectly legal so long as it is not done on city property, as Benetton, Donna Karan, Giorgio Armani, and Calvin Klein all know.

Commercials are even making their way into restrooms. Here in the last refuge of privacy such cleverly named firms as Privy Promotions, In-Stall Ad Systems, and Headlines USA find a really captive audience for their framed ads, called indoor billboards in the trade. Beer companies have experimented with messages over urinals to the effect that it is now "time for more Coors" or "put used Bud here," but the idea has not caught on. However, the *Minneapolis Star Tribune* has had success advertising its singles columns in the bathrooms of trendy restaurants. So it is simply a problem of matching the message to the medium.

No destination is safe. The Russian government has even sold space inside Red Square. For something less than $1 million your message can be part of the May Day celebration. Coca-Cola and Pepsi are already in Pushkin Square. For $100,000 the side of GUM, the largest department store in the world, is yours. Lenin's tomb is off-limits, but above Lenin's tomb is OK. For about $30,000 you can float a blimp. Who's itching to get onto Russian space? The usual suspects: AT&T, Reebok, Sara Lee, and of course the ever-present tobacco companies.[2]

Finally, no matter where you go in this world or beyond, when you get home, your credit card bill for the trip will eventually appear. When it does, it may have that tear-off tag on the envelope upon which is printed yet another ad.

Almost as interesting as where advertising is, is where it might be. Here are some of the more interesting venues contributed by advertising men and women who make hundreds of thousands of dollars thinking up and trying out some of these locations:

- Subway tokens.
- The backs of chairs in commuter trains.
- The Gateway Arch in St. Louis.
- Postage stamps and paper currency.
- In place of the telephone dial tone.
- Polo ponies.
- The bottom of golf holes, to be observed while putting and then while removing the ball.
- Self-serve gasoline pumps. Messages scroll along with the amount of gas pumped.
- Rural mailboxes. Although the Postal Service prohibits advertising on boxes, John Deere has produced a green and yellow version that retails for about $50.
- Astronauts' uniforms.
- Postcards. Laden with advertising, they are given to patrons by restaurants.

2. Nor would you be ad free in outer space. For $500,000 NASA agreed that Columbia Pictures could cover a rocket with an ad for Arnold Schwarzenegger's *Last Action Hero* (the movie bombed before the missile flew). And Joel Babbit, an Atlanta ad exec, almost succeeded in launching a billboard high in the heavens. The space billboard was to be an unfolding screen set in geosynchronous orbit 250 miles above the equator; in the evening it would appear to be about the size of the moon—just right for a logo. The usual suspects were interested, but the U.S. Department of Transportation nixed the idea. Babbit went on to head Whittle's Channel One.

- School buses.
- Slot machines. Why should they come up cherries and oranges? Why not boxes of Tide?
- Catalogs. This has been done, most notably by *The Sharper Image*, but the reverse is almost as interesting—a recent *Lands' End* catalog included a story by David Mamet.
- Video games. "Cool Spot" is a game like "Pac Man," except it stars "Spot," the 7-Up mascot; "Yo! Noid" is a game centered around the Domino's Pizza character. "Mick and Mack: Global Gladiators" has a black hero who battles pollution. To get from level to level the player has to collect golden arches passed out by a gate-tending Ronald McDonald.

And here are some suggestions about where to put ads from my students, who make nothing . . . yet:

- Dolls that speak when you pull a string.
- Elevators. The buttons would light up LED displays.
- Football helmets and as football team names—Exxon Oilers, Charlie the Tuna Dolphins, Jolly Green Giants.
- Red lights, within the blink.
- Hospital ceilings.
- Shower heads.
- Compact discs.
- Food, such as logos burnt onto toast served in a restaurant.
- Condoms.
- Airplane window shades.
- The bottoms of jars.
- Tennis courts.
- Checks.
- Bar stools.

It may be of some comfort to critics of this use of the human imagination that a new advertising medium has begun appearing *inside* advertising agencies. Called Media News, it appears on a never ending fifty-four-by-eight-inch alphanumeric display similar to the Dow Jones market ticker. Running across the board is information interspersed with thirty seconds of commercials. Advertisers pay $5,000 for thirteen weeks of ads in a medium described by its creators as "invasive without being aggravating." Poetic justice?

The rise of place-based (as it is known in the trade), in your face (as it is experienced), or new media (as it is presented to the public) follows the principle that where blank space exists, there shall advertising be. The triumph of Adcult is attributable not so much to new products as to new media reaching new audiences. Each new invasion by commercialism is greeted with an out-cry, followed by tentative acceptance, assumption, and expectation. And finally, of course, neglect.

To appreciate how advertising went from being the cart to the horse is to appreciate how profoundly radio and television differ from other media. As in the child's game of paper-rock-scissors, each print medium, be it newspapers, magazines, trade cards, billboards, or whatever, had strengths that over-powered the others. And each had weaknesses. Adcult introduced a new medium—electrons swimming about in the electromagnetic spectrum—that trumps all the rest, at least thus far. The obvious distinction between print and electronic media is that more plasma can always be added to print: more sheets, bigger pages, more inserts, more billboards. But it is impossible to increase the broadcast hour. It will always have just sixty minutes.

But there are ways around this too, such as expanding the advertising pod, introducing infomercials, and product placement. More important, electronic media vastly increase the reach, the tonnage, the penetration of commercial communication, drawing millions of new audience members together to be shipped off for first a word, then an image, from the sponsor. Almost everyone can hear and see; relatively few can or will read. Because this shift from word to sensation occurred so rapidly halfway through the twenti-eth century, and because the shift has been so profound in carnivalizing cul-ture, it might be well to set it in a historical context.

PRINT AND BOOKS

If it plese ony man spirituel or temporel to bye ony of two and thre comemoracios of Salisburi use enpryntid after the forme of this present lettre whiche ben wel and truly correct, late hym come to Westmonester in to the almonestrye at the reed pale and he shal have them good chepe. Supplico stet credula. [Please do not remove this notice]

• WILLIAM CAXTON, HANDBILL ADVERTISING PUBLICATION OF RULES
FOR EASTER POSTED ON LONDON CHURCHES, 1478

Although the history of the courtship of advertising and newsprint is rather like the history of Donna Julia in Byron's *Don Juan*—"And saying she would ne'er consent, consented"—the history of advertising and book publishing is far more amiable. Initially, publishing and advertising were joined at the press. Book publishers, from William Caxon to modern university presses, have advertised forthcoming titles in the flyleaves and on dust jackets. Although we may be startled when Christopher Whittle markets his Larger Agenda Series of books (Big Ideas, Great Writers, Short Books) by inserting advertising in what is essentially a long magazine article, he is actually behaving like a traditional book publisher. When Whittle published William Greider's *The Trouble with Money*—ninety-four pages of text and eighteen pages of Federal Express ads—book reviewers turned away, aghast. But when Bradbury & Evans published Charles Dickens's *Little Dorrit* in 1857, no reviewer or reader blanched at seeing the bound-in ad section touting Persian parasols, smelling bottles, portable India-rubber boots, and the usual array of medicines.

Books were not historically an advertising medium for a simple reason: there wasn't much to advertise, and once there was a surplus of mass-produced objects at the end of the nineteenth century, there were less expensive media to use. The death knell to book advertising is still being rung not by publishers but by the postal service. Put an ad in a book and it no longer travels at fourth-class book rate but at third-class commercial rate. A prediction: advertising will return to books. UPS, FedEx, and the other commercial carriers make no such distinction about content, only about weight and size.

Ads are not in books for another reason. Since Dr. Benjamin Spock fought Pocket Books to have cigarette ads removed from his baby-care book in the late 1940s, the Authors' Guild has inserted a no-advertising clause in its boilerplate contract. What would it take to reverse this? Not much, I suspect. To find out, I wrote this letter to university press editors. I thought they would be the most sensitive to this question, because they are often in financial straits (and, as opposed to trade publishers, they always answer their mail, no matter what you ask them):

Dear [University Press Editor],

I need your help! I am writing a book on advertising in American culture, and I'm especially interested in how commercial messages find their way into new spaces.

One of the few venues relatively free of advertising is the university press book. My question is: what would it take for you to let a little bit of advertising appear inside your "product"? Or would this be like being "just a little pregnant"? Many university presses will announce other books on the jacket covers, and (like PBS) they will allow public thanks to be made to the Mellon Foundation (or the Pepsi Foundation) for Subventing This Most Important Publication. But would you allow Pepsi-Cola to put a little trademark image on the copyright page of one of your books? What if Pepsi totally paid publication costs for The Book We've All Been Waiting For, and what if this book had nothing to do with soft drinks? Assume that you wanted to publish this book, and it would sell only a few hundred copies, and, if you didn't publish it, this information won't get out . . . ever. And it is about your favorite subject with lots of color plates, all prepaid.

Continuing with this hypothetical: What if Podunk State University Press or, better yet, Cambridge University Press started allowing little Pepsi logos to appear inside their books—not just on the copyright page but, say, on the chapter heads? And what if Pepsi said they would fund some of your other list with no images in exchange for good position in a few? I know this is a slippery-slope question, but I'm interested in knowing whether you ever think about these issues and, if you do, how so. Commercial publishers do. Not only are trade books cross-marketed with other products like movies and cosmetics, but a few years ago a Beth Ann Herman put a Maserati "whose v-6 engine had two turbochargers, 185 horsepower and got up to 60 in under 7 seconds" into her novel Power City in return for a publication party at Wilshire Maserati in Beverly Hills. Who gets hurt? The movie industry claims that product placement keeps the ticket prices down. You know your books are too expensive to begin with, only libraries can buy them. The "cost externalization" (as the economists say) of advertising will lower the price, expand your market, enlarge knowledge.

I know these questions are a nuisance but if you ever think about these matters—in fact, if you've ever had to deal with these matters—I'd be most interested in hearing how they got resolved.

The responses were instructive. The premier presses acknowledged the possibility that advertising could subsidize their product. The idea that advertising could drop the price of a $40 book to, say, $30 was at least worth considering. These presses see themselves as selling books to libraries and to readers. However, to the middle-echelon presses the idea was sacrilegious. How could they compromise their academic integrity? They sell primarily to academic libraries, and these libraries are notorious for paying outrageous prices for sometimes less-than-mediocre product.

Still, the future is clear. There is not much to separate "Made possible by a grant from the National Endowment for the Humanities" from "Made possible by a grant from Coca-Cola." Getting inside the text will probably be the work of conglomerated book publishers and will be done in the name of making the product more affordable to all. University presses will follow, from the top down. After all, this is exactly what happened with newspapers.

Print and Newspapers

It is the advertiser who provides the paper for the subscriber. It is not to be disputed, that the publisher of a newspaper in this country, without a very exhaustive advertising support, would receive less reward for his labor than the humblest mechanic.

• ALEXANDER HAMILTON, FOUNDER OF THE *NEW YORK EVENING POST*, 1803

In the language of Madison Avenue, newspapers would have eaten the advertising lunch of book publishers, if only books had had one. But books were barely able to advertise themselves. What did "advertisements" in early newspapers advertise? Ship landings, forthcoming plays and books, lost slaves, apprentices and dogs, freak shows, and, most important for the future of branded goods, patent medicine. Sugar, coffee, liquor, biscuits, hats, and whatnot were all sold unbranded until the late nineteenth century. Not only were there few surpluses (ads for acreage were common in America, rare in England), and not only was there little disposable income, but the medium was prohibitively expensive. Rag paper, slow-drying ink, and hand presses made newspaper reading a community activity, usually limited to a pass-around sheet at a coffee house. Until the mid-nineteenth century, books often carried more advertising than newspapers.

The concept of news as a commodity is a modern development, in part a result of advertising's need for a stable context. The fears of the Tories that the Whig "rags" would destabilize their power resulted in the confiscatory tax acts of the early eighteenth century. Although they thought it unfair to tax the paper or the content, the British taxed the advertisements. The stamp tax on English newspapers and magazines, although small (amounting to one pence per page and one shilling per page of advertising, regardless of size), was essentially ruinous. In the United States no tax had been applied, and newspapers flourished. In 1765 the British attempted to export the tax and, in a sense, wrought the First Amendment to the Constitution, which makes no distinction in personal, political, and commercial speech—something advertisers still mention in reverential tones.

All free-speech panegyrics aside, newspapers revived in the late eighteenth century more because the price of production fell than because the hackles of right-thinking people rose. Given a choice between inexpensive entertainment or expensive freedom, we know how we have responded. More bread and circuses. The major beneficiaries of the Stamp Act in Britain were the forerunners of place-based, in-your-face media: the handbill, the broadside, trade cards, the billboard, and especially the poster. Like fluids dammed up in one conduit, all manner of advertising effluent appeared after the stamp taxes were imposed. London was literally papered over nightly with posters; sandwichmen appeared, often in sequence (forerunners of Burma Shave); and even animals were festooned with messages on their sides and tails. In fact, signs were so numerous in London that in 1839 the Metropolitan Police Act attempted to control their proliferation with predictable failure. The tension was relieved, however, by changes in the media.

Within thirty years the price of newsprint plummeted almost 50 percent. In 1850 the French developed chlorine to bleach rags. Until then paper makers could use only white cloth. Now almost all fabric could be "pulped." Next came the invention of machinery to make paper in endless sheets. By 1875 wood-based paper, fast-drying inks, and the rotary press had made the production of newspapers so inexpensive that publishers *had* to find a large audience or the economies of scale would work in reverse. Once it was possible to produce eighteen thousand impressions per hour instead of three thousand, with no difference in cost, everyone's best interest would be served by expanding circulation. Thus newspapers had plenty of space for advertising and plenty need for it. Ironically, the recalcitrant parties were the publishers. James Gordon Bennett, publisher of the *New York Herald*, the leading advertising medium in the United States, kept advertisers penned up by the infamous "agate rule." He rigorously restricted ads to single-column width and 6-point type. At first this produced tiny ads, but eventually advertisers managed to rise from this Procrustean bed. The results can still be seen occasionally in the classified sections.

♦ How to look big in small type: in the *New York Herald* in 1885 and in the *New York Times* today.

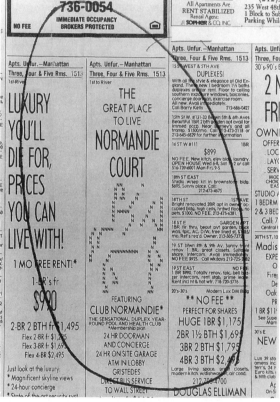

Such advertising was all over the front and back pages of American newspapers. It was as short lived as it was ugly. Advertising would break free of the agate rule as it would almost all other restrictions. Not only were such contortions an embarrassment to publishers who had tried to pretend ads were secondary, but they encouraged readers to look at exactly those spots to see clever new ways of expression. In addition, and in retrospect far more important, the appearance of arresting print imagery encouraged a new livelihood—the buying and selling of space in a number of papers for running identical messages for the same products.

In the mid-nineteenth century Volney Palmer in Philadelphia sent letters to postmasters to be forwarded on to local newspapers offering to buy space sight unseen each week for an extended period of time. He then made the promise that has profoundly affected each new medium since. He would pay cash up front. Palmer then marked up the cost of that space and sold it to a client. At almost the same time George Rowell did the same thing in the Boston area: he bought "squares" of blank space at wholesale, sold them at retail.

Thus the advertising agent came into being, and thus began the bizarre system of remuneration that paid the agent a percentage of the purchased space. Once the newspapers admitted they preferred not to sell their space on their own—such commerce was still the dirty little secret of publishing—they happily paid a commission of about 15 percent to someone who would. From this evolved the pattern of the media's in effect *paying* the agent to sell their space. Only later did agents suggest to their clients that they could also fill the space with varying copy. In an apocryphal advertising story of the early days a young salesman reported to his agency boss that he has saved the client money by negotiating a lower ad rate. The boss replied, "You're fired."

Until the Civil War the major nationally branded products were patent medicines. The sons of Lydia E. Pinkham had more to do with the dispersion of American culture than did the sons of the pioneers and the daughters of the Revolution put together. Her Vegetable Compound (composed of almost 40 percent alcohol along with a root mixture of laudanum), and those of her numerous competitors, produced almost half the national advertising in the 1890s and hence almost half of agency income. The outrageous claims of many of today's over-the-counter nostrums (fast, Fast, FAST!) find their inspiration in the early free-for-all of unregulated promise-the-moon advertising. Soon there was yet another piper to pay. As media became more dependent on advertisers, ad agencies lobbied for something far more subtle and important—control of content—not because they had a political agenda but because they wanted particular audiences to see their ads.

By the 1880s advertisers had begun to exercise their power. The sectionalization of the newspaper and the institution of the "jump" (or broken story, which forces the reader to leave the first page and plow through pages of ads to find the continuation) were innovations demanded by advertisers. In the economic battles of Joseph Pulitzer and William Randolph Hearst the lofty principles of newspapering were let go like a smelly fish. Newspapers could make money not by increasing circulation but by increasing the advertising load. First, they allowed display advertising, then they cut loose whole sections, supposedly to meet reader demand but in reality to service advertisers. So groceries sponsored food sections, automotive sections went to car dealers, real estate to brokers, and travel to agents. Later, of course, entertainment sections would carry movie ads and the Sunday TV books would list the week's shows. Initially, the newspapers resisted both, just as they had refused to print radio schedules in the 1920s, but the control was moving from editor to publisher to advertiser.

Does this catering to the advertiser continue? I will discuss actual influence on content later, but in terms of format the answer would have to be a resounding "you bet." Although it is unfair to pick on *USA Today*, this Gannett newspaper has had a profound influence on what newspapers look like. *USA Today* aspires to be what newspapers have feared most—and to which they have lost most of their readers and advertising—in the last forty years: television. That's one reason it's so colorful. The other is that color is the greatest single determiner of recall in print advertising. Color ads produce sales 83 percent greater than black and white, 74 percent of readers want color, and, more important, 90 percent of readers aged eighteen to twenty-five want color. Twelve percent of American papers could publish in color in 1979; now more than 97 percent of newspapers have color presses. Even the *Wall Street Journal* will succumb. Perhaps *USA Today* is an unfair example of an advertiser-driven newspaper. After all, it even sells the ears, the upper righthand tabs of the inside sections (themselves appropriately ad driven: Money, Sports, and Life). Those little corner triangles now carry long-running ads for Northwest Air and Wrigley chewing gum. I called the *New York Times* to ask if it would ever consider doing this. Absolutely not. But of course they've sold agate at the bottom of page one for years.

How exempt is the *Times* from commercial pressure? One of the major reasons the New York Times Company purchased the *Boston Globe* was not only to provide its advertisers greater penetration of New England but to get access to the *Globe*'s color press technology. The *Times* had its own color presses coming on line, but they were difficult to operate with long press runs. In 1992 the *Times* was gradually working color into the *Book Review* before spreading it to the rest of the paper. And what of the inside sections? Read between the lines of this interview between *Advertising Age* and A. M. Rosenthal (who presided over the revolution at the *Times* in the 1970s as the paper went from two to four sections):

> We satisfied advertisers and potential advertisers by giving them what we promised to give them. In the news sections, we promised to give them the best news we had. In the "Living" section, we said we'd give them the best food reporting they could ever have. And we did. In order to get advertisers we gave them more circulation. We gave them whole new audiences. We invented "Science Times" for the computer audience. "Science Times" was my baby. The business department was not hot for it, they didn't want it. They wanted a fashion section on Tuesdays, but I felt that would tip the paper and I fought it. And in the end, I went ahead with "Science Times." I knew it was a Timesy subject. But there were no ads. Then one day a man came in to me from the advertising department and he said, "Abe, would you consider having a computer column?" I said, "Computer column? Yeah." And he said, "I think it might bring in a little advertising." I said, "Next Tuesday." And we did. I always believed, you know, if somebody gives you a good idea, take it right away and say you're glad you thought of it. But he was right. And we got a lot of computer advertising.   • (Wolf 1993:25)

Little wonder that Mike Doonesbury in August 1993 offered this pitch in Gary Trudeau's strip. In the Sunday strip, Mike, who works at an ad agency, appears first; the succeeding panels open with these words: "Your Ad Here,"

"This Space Available," "Your Personal Message Here," "Your Classified Ad Here." Although Mike is humorously offering about half his cartoon space for rent, newspaper publishers seriously offer about 70 percent of theirs. Just as the five hours of the Super Bowl include only about twelve minutes of actually moving the ball, so the daily city edition of the *Times* carries only a few pages of "news" relative to the bulk of ads. Nationally, 80 percent of all newspaper revenues come from advertising: 52 percent from retailers, 35 percent from classified, and 13 percent from national clients like airlines.

Of course, without advertising the *Times* would cost more than $4. The only way to increase revenues without upping the price, or adding advertising space, is to increase circulation. First-copy costs are stupendous. Ironically, economies of scale are such that to increase the "reach" of this medium and lower your last-copy cost, you also run the risk of alienating core readership. This Hobson's choice for the publisher has proved good for the advertiser. It means that papers tend to self-censor to provide a bland and unobtrusive plasma as they seek to maximize their profits. The blandness of American newspapers today is partially the result of this economic behavior.

Print and Magazines

The first thing ye know here won't be as manyu pages iv advertisin' as thre are iv lithrachoor. Then people will stop readin' magazines. A man don't want to dodge around through almost impenethrable pomes an' reform articles to find a pair iv suspenders or a shavin' soap.

Another thing, th' magazines ought to be compelled to mark all lithrachoor plainly so that th' reader can't be deceived.

• FINLEY PETER DUNNE, "MR. DOOLEY ON THE MAGAZINES," 1909

If the relationship between advertising and newspapers is like that of Don Juan and Donna Julia, advertising's relationship with magazines is that of Petrucchio and Kate. Before magazines capitulated at the turn of the twentieth century, they fiercely defended their pages from commercial contamination. George Rowell, the Boston advertising agent, stood dumbfounded as Fletcher Harper spurned his offer of $18,000 for the back page of *Harper's*. Rowell was buying space not for some outrageous patent medicine but for the Howe Sewing Machine. Another time Rowell asked Harper for circulation figures, only to be told they were none of his business. In addition, to punish the effrontery Harper refused to accept any of Rowell's placements for months. When *Harper's* did accept ads for products other than its own books, it put them in an advertising ghetto in the back pages.

Harper's behavior was by no means extreme. For a number of reasons he felt he had to defend not only his "privileged space" but also his readers. It is hard for us today, when magazines are sold as disposable products that are discounted, reformatted, and repackaged almost monthly, to realize that magazines were once treasured. They were saved to be passed on to future readers. In the eighteenth century and most of the nineteenth the relationship between editor and reader was one of sage and student. Magazines mimicked not newspapers but books. In fact, magazines are still called books in the trade. The intimate connection that joined author and reader in the "gentle reader" motif was carried across media from the novel to the magazine. In the United States many early magazine publishers were book publishers—*Scribner's*, the *Atlantic*, *Harper's*—who used the monthly or bimonthly magazine as a way to maintain this contact. Publishers saw themselves as gatekeepers and often even had their own columns, with a title like "At the Editor's Desk," from which they commented on the passing scene. Because their income was almost totally subscription based, it was little wonder that Harper could spurn Rowell.

There were other reasons for the magazine's arm's-length relation with commerce. Where newspapers were local, magazines were national. Until branded products were distributed across the reading area, it made no sense to advertise. Like the railroads, which carried products to the hinterlands, magazines would become a central part of the distribution stream. Because books were one of the few truly national products, many pre–Civil War magazine ads were what were called reading notices. These bits of puffery were scattered through magazines, usually touting books from a publisher who had contracted with the magazine for space. In fact, the first ad in an American magazine was an 1871 four-line reading notice in the *General Magazine and Historical Chronicle*. Often books carried reciprocating ads for magazines. But not always. Sometimes the magazine publisher just wanted to pass along hints for good reading to his gentle readers.

War probably has the greatest influence on media and hence on advertising. As we will see with radio in World War I and television in World War II, the Civil War transformed magazines. For the Civil War left in its wake a vast surplus of goods: canned goods, clothing, shoes, guns, blankets . . . that had been produced by machinery that now could not be turned off. New branded products were appearing using the same machine technology. Products like Royal Baking Powder, Ivory Soap, and Bakers chocolate, then Kodak and Gillette, and finally all manner of branded objects like bicycles and farm implements needed a national medium for efficient promotion. Always in the wings, waiting patiently to buy whatever space it could, were Lydia E. Pinkham and her cohorts. The patent medicine industry grew like Topsy as developments in health care spread what had been learned in battlefield hospitals. By the 1870s *Harper's*, the *North American Review*, *Scribner's*, and their ilk were almost as heavy with "medicine" ads as physicians' journals are today.

Why and how magazines tumbled into the pockets of advertisers is an interesting prefiguring of what would happen with radio and television. At the end of the nineteenth century, advertising agencies —most important were J. Walter Thompson and N. W. Ayer—were pleading with magazine publishers not just to let them out of the advertising ghetto but also to allow them to help expand and direct the magazines' circulation. National manufacturers understood that they had to advertise to take advantage of the economies of mass production. The Postal Act of 1879 had created a special mailing rate for magazines, allowing them to be distributed at advantageous rates even though they carried advertising. And, most important, the economy crashed in the 1890s.

Up in Maine, Frank Munsey profoundly changed American culture. One of his magazines, *Munsey's Magazine,* was headed to bankruptcy. The magazine was going deeper into debt with each issue. Munsey already owed more than $100,000, so if it failed, he was stuck. If he continued to print, however, he would be stuck worse. In an act of intuitive genius in 1893 Munsey cut the price of his magazine from 25 cents to 10 cents and upped the circulation from forty thousand to two hundred thousand. What made up the difference was advertising. He maintained his ad rates at $1 per one thousand readers and guaranteed the audience. For the first time, instead of delivering his magazine to subscribers, he was delivering his readers to advertisers. It was a lesson not lost on the *Ladies' Home Journal, Cosmopolitan, McClure's,* and others, which quickly followed suit. Not only did ads rapidly start moving to the front of the book, and not only were they being placed in the middle of editorial material, but they became the profit center of publishing, replacing subscriptions. As the great benefactor of Munsey's action, Cyrus Curtis, told an audience of advertisers, "Do you know why we publish the *Ladies' Home Journal*? The editor thinks it is for the benefit of American women. That is an illusion, but a very proper one for him to have. But I will tell you; the real reason, the publisher's reason, is to give you people who manufacture things that American women want and buy a chance to tell them about your products" (Wood 1958:211).

In 1900 *Harper's* carried a greater volume of ads than in all its twenty-two previous years. George Rowell had the last word. Fletcher Harper was now dependent on advertising. This process didn't stop. In 1908, 54 percent of *Harper's* 137 pages carried advertising; by 1947, 65 percent of its 208 pages had been given over. Curtis had claimed that once he got a circulation of 400,000 for his *Saturday Evening Post,* he could afford to give the magazine away to anyone who would pay postage. He was right. The magazine grew so plump on advertising that it was bought, newly published but undistributed, as scrap paper. By December 7, 1929, the *Post* weighed in at two pounds. Its 272 pages contained 21 hours of reading matter, showcased 214 national advertisers, and took in an ad revenue of $1,512,000. The battle for ad placement inside the covers was fierce. The Campbell Soup Company scored a coup when it contracted to perpetually purchase the first page immediately following the editorial matter, a place still called the "Campbell Soup position" because it gets the greatest attention.

Publishers tried anything that would increase the effect of the advertising: common page size; the halftone image; process engraving; ads separating text in innovative ways; cartoons; cover illustrations—so important for newsstand sales—by the likes of Frederick Remington, James Montgomery Flagg, N. C. Wyeth, Cole Phillips, and Maxfield Parrish; the use of black-and-white photography, then color, sweepstakes, and finally discounted subscriptions. Magazine publishers even submitted to the very indignity Rowell suggested to Harper: they established the Audit Bureau of Circulation to provide agencies with the numbers that they needed in order to run the magazine business.

Have matters changed as magazine publishing has been subsumed into Adcult? Have a look at the *New Yorker*, which is to magazines what the *New York Times* is to newspapers. When the magazine was founded, both Harold Ross, the editorial power, and Raoul Fleischmann, the publisher, hoped to avoid the fall into the advertiser's pocket. In 1933 they published a Code of Practice. In it they articulated the highest ideals: "Great advertising mediums are operated for the reader first, for profits afterwards." They rearticulated this credo in an interoffice memo: "We must all bear in mind always that our first obligation is to our readers and our second obligation is to our present and past advertisers" (Peterson 1979:55). They were not kidding. The *New Yorker* turned down ads that were in poor taste and for "unappealing" products. It was said that the magazine did not sell advertising space, it accepted it. Fairfax Cone, of the famous Chicago agency Foote, Cone & Belding, used to tell the story of how the *New Yorker* refused his sweater ad for Marshall Field & Company because it had already run an ad for a similar sweater from a different store.

There is no doubt the *New Yorker* had become predictable by the 1980s, even stuffy. Eustace Tilley, the February cover dandy, really seemed to be in charge. The magazine was in trouble for more than predictable content. In the golden days of the 1960s the magazine had carried more ad pages than any other consumer magazine, an average of 115 per issue. The number had fallen to the upper thirties. Si Newhouse, who had purchased the magazine from Fleischmann, brought in a book editor, Robert Gottlieb from Alfred A. Knopf, but things only got worse. E. B. White wannabees were still writing thirty-thousand-word articles on grain, it was running too many "a friend writes . . . " pieces, and it was featuring a growing diet of postmodern fiction that simply could not be read in the bathtub. Other magazines, like *New York* and *Vanity Fair*, were poaching the *New Yorker*'s readership. Although Newhouse's Advance Publications does not make its financial statements public (nor do most magazine publishers; if they are public companies like Time Warner, they bunch them together so the advertising agencies will not know profit and loss, although they will know circulation), industry observers calculated that the magazine was losing $10 million a year.

Newhouse could have done what Frank Munsey did and cut his subscription rates, but instead he replaced Gottlieb with Tina Brown. The publishing world of Upper Aesthetica wailed that the barbarians from Lower Vulgaria were on the loose. Brown would tart up the magazine: it would soon resemble the gossipy *Vanity Fair* with its adulation of celebrity, the writing would degenerate into fawning breathlessness, there would be too much color and too many photographs, the covers would be sensationalized (remember, this was the woman who ran the cover of a naked and pregnant Demi Moore), and, especially, Brown would sell out to the advertisers. After all, at *Vanity Fair* Brown had courted Calvin Klein with a famous fawning puff piece and supposedly pried his infamous "poly-bagged outsert," a 116-page jean ad, away from *Rolling Stone.*

Since Brown took over in October 1992, the taste of the *New Yorker* has moved a bit downtown. Eustace Tilley would have arched his eyebrows over her covers that show such edgy scenes as a weird hippy in a hansom cab with the high-hatted driver traversing Central Park, a black woman kissing a Hasidic man, or a kid in Arab garb jumping onto a sand figure of the World Trade Center. He might also be distressed by full-page comics and full-page photographs, the replacement of the coy table of contents with an informative one, the punchy writing, and the topicality of subject matter. Tina Brown's first table of contents and the facing page, her visibility in direct mailings, and the willingness to cross-market the magazine say much about the powers of Adcult.

But Eustace Tilley would have to confess that Tina Brown has saved the magazine. Her style has brought in advertising. Her first issue carried eighty-five pages of ads—almost double the previous year's issue—from the likes of Calvin Klein, Ralph Lauren, and Elizabeth Arden. She has changed the audience. According to Simmons Market Research, readership is up 13 percent from the Gottlieb era; more important, median household income is up 12.5 percent to $61,515; more important still, the median readership age has dropped to 46.1 from 47.7. And most important of all, the magazine increased ad pages 16.9 percent while raising the base rate. Because some 60 percent of magazine revenues are from advertising, the Talk of The Town is the talk of the street or, better yet, the talk of Madison Avenue.

That newspapers and magazines are, in the current bafflegab of modern times, members of a victim class is arguable. They are remnants of a print culture in which selling was secondary to informing. Survivors have replaced their interest in their reader with the more modern view of the reader as commodity. Like the electronic media, print has become but a subdivision of the conglomerate—huge networks like Scripps-Howard, Time Warner, the Tribune Company, the New York Times Company, News Corp., the Washington Post Company, Times-Mirror, Meredith, Advance Publications, and Paramount Communications that own newspapers, magazines, television and radio stations, and sometimes movie studios and sell advertising space in all their properties. Because advertising flows to the medium that provides the target audience at the lowest cost, the consolidation of print into more efficient oligopolies is one result of the rise of Adcult.

◆ Tina Brown
takes over the
New Yorker and
Eustice Tilley
takes a rest.
Highcult enters
Adcult.

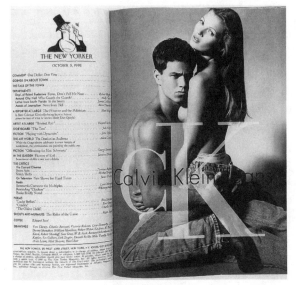

*Hold the presses...we have a great deal
for James B. Twitchell!*

James B. Twitchell
English Dept
University Of Florida
Gainesville, FL 32611-0000

◆ Even the cover is for sale: not a single fold-out but a French door.

The struggle to find the largest targeted audiences has led to two interesting extremes. On one hand are magazines that are pure advertising, like *Colors* from Benetton, *Le Magazine de Chanel*, or *Sony Style*, which remove the line between advertising and content so that you cannot tell what is text and what is hype. On the other extreme are magazines like the reincarnated *Ms.* or *Consumer Reports*, which remain ad free for political or economic reasons. Meanwhile the rest of magazine culture aspires to the condition of women's magazines, in which the ratio of advertising space to print space is about ten to one and to the editorial condition of newspapers, which is as bland as vanilla.

PRINT AND TRADE CARDS

It will cure entirely the worst form of Female Complaints, all Ovarian troubles,
Inflammation, Ulceration, Falling and Displacements of the Womb and the consequent
Spinal Weakness, and is particularly adapted to the Change of Life. It removes faintness, flat-
ulency, destroys all craving for stimulants, and relieves weakness of the stomach. It cures

Bloating, Headaches, Nervous Prostration, General Debility, Sleeplessness, Depression and
Indigestion.

• TEXT SIDE OF A TRADE CARD FOR LYDIA E. PINKHAM'S VEGETABLE COMPOUND, 1880

Print, no matter how it is configured, is usually an inefficient advertising form
for most Fast Moving Consumer Goods. Not only do you have to be literate
to experience it, but you can always turn the page and escape. Not so the electronic media, especially in the halcyon days before the radio "scan" button
and the TV remote-control clicker. However, there was a quasiprint medium
along the way to Adcult that should be considered, if only because it shows in
slow motion how energetic and explosive advertising can be when it carries
only its own weight. The trade card is the forgotten cousin in the media family, the missing link, living at the edge of old-fashioned print and new-fangled
electrons. Although the newspaper and magazine have to carry the weight of
news and information, the trade card was a pocket billboard.

The trade card was the first of the "free" entertainments. The modern
business card is essentially an announcement of where you and your service
are located. The reverse side is blank. What a waste of space. In the eighteenth
century the "reverso" often carried engraving appropriate to the information
side. As engravers developed their craft, some of them—William Hogarth, for
instance—produced such fine engravings that the cards were valued even
then as collectibles. In the 1790s a Bavarian inventor learned that he could
vastly expand the artistic possibilities by using specially prepared blocks of
limestone, a greased crayon, and water. The engraver could draw rather than
carve the images. By the 1820s lithography had replaced engraving. It was easier, faster, and far more expressive. It was also more expensive. The innovations in paper and printing that revolutionized publishing also helped the
trade card. But what revolutionized lithography and transformed magazines
and newspapers was the application of color. Chromolithography allowed the
mass production of images using different colors from differently inked
printing stones.

Trade cards were produced by the thousands. Once the lithographic
"stones" were replaced by zinc plates and steam power applied to the presses,
trade cards were produced by the hundreds of thousands by the 1880s.
Because newsprint was so expensive and because magazines and newspapers
were still hesitant to sell their space to any commercial interest (let alone to
any company of questionable pedigree), companies with newly branded
products started using the cards as hand-to-hand advertising. Who was first
in line? As usual, the patent medicine companies.

The cards were distributed by drummers, who carried packages of the
cards along with the products. The cards would be there on the counter of
your local general store, free for the taking. Merchants liked them because
their names were often printed on the back, and the companies liked them as
a way of branding parity items like biscuits, soap, flour, and the like and

because the cards showed retailers that the manufacturers cared enough about them to advertise their services. Children were the major collectors of the cards. Precursors of Saturday-morning television ads, the cards often alerted children that a word to their mothers might be in order if they wanted her to buy a particular product. Manufacturers later stuck the cards in the packaging of products as part of a series to be collected. Many early brands of cigarettes sold because the smokers cared more about collecting cards—called stiffeners because they held the package upright—than favoring a particular taste. The cards featuring buxom burlesque queens were so popular that they sprang loose to become "bachelor cards" that collectors had to purchase, as well as small calendar cards, a vestige of which can still be seen on garage walls today as the girlie calendar. Still later, companies mailed decorated trade cards to customers as a way of saying thanks. From this came the modern tradition of sending Christmas cards, a rare example of a commercial practice co-opted by individual use.

Many cards are works of high lithographic art. The most arresting are for patent medicines, in part because creating scenes of utopian good health can be so colorful and in part because there were so many competitors that the advertising had to be eye catching. By the 1880s the patent medicine industry was spending almost 40 percent of its gross on advertising, producing more than half the cards in circulation. Because the medicines were indistinguishable, the cards had to innovate. Like the blue jean advertisers today, companies had little to lose by being outrageous. Next in popularity was thread, a product for which branding is especially crucial. After thread came soap, which

◆ Quid pro quo in action: amusement on the front of the trade card, ad on the back.

We will not weary you with statistics
telling how Messrs.

J. & P. COATS

make their

BEST SIX-CORD SPOOL COTTON,

or how much they make daily, neither will we presume to give an opinion as to its quality. It is more important for you to find out:

Whether the thread is strong and will save you time and annoyance?

Whether it will run on your Sewing Machine?

Whether the colors will match all the fashionable shades, and work well on silk goods?

The only possible way to arrive at the truth is to

Use the Thread Yourself!

You will then know, why it is called

BEST

SIX-CORD SPOOL COTTON.

had the same problem, with Ivory, Pears', and Sapolio in a fierce battle, and finally the commercially prepared foods like the breakfast cereals of Post, Quaker, and Kellogg as well as the machine-packaged foods of Swift and Libby, McNeill & Libby. These brands, many of which are now household names, were created not in print but on the backs of trade cards.

The trade card disappeared almost as quickly as it had come. It was doomed for a number of reasons: as pulp-based paper led to lower printing costs, magazines started accepting advertisements; photography and later halftone printing allowed high-quality images to be mass-produced on inexpensive stock; postal regulations reduced fees on second-class mailings so that in the 1880s magazine circulation increased by almost 100 percent; and printers soon learned how to mass-produce lithographed illustrations that could be bound into the magazine during the print run. The descendants of the trade cards remain now, almost totally free of their commercial roots, as Christmas, birthday, and Valentine's Day cards, as well as illustrated postcards and advertising cards distributed free in big-city restaurants.

But what really doomed the advertising trade card was one of the central forces in creating Adcult. The makers of branded products learned at the hands of ad agencies that you do not advertise to the retailer if you can advertise to the end-user. This lesson was one of the crucial turning points in the rise of Adcult and would become central in the development of electronic media. In the old days a customer went into the store and asked the store manager for a product: "Give me some soap." If the drummer had done his job, he would have "beaten the drum" for your product. The storekeeper would say, "Here, have some Sapolio." The trading card encouraged this by associating the store with the product. Alas, this interchange gave storekeepers financial power over the producer. Storekeepers could pocket the added profit of the producer's mass production and advertising expenses by raising the markup *in* the store. In Adcult the object is for customers to walk into the store and say, "Where is the Sapolio?" and turn on their heels if not satisfied. From the manufacturer's point of view the key is to force storekeepers to stock the manufacturer's branded product and to make the storekeepers pay the highest wholesale price.

If you want to see this early Adcult interaction unfolding today, look at the numerous ads for pharmaceutical products flooding print media. Whereas the drug companies used to target the pharmacy or the doctor for prescription drugs, now they have wised up and are heading for the end-user. If they are successful, the patient approaches the doctor and says, "I need Rogaine. I need Proscar. I need Prozac." There is a downside in this interchange, however, *if* storekeepers can use the manufacturer's advertising to advantage. Witness the success of Wal-Mart. The genius of Sam Walton was that he realized that the store as store is unimportant. Who cares if the store name is Sears or Sam's? Walton prevailed by carrying branded products but always at the lowest price. Make your deals with the manufacturer, not with the customer, but let the manufacturer do all the advertising. Walton rarely advertised his stores, and he never passed judgment on what they sold or tried to predict what they might sell. What he advertised was "everyday lowest price."

ℛADIO AND ADVERTISING

One of the chief pretenders to the throne of God is Radio, which has acquired a sort of omni-science. . . . I live in a strictly rural community and people here speak of "The Radio" in the large sense, with an overmeaning. When they say "The Radio" they don't mean a cabinet, an electrical phenomenon, or a man in a studio, they refer to a pervading and somewhat godlike presence which has come into their lives and homes.

• E. B. WHITE, "SABBATH MORN, 1933

If surplus is the mother of advertising, war is the mother of surplus. This statement is as simpleminded as it is true, for what it takes to fight a modern war is the production of certain otherwise useless objects in such quantity that you can last longer than your opponent. Alas, when the conflict is over, the market for these products is glutted. Now the commercial battle begins because industry needs to get rid of the surplus. Whereas the Civil War produced a surplus of what are now ordinary items of underwear, canned food, and utensils, the First World War produced a surplus of technical things like gears, bearings, binoculars, engines, gunpowder, and radio receivers. Although the story of how those receivers were disbursed has been told before, it is usually told in terms of American industry applying its willpower to overpower the patent contentions of various inventors or to manipulate the votes of politicians. So the story that we usually hear centers on industrial development (or capitalist exploitation): the role of AT&T, Westinghouse, General Electric, and their conglomerated offspring, RCA, the Radio Corporation of America. A tale less often told centers on Madison Avenue and the never ending role of a burgeoning Adcult in colonizing new media.

To treat symptomatic benign enlarged prostate:
Only one medicine can shrink the prostate.

PROSCAR.
(FINASTERIDE)

Until recently, there wasn't a medicine that could help the condition known as symptomatic benign prostate enlargement or BPH. But now there is PROSCAR, the first oral prescription medicine that can shrink an enlarged prostate.

However, it is important to know the following: PROSCAR doesn't work for everyone. Even though your prostate may shrink, you may not see an improvement in urinary flow or symptoms. And you may need to take PROSCAR for 6 months or more to see whether it helps you.

How PROSCAR can shrink an enlarged prostate.

As a man ages, a key hormone can help cause the prostate to grow. PROSCAR actually blocks the production of this hormone, so it helps shrink the prostate to a smaller size in many men. As a result, some men treated with PROSCAR experience an increased urinary flow and an improvement in urinary symptoms.

Why you should see your doctor soon.

Your doctor has several options for the treatment of symptomatic BPH: watchful waiting (monitoring the condition with regular checkups), medication, or surgery. It's important to see your doctor because the problem doesn't usually get better by itself. In many cases, the prostate continues to enlarge and the symptoms may get worse. So if your urinary symptoms are bothering you, have your family doctor or a urologist assess your condition and ask if PROSCAR is an appropriate treatment for you.

It is also important to have regular checkups. *While benign prostate enlargement is not cancer and does not lead to cancer, the two conditions can exist at the same time.*

Remember, only a doctor can evaluate your symptoms and their possible causes. So, if your urinary symptoms are bothering you, don't wait any longer. You may find that your enlarged prostate can be made into a smaller problem.

For more information about prostate enlargement and PROSCAR, call 1-800-635-4452 today.

TABLETS
PROSCAR 5mg
(FINASTERIDE)

◆ MERCK

©1993, Merck & Co., Inc.   Please see patient information on the following page.   J3P088/7015-PSA781

◆ The holy grail of Adcult: encouraging consumers to insist that they be supplied with the branded product.

Broadcasting is to media what mass production is to objects. For about thirty years in the middle of the twentieth century, *broad*casting, literally the casting out of seed in handfuls rather than the placing of it in rows, created a radically new culture, Adcult. Although the hands that cast the seed belonged to the transmitter owners of the nascent "networks," to be known acronymically as NBC, CBS, and finally ABC, the power behind the hand that determined what seed to use and where to throw it was the advertising agencies'. These institutions essentially ran the show. What happened with radio is the crucial step in the development of Adcult and in the modern carnival culture that followed. For decisions made by advertising agencies about how to use radio waves determined how television would be developed, and, as television goes, so goes culture—all culture, all around the world.

After World War I, Westinghouse had a materiel surplus—tubes, amplifiers, transmitters, and crystal receivers. The navy had encouraged wireless as a way to communicate with ships at sea (the *Titanic* tragedy in 1910 might have been avoided had wireless operators been on duty), and the army had used it as a way to direct troops in the trenches (using barbed wire as antennae). Once the war was over, Westinghouse was stuck with tons of radio materiel. So in November 1920 it started radio station KDKA in Pittsburgh. Once transmitters were built, Westinghouse could unload its receiving apparatus. And you could even make a receiver at home. All you needed was a spool of wire, a crystal, an aerial, and earphones—all produced by Westinghouse. The hobbyist supplied the patience and a cylindrical oatmeal box. By July 1922 four hundred stations had sprung up.

No one seemed to care what was on the air so long as something was. When stereophonic sound was introduced in the 1950s, the most popular records were not of music but of the ordinary sounds of locomotives and cars passing between the speakers. People used to marvel at the test patterns of early television, and monks doubtless stood in awe in front of the first printed letters. Great plans were being hatched for radio, however. Universities would take advantage of this new way to disperse their respective cultures by building transmitters. A utopian world was in the offing, a glimpse of which you can see in the 1926 cover of *Radio Broadcast* magazine.

The problem was that everyone was broadcasting on the same wavelength. When transmitters were placed too close together, the signals became mixed and garbled. AT&T suggested a solution. The company would link stations by using its telephone lines, and soon everyone would hear clearly. AT&T envisioned tying some thirty-eight stations together in a system it called "toll broadcasting." The word *toll* was the tip-off. Someone was going to have to pay. The phone company suggested that time could be sold to private interests and called this subsidy "ether advertising." The suggestion was not an immediate success. Secretary of Commerce Herbert Hoover, considered a presidential possibility, warned that it was "inconceivable that we should allow so great a possibility for service . . . to be drowned in advertising chatter" and that if

HOW TO BUILD THE R. B. "UNIVERSAL" RECEIVER

How "Television" Works—More About the R. B. "Lab." Circuit—What the Future Holds for the Radio Industry—How the Barometer Affects Radio—A Non-Radiating Circuit for Beginners—What's the Matter With Announcers?

Doubleday, Page & Co., Garden City, New York

◆ The 1926 cover of *Radio Broadcast*: the utopian vision of mass media precedes the sad reality of commercialism.

presidential messages ever "became the meat in a sandwich of two patent medicine advertisements," broadcasting would be destroyed (Barnouw 1978:15). Such Cassandras were uniformly ignored. This would never happen. The universities would see to it with their responsible use of education.

In 1922 AT&T started WEAF (for wind, earth, air, and fire) in New York. WEAF tried all kinds of innovative things, even broadcasting live from a football stadium. The station tried letting companies buy time to talk about their products. Such talk was always done in good taste: no one mentioned where the products were or offered samples, store locations, comparisons, or price information—just a few words about what it was that the advertiser offered—and such discussions never ever were held during the "family hour" (from 7 to 11 P.M.) At 5 P.M. on August 28, WEAF even let a Mr. Blackwell step up to the microphone and say his piece about a housing development. He spoke only once. This is what he said, and it is every bit as important as "Come here Mister Watson, I need you," only a bit longer. It was to be the "May Day" distress call of high culture.

It is 58 years since Nathaniel Hawthorne, the greatest of American fictionists, passed away. To honor his memory the Queensboro Corporation has named its latest group of high-grade dwellings "Hawthorne Court." I wish to thank those within sound of my voice for the broadcasting opportunity afforded me to urge this vast radio audience to seek the recreation and the daily comfort of the home removed from the congested part of the city, right at the boundaries of God's great outdoors, and within a few miles by subway from the business section of Manhattan.

This sort of residential environment strongly influenced Hawthorne, America's greatest writer of fiction. He analyzed with charming keenness the social spirit of those who had thus happily selected their homes, and he painted the people inhabiting those homes with good-natured relish. . . .

Let me enjoin upon you as you value your health and your hopes and your home happiness, get away from the solid masses of brick, where the meager opening admitting a slant of sunlight is mockingly called a light shaft, and where children grow up starved for a run over a patch of grass and the sight of a tree. Apartments in congested parts of the city have proved failures. The word "neighbor" is an expression of peculiar irony—a daily joke. . . .

Let me close by urging that you hurry to the apartment home near the green fields and the neighborly atmosphere right on the subway without the expense and trouble of a commuter, where health and community happiness beckon—the community life and the friendly environment that Hawthorne advocated. • (Archer 1928:397–98)

Three weeks later the Queensboro Corporation had sold all its property in Hawthorne Court in Jackson Heights, Queens.

Nibble, nibble. The mice would not be kept long from this kind of cheese. William Rankin, an ad man, bought one hundred minutes of time to discuss Mineralava moisturizing soap, just to see if radio was for real. It was, and he soon enlisted his other clients, like Goodrich and Gillette, to have a go at broadcasting their message. AT&T kept the cheese squarely in view. The phone company even insisted on paying the 15 percent commission directly to the advertising agency, just as had been done with print media. In so doing AT&T reinforced the connection between the agency and the medium, at the expense of the connection between the agency and the client. Not to put too fine a point on it, AT&T essentially bribed the agencies. As opposed to print, there was no dickering, no paperwork, the commission was yours if you got the client to buy the time. The station would even throw in an announcer. Remember, this was a way to sell radio equipment, not some sponsor's surplus product.

The most pressing problem was to find out what listeners wanted. When David Sarnoff's NBC, the broadcasting arm of RCA, absorbed AT&T's WEAF, he pledged to "invest in the youth of America" with "better programs permanently assured." He kept his word. When NBC went on the air November 15, 1926, it was with a four-hour extravaganza from the grand ballroom of the Waldorf Astoria. Sarnoff engaged Walter Damrosch to conduct the New York Symphony and the Metropolitan Opera's Tito Ruffo sang the arias, Will Rogers impersonated Calvin Coolidge, and soprano Mary Garden warbled "Annie Laurie" from her apartment in Chicago. But to be honest, he kept his word only for a while. Sarnoff thought that if you had good programs, you could sell a lot of radio sets. He should have listened to Frank Munsey. What you need to do is to forget selling sets and start selling advertising. Sarnoff learned this the hard way. He had to compete with William Paley.

The bloom was already off the radio rose by the late 1920s. A new development, popular music, had elbowed aside classical, and advertisers had cleverly been attaching their clients' names to these musical groups. There were the Goodrich Silvertown Orchestra, Cliquot Club Eskimos, Gold Dust Twins, Ipana Troubadours, A&P Gypsies, Kodak Chorus, but this gratitude factor, or indirect selling, didn't do more than put your name out there. It didn't *sell* your product. What it was selling was popular music. The key to advertising success is to make your customers force your product into the store. Worse yet, the American Society of Composers, Authors, and Publishers (ASCAP) started to demand license fees for playing this copyrighted music, something Mozart and Beethoven didn't do. If you wanted to broadcast popular music, you would have to pay. This economic conundrum could be resolved by educating listeners to crave the supposedly self-evidently superior classics or by giving the public more of "what it wanted" but somehow increasing advertiser control.

William Paley, suave, elegant, Ivy League–educated son of a Jewish cigar merchant, knew behind which door was the lovely lady and behind which door was the tiger. Although he would spend much of his life pretending otherwise, he confessed in 1934 that a radio program "must appeal to either the emotions or the self-interest" of a listener, "not merely to his intellect." Hence radio broadcasters "cannot calmly broadcast programs we think people ought to listen to if they know what is good for them" (Smith 1990:91). The Tiffany Network—

✦ September 1926: RCA promises in this full-page ad, "If the public will make known its views to the officials of the company . . . we are confident that the new broadcasting company will be an instrument of great public service."

CBS—was built precisely by pandering to the tastes not only of the common listener but to the advertising agencies.

After the stock market collapsed in 1929, Paley purchased the United Independent Broadcasters, a money-losing loose federation of stations headquartered in Manhattan. Only one show in five had a sponsor. Coming from a tobacco family, he knew firsthand that advertising was central to the branding of what are essentially interchangeable products. One of his first acts was to sign up Paul Whiteman and his symphonic jazz orchestra. Paley paid Whiteman the unheard-of salary of $5,000 a week and $30,000 to the band to create *The Old Gold Program.* Paley knew how to sell tobacco. You don't sell cigars, you sell Old Gold cigars. He knew this because his family company had sponsored a half-hour radio show called *The La Palina Smoker* in which a sultry Miss Palina cooed the virtues of men who smoked the Palina (from *Paley*) cigar. Within months business had boomed. Sales jumped from four hundred thousand cigars a day to one million.

Now in New York the first thing Paley did was to visit John Orr Young and Raymond Rubicam to find out if radio had a future as an advertiser-supported medium. They introduced him to Tony Geohagan, an expert on radio, and from there he made his way to arguably the most incredible man in the history of American popular culture, George Washington Hill. Hill controlled the American Tobacco Company. Much maligned (Hill was the prototype for any number of villainous roles in the movies, most notably as played by Sidney Greenstreet in the 1947 adaptation of Frederick Wakeman's *The Huckster*), he did have some eccentricities. He spat, poured water on underlings, and decorated his Cadillac limo with Lucky Strike posters. But he too knew how to sell tobacco. NBC thought he was a vulgarian. Paley, desperate for advertisers, found him less vulgar. He even gave Hill a tip: cigar smokers liked military music. Why not sponsor a military band? Hill bit, later claiming the idea as his own. Hill sponsored *The Cremo Military Band Program* on CBS. Between numbers the announcer not only mentioned the price (breaking a taboo) but repeated this delightful slogan: "There is no spit in Cremo." Not tasteful perhaps, but effective.

Over at NBC Sarnoff was still thinking of radio as a piece of furniture. Paley knew better. This thing was a programming device, and if you could program it successfully, you would capture an audience that you could then rent to advertisers. It behaved like a magazine, except that everyone could read it at the same time. One of Paley's habits was to keep buying stations, especially in the West. Whereas NBC forced its affiliates to buy programs, CBS would provide a few hours of programming free to its stations—"sustaining programs"—in return for which they would carry the network advertising. Although it might seem that *sustaining* referred to the individual stations, in truth it referred to the New York headquarters. Paley's idea of public service was William Paley.

Paley also instituted an option clause that gave CBS the right to commandeer local programming if New York could sell the time for the network. So

Paley could promise a time, say, 8 P.M. Friday to an advertiser with the guarantee the ad would be heard all around the country. Meanwhile NBC had to negotiate each and every time with each and every affiliated station. Sponsors love nothing more than the knowledge that they control a certain amount of space or time each week. Agencies love it even more. After all, by the way they are compensated this means a steady cash flow from their client. They produce one ad but are paid as if they had produced hundreds.

Paley understood the radio food chain. Let the agencies create the programs for the client. Guarantee them their time. Let them have not just time blocks, as with the *Maxwell House Hour, Palmolive Hour,* the *General Motors Family Party,* and *Cities Service Orchestra,* but give them entire nights, as Ford was considering with Sunday. As a service to advertisers, CBS pioneered block programming in which all the shows of a type appear together, as with soap operas at midday or action-adventure at early evening. When William Benton of Benton & Bowles integrated commercials with the show, Paley embraced it. So you have the *Palmolive Hour* with Paul Oliver and Olive Palmer. Paley knew better than to second guess the client's choice of genre. For instance, the soap opera, the hard-sell creation of Blackett-Sample-Hummert, provided hours, days, weeks, years of programming. Paley embraced it. He was not a gatekeeper, he was a programmer. If people wanted escapist fare like police shows, quiz shows, bebop; if they preferred singing commercials to symphonic music; jive-talking announcers to high-culture "introducers," fine— "give" it to them. If DuPont wanted to sponsor a self-serving history show called *Cavalcade of America* put together by BBDO, that never mentioned gunpowder, blacks, labor unions, and women, so be it. If the client wants to have singing commercials integrated into the show so that the original words seem to refer to some product, that's all right too.

"Giving the public what it wants" had its price. Like television today soon the messenger was being blamed for the message. Commercial radio broadcasting was "dumbing-down" American culture with its incessant repetition of mindless humor, maudlin sentimentality, exaggerated action, and frivolous entertainment. Proving yet again the power of Gresham's Law when applied to culture, radio programming by the 1930s was selling out to the lowest common denominator. Typical of highcult outrage was James Rorty, erstwhile BBDO copywriter-turned-snitch for such leftward-leaning periodicals as the *New Republic*:

> American culture is like a skyscraper: The gargoyle's mouth is a loudspeaker [the radio], powered by the vested interest of a two-billion dollar industry, and back of that the vested interests of business as a whole, of industry, of finance. It is never silent, it drowns out all other voices, and it suffers no rebuke, for is it not the voice of America? That is this claim and to some extent it is a just claim. . . . Is it any wonder that the American population tends increasingly to speak, think, feel in terms of this jabberwocky? That the stimuli of art, science,

religion are progressively expelled to the periphery of American life to become marginal values, cultivated by marginal people on marginal time?

• (1934:32, 270)

But wait! What about those universities? Weren't they supposed to make sure the airwaves would be full of "the best that had been thought and said?" Although there were more than 90 educational stations (of a total of 732) in 1927, by the mid-1930s there were only a handful. What happened? The university stations had sold their licenses to executives like Paley, and these stations had been merged into the burgeoning networks—called nets or, better yet, webs—emanating from Manhattan. In one of the few attempts to recapture cultural control from commercial exploitation, the National Educational Association (NEA) lobbied Senators Robert Wagner of New York and Henry Hatfield of West Virginia to reshuffle the stations and restore a quarter of them to university hands. The stations would forever be advertising free, making "sweetness and light" available to all. The lobbying power of the NEA met the clout of Madison Avenue. No contest. The Wagner-Hatfield bill died aborning, defeated almost two to one.

One reason the Wagner-Hatfield bill floundered so quickly was the emergence of a new cultural phenomenon, the countrywide hit show. Never before had an entertainment been developed that an entire nation—by 1937 more than three-quarters of American homes had at least one radio—could experience at the same time. *Amos 'n' Andy* at NBC had shown what a hit show could do. Sarnoff thought a hit was the way to sell radios, and he was partially right—more than one hundred thousand radios were bought just to listen to the minstrel antics of white men in black face. But Paley knew better. Hits could make millions of dollars in advertising revenue. Although not yet called a blockbuster (that term would come with the high-explosive bombs of World War II), the effect of a hit was already acknowledged as concussive. One hit could support hundreds of programming failures.

If agencies were having trouble finding hits, the network could help. Paley knew more than they did about the tastes of the audiences he could deliver. The network could even offer legal advice. Paley encouraged Correll and Gosden (Amos and Andy) to incorporate, break their NBC contract, and enter a long-term contract with him. For a while Sarnoff thought he could put a stop to talent raiding by promising not to raid CBS. But Paley wouldn't stop. After he signed NBC prize Jack Benny, Paley and Sarnoff met. Sarnoff said, "Why did you do this to me, Bill? I thought we had an agreement not to raid each other's talent." After a pause, Paley replied curtly, "I needed them."

Paley never forgot that above the broadcast studios at Radio City was the Sponsor's Booth. An early CBS sales brochure, "You Do What You're Told," prepared to convince agencies of the directive power of radio, made the pitch:

When the dentist says "Open your mouth," you open, don't you? When your wife says, "Tuck her in tight," you tuck, don't you? So too with "don't go yet"—"shake hands with Jim Brown"—"come right in."

We may not be happy about doing what we're told, it may not make us feel good, but, the brochure continues, now in nursery-rhyme fashion:

> Seven times
> Eight times
> Nine times out of ten
> People do what they're told
> > • (Barnouw 1978:188)

The key to radio selling, which Paley never tired of stressing, was that the reader can turn a magazine page with ease, but it is an effort to turn the dial. In the generation before the transistor, and two generations before the electronic search and scan buttons were developed, once listeners had turned the machine on and tuned to your frequency, they were yours. By 1938 radio had surpassed magazines as a source of advertising revenue.

CBS would provide listeners for the advertiser, and it would guarantee they were really there. No other network was so obsessed with audience measurement. The ad agencies had forced newspapers and magazines to measure their circulations. Let other networks wait for the Crossley Reports; Paley would deliver such information (albeit often rejiggered with a CBS bias) as a service. In the 1940s he hired Frank Stanton from the N. W. Ayer Agency, because Stanton was one of the first to really find out where the audience was at particular times. Stanton had written on audience measurement at graduate school, he had attempted to construct a crude audiometer complete with waxed tape and stylus, and he had built prototypes and surreptitiously installed them in listeners' homes. More important, he took the next step. He would drop by later to interview listeners and compare what they claimed to listen to and what they did indeed listen to. The two bits of information were often contradictory. They still are. Almost half as many people who claim to "regularly watch" PBS really do. Radio could sell only if there were listeners, and CBS had to produce them. It did. CBS finally displaced NBC as the number one radio network in 1949, capturing twelve of the top fifteen prime-time shows—an advantage later carried over to television.

His largely fictional 1979 memoir *As It Happened* notwithstanding, Paley had no such talent for television. He vetoed the first version of video put forward by his own resident genius Peter Goldmark, and he had no intuition for programming images. He even despised his own hit show of the 1970s, *All in the Family*. No matter. The game was the same. Plant some entertainment, harvest an audience, take the audience to market, sell it to the highest bidder. Other programmers were not so sanguine. In 1927 Lord Reith said at the founding of BBC radio, "He who prides himself on giving what he thinks the people want is creating a fictitious demand for lower standards which he will then satisfy." Aim high, improve standards, speak the proper BBC language, dress your radio news reader in formal attire, noblesse oblige. William Paley cast his lot with the Will Rogers school of thought: no one ever went broke underestimating the taste of the American consumer. Rupert Murdoch, Paley's cultural successor, continues the defining sentiment of Adcult: "Anybody who, within the law of the land, provides a service which the public wants at a price it can afford is providing a public service" (Whitney 1989:C24).

In truth, Paley or no Paley, television never had a chance to be anything other than the consummate selling machine. It took twenty-five years for radio to evolve from wireless; it took only five years for television to unfold from radar. And although it took a decade and the economic depression to allow advertiser control of the radio spectrum, it took only a few years and economic expansion to do the same with television. Advertisers rested during the war. They had no product to sell. No surplus means no advertising. Even President Truman had mentioned the unmentionable. Advertising costs should be deleted as a deductible business expense or at least reduced from its 100-percent range because there was no need to advertise. In Adcult the loss of deductibility has always the been the cross to the vampire. Given a choice between paying taxes or using those monies to buy advertising, albeit worthless advertising, most companies would choose the latter. At least such advertising can make the company feel good about itself.

As a consequence the agencies offered to turn their attention to the war effort if Truman would turn his elsewhere. The War Advertising Council encouraged the purchase of war bonds, donating blood, the thrill of enlistment, and, most interesting in terms of how they would later behave, encouraged women to enter the workforce. All pro bono, as the modern reincarnation of the War Council, the Ad Council, likes to say, almost truthfully. At the same time, to protect their billings, the agencies encouraged their clients, plump with cash that they did not want taxed as excess profits, to continue to buy media space and fill it at least with high-minded programming. So GM supported the NBC Orchestra, U.S. Rubber backed broadcasts of the New York Philharmonic, and Allis-Chalmers underwrote the Boston Symphony. The agencies still collected their 15 percent like clockwork. To be sure, they did some product advertising of the "There'll be a Ford in your future" variety, but most of it was half-hearted. Some print work was sensational, but most war advertising did not go into print because paper was crucial war materiel. Most of it went into radio.

Although radio did not just survive but prospered during the war, the new kid on the block was too tough to beat. From the first narrow broadcast, television was going commercial. The prophetic Philo T. Farnsworth presented a dollar sign for sixty seconds in an early public demonstration of his television system in 1927. Once Hazel Bishop became a million-dollar company in the early 1950s, the result of television advertising, the direction of the medium was set. It would follow radio. Certain systemic changes in both broadcast media did occur; most important, the networks recaptured programming from the agencies. Although this shift away from agency control

took scandals to accomplish (most notably the quiz scandals rigged by ad executives, not networks), it would have happened anyway. Simple economics made it less expensive to sell time by the ounce than by the pound. The nets could make more by selling minutes than by selling half- or full hours. Only the behemoths could afford time chunks for their *Philco Television Playhouse, Kraft Television Theater, Firestone Hour,* or *U.S. Steel Hour.* What about all the little companies? Magazines maximized ad revenues by selling space by the partial page; why not television?

Paradoxically, the ad agencies balked at first. The ad industry was probably the most conservative social force of the 1950s. It was no happenstance that much of the red scare and McCarthyism came from the rep ties and wing-tips of Madison Avenue (Young & Rubicam, to be specific). But once the agencies realized that giving up programming was in their best economic interest, they fell in line. After all, more sponsor buying means more agency billing, means more income flowing down Madison Avenue. Having the networks produce the shows meant that they also had to produce and guarantee the viewers. In the polite language of the time these guarantees were called assurances. The Federal Communications Commission (FCC) didn't mind how time was sold. Since 1934 the federal agency had almost always been compliant if a change would benefit an expanding marketplace. Now the nets

• World War II is on. Read this in 1942 and you'll never again complain about the lousy service on the New Haven Railroad. And after the war you'll buy a car from GM.

could sell one-minute insertions, six per hour, and they could sell them as part of a time period, not part of a show. The agencies could resell them to anyone, just as newspaper space brokers did in the nineteenth century. The motto of this new medium became Programs Are the Scheduled Interruptions of Marketing Bulletins. How could it be otherwise?

TELEVISION AND ADVERTISING

In day-to-day commerce, television is not so much interested in the business of communications but in the business of delivering audiences to advertisers. People are the merchandise, not the shows. The shows are merely the bait.

• LES BROWN, *TELEVISION: THE BUSINESS BEHIND THE BOX*, 1971

Call television whatever you want—"idiot box," "American dada," "Charles Dickens on LSD," "plug-in drug," "chewing gum for the eyes, "the bland leading the bland," "summer stock in an iron lung," "dream machine," "vast wasteland," "white noise for the brain,"—this electronic medium is the greatest advertising medium ever concocted, bar none.

Television is *the* primary force in Adcult. Whereas growing up generations ago was defined by a progression of books read, for my parents by movies seen, for those of us born since World War II it has been marked by a progression of television jingles memorized. Print took about two centuries to gain currency as communal memory, photography was in general use after 1900, the telephone took half a century to become part of everyday life, radio was absorbed in thirty-five years and movies in twenty. Television happened overnight. At some mysterious point in the 1950s television ceased to be just an odd-looking gizmo—a radio running a picture track—and entered the bloodstream. It became part of our nervous system.

In our culture most people watch television for most of their "free" time. After sleeping and working, watching images on a video tube is what we do with ourselves. It is our favorite way to pass time. More than 95 percent of American households have at least one television set, and it is on more than six hours a day. We spend the equivalent of a day a week watching it. Well over eighty million households have this thing as part of their lives, and asked if they would give up the thing or a family member, most respond that the thing stays. More American households have televisions than have indoor plumbing. The New York state legislature passed a bill stating that television is a "utensil necessary for a family." The experience of watching this utensil has become the social and intellectual glue that holds us together, our "core curriculum," our duomo. Television has co-opted many of the ceremonies of American life. Religion, politics, and sports have gone into the box. "Did you see . . . ?" has replaced "Do you know . . . ?" "Did you read . . . ?" or "Have you heard . . . ?" Television displays most of what we know and much of what we believe.

And who decides what is displayed? For a while the networks had in-house censors. No longer. The only gatekeepers are the advertising agencies.

They have their own ever alert watchdogs whose job is not to protect the viewer but the sponsor. The Advertising Information Service, which is owned by twenty-one large advertising agencies, employs twenty people to screen shows for problems. Examples of what they do: a scene in which wild dogs chase a girl on an episode of *Little House on the Prairie* was cut because one of the sponsors was Puppy Chow. No cat food commercials appeared on *Alf*, because the alien threatens to eat the family cat. General Motors wants to be sure that none of its commercials is in the neighborhood when Michael Moore is touting his anti-GM movie *Roger and Me.* The Advertising Information Service is not in the least concerned about the steady infiltration of product placement in prime-time television. Quite the contrary. Its staff checks to be sure that Coca-Cola has a red coke machine in the series *TV 101*, that Alf is eating only Hershey bars, that Oneida silverware is identifiable on the tables of *Dynasty* and *Dallas*, and that Budweiser beer is drunk at Roseanne's house, whereas Stroh's is served over at *Cheers.*

This all sounds rather ominous to those who vibrate while reading *Brave New World*, but I think it is not. The agencies have no agenda other than to assure the sponsor that the network is providing the audience as promised. Audience share is the commodity that ABC, CBS, NBC, and Fox sell—not the shows. Or, seen another way, production companies sell video sequences to the networks, which broadcast them in order to rent the attention of the audience to advertisers. No one in the business pretends otherwise. Robert Niles, vice president of marketing for NBC, puts the matter like this: "We're in the business of selling audiences to advertisers. They [the sponsors] come to us asking for women 18 to 49 and adults 25 to 54 and we try to deliver" (Harmetz 1986:21). Niles's predecessor, Sonny Fox, now an independent producer, makes the point more politely at a lecture series sponsored by the Annenberg School at the University of Southern California: "The salient fact is that commercial television is primarily a marketing medium and secondarily an entertainment medium" (Andrews 1980:64). And Roger King, in charge of syndication for King Brothers (*Wheel of Fortune, Jeopardy*), contends, "The people are the boss. We listen to the audience, see what they want, and try to accommodate them. I know it sounds simplistic, but that's exactly what it is" (Dunkel 1989:80). Or here is Arnold Becker, erstwhile vice president for research at CBS: "I'm not interested in culture. I'm not interested in pro-social values. I have only one interest. That's whether people watch the program. That's my definition of good, that's my definition of bad" (Andrews 1980:64).

Just as tax collection is the unacknowledged heart of government, audience measurement is the heart of Adcult. It starts with Rowell's *Directory* for newspapers, continues to the Starch Ratings and Simmons Market Research for magazines, the Crossley and Arbitron surveys of radio, and comes full flower with the Nielsen ratings for television. Because the networks cannot depend on copies sold, coupons returned, or gross receipts at the box office, programmers have to guess at the audience. In radio days AT&T noted that calls dropped 50 percent during *Amos 'n' Andy,* and water departments found that pressure decreased in the evening on the half hour, but these were hardly sophisticated counters. In the mid-1930s two professors at the Massachusetts Institute of Technology (MIT) developed an ingenious device called the Audimeter that measured where and when the dial on a radio was moved. Each time the dial was turned, a mark appeared on a moving spool of paper so a history of specific listening habits could be constructed. Not only could the Audimeter provide a quantitative measure of audience, it could also tell who was listening to what. Hooking the meter up to Junior's set, or to Granny's set, would produce a different chart and let a station know what percentage of its audience was working class, male or female, adolescent, retired, or whatever profile it wanted.

In 1936 A. C. Nielsen purchased the Audimeter, and the history of Adcult was forever changed. Nielsen gathered and sold audience profiles. Because broadcasters are in the business of selling the attention of an audience to advertisers, here was a way to tell where the audience was and how long it would pay attention.

Nielsen was soon able to determine precise audiences using what still seems a ridiculously small sample. The Nielsen rationale: imagine 100,000 beads in a washtub; 30,000 are red and 70,000 are white. Mix them thoroughly, then scoop out a sample of 1,000. Even before counting, you are sure that not all beads in the sample will be red. Nor would you expect the sample to divide exactly at 300 red and 700 white. The mathematical odds are about 20 to 1 that the count for red beads will be between 270 and 330—27 percent to 33 percent of the sample. This is called a rating of 30, plus or minus 3, with a 20 to 1 assurance of statistical reliability.

Nielsen deals with two sets of numbers: ratings and shares. A rating is the percentage of the total television households in an area that are tuned in, whereas the share indicates the percentage of viewers already watching who are tuned to a particular program. Advertisers can now know within an hour how large their audience was. Although some find it hard to accept the idea that a sample of three thousand families represents two hundred million viewers, statisticians respond that the next time your doctor wants to do a blood test, don't let her take only that smear—make her take all of it.

The A. C. Nielsen Company always makes clear that it does not provide a pure rating but rather a "statistical estimate." Nielsen also makes clear that the process is not at all like polling, which requires prediction. Nielsen has no interest in how an audience plans to act, or expects to act, or pretends to act; it wants only to calculate the act itself. The networks, in consultation with the agencies, have five age categories in their demographic analysis: up to 11 years of age, 12–17 years of age, 18–34, 35–55, and older than 55. The heaviest watchers are the youngest and oldest viewers, but unfortunately for TV critics, they are the smallest consumers. Those with the most disposable income are aged

35 to 55, but those who are most willing to part with it are aged 18 to 34. In the 1950s only those aged 35 and older had access to sets and so programming was for them. Essentially, the history of TV programming has been the shifting downward of sophistication as more people could afford sets and younger audiences had more income and hence more attraction to advertisers.

To measure the television "acts" the Nielsen company started using two systems. First, it installed a Storage Instantaneous Audimeter, a box the size of a cigar box, in seventeen hundred houses. This device measures dial switching as an electrical impulse sent over telephone lines to a computer in Dunedin, Florida. However, the system does not record *who* is watching, so a separate sample is taken by asking as many as twenty-six hundred respondents to fill out a diary of their week's viewing. This group is chosen at random and one third is shifted each week. The diary is the weak link. Most families choose one person to fill it out. That person is usually an adult female and too often, say the ad agencies, she constructs a diary of what she would like to have seen or what she would like to keep on the air. While watching the thirty-seventh rerun of *Gomer Pyle* there is an understandable temptation to write down the *Carnegie Hall Special*. This halo effect has protected many family shows, such as the *Cosby Show*. The advent of cable and the complexity caused by having almost 50 percent of households able to receive more than twenty channels proved to networks, ad agencies, and sponsors that the system would have to change.

The English, who produced such dystopian masterpieces as *1984*, provided the solution—a passive mechanical eavesdropper. After all, the Brits have a history of elegant snooping. BBC radio introduced audience counting with its Listener Research Department. In the early 1980s a small corporation called Audits of Great Britain introduced the dreaded and ballyhooed Peoplemeter. The Peoplemeter combines the functions of the Audimeter and the diary in yet another little cigar box that sits atop the set like a religious icon. The Peoplemeter is operated by a hand-held remote-control wand. The metering function acts as it did under the Nielsen system, but the diary function is activated when each family member enters a number on the wand whenever she or he is watching the set. The Peoplemeter is now in four thousand demographically profiled households, and these four thousand essentially control what stories the rest of us will see. To be sure, this system has its quirks. It favors those who are not frightened by electronic gadgetry—the young and urban—and it will be neglected and abused. Junior may enter Mom's number to preserve his professional wrestling, and Mom may want to preserve reruns of *Family Ties*. So the R. D. Percy Company of Seattle is promoting still another solution. Its Voxbox is a totally passive system that records the number of people in the room on the basis of body heat and body mass. When the television is turned on, the Voxbox records. If someone leaves the room, a message on the screen asks who remains. Supposedly, that person will tattle.

A still newer generation of passive meters is on the horizon. The state of the art features a cameralike recorder programmed to recognize faces and note which members of the family watch. Called smart-sensing technology, this is the method used by the military to distinguish between warplanes. Every seven seconds the infrared sensor scans the space in front of the television looking for patterns of light and dark, the shine of nose, the line of mouth, and if any new object is noted, it makes more detailed scans at higher and higher resolution and compares this information with stored data. The unfamiliar would be scored as "visitor." When a match is made, the information is instantaneously sent over phone lines to the Nielsen computer. No one in the media seems particularly concerned about Big Brother.

Ironically, after more than thirty-five years of cooperation between the networks and the advertisers in the use of the Nielsen system, it was the networks that balked at the Peoplemeter. No wonder; one of the most glaring facts the Peoplemeter showed was how much market share the networks have lost to the independents in the cable networks. In the first three months of use the Peoplemeter showed a still more startling trend: millions of viewers were abandoning not just the networks for cable or for rented videocassettes but were simply shutting their sets off.

ABC threatened to drop the Nielsen altogether, as did a halfhearted CBS. Why pay millions of dollars a year to be told that their commercials were not being consumed? CBS was especially concerned because it uses a system of "make-goods," which guarantees to provide free time on other programs if the contracted market share is not delivered. To make matters worse still, women aged twenty-five to fifty-four, an audience CBS prided itself on entertaining, were wandering away in droves. The advertisers didn't care about the networks' problems. With thirty-second spots costing $80,000 to $500,000, who could be concerned about the digestive problems of network executives? The real alliance is no longer between network and sponsor, as it was in the days of the *Firestone Hour* and the *Kraft Theater*, but between worldwide sponsor and worldwide advertising agency.

The tantalizing next step of tying consumption of advertising for Product X to the consumption of X has proved elusive. This step is called Single Source Data and involves correlating the results of the Peoplemeter with the bar-code scanner down at the local A&P. This is the holy grail of Adcult. A number of large companies—most important is Arbitron's ScanAmerica—have tried to complete this circuit, either by having Mom's code entered at the grocery store or by having her pass a wand over her purchases once she gets home.

Paradoxically, the introduction of ScanAmerica didn't disturb what few gatekeepers are left in Adcult. Walter Goodman of the *New York Times* was one of the few to sound the alarm. He wrote,

> But suppose the measurements were perfected? How comforting would that be to citizens of a democracy? Listen to one of the futurists for Arbitron wax enthusiastic about gadgets that would register not only what people watch but

also what they buy: "You could see that a particular group of programs might deliver heavy users of spaghetti sauce and therefore I might approach the manufacturers of spaghetti sauce and point out that I am a very valuable station to you because I can deliver the audience that's heavily involved with your product." Anybody out there who feels heavily involved with spaghetti sauce and doesn't mind being delivered? • (1992:C18)

Goodman need not be overly concerned. Single Source Data hasn't worked. Yet. As is typical of the world of Adcult the problem is too much data, too little understanding. Advertising agencies, although they would never admit this publicly, are breathing a sigh of relief. With $30 billion of ad sales resting on such numbers, no one wants to be told what many suspect: a huge fraction of advertising money is wasted—far more than the half that Lord Leverhume and John Wanamaker suggested. Nielsen is still trying to perfect its system but not trying very hard. After all, it is paid by agencies as well as the media.

Actually, no one on Madison Avenue is very happy with television these days. True, cable has allowed networks to narrowcast to demographic target audiences, or niches, and it is true that cost per thousand has dropped as competition has increased, but the fact of the matter is that, although the machine is everywhere and always on, no one really pays it proper attention any more. Although advertising dollars were constant between 1980 and 1990, about 20 percent of total expenditures, and although they still reached about 98 percent of the audience, that audience has so fractured into network, cable, and independent that fewer people are likely to watch one ad. To reach one hundred gross rating points (a common measure of media weight), it now takes nine spots to do the "work" of six. There are simply too many ads and too many short (fifteen-second) ads. The networks are broadcasting about six thousand commercials a week, and more than a third of them are these shorties. It doesn't take a genius to know that if you double the ad pages in your magazine, and then make many of them quarter-page ads, any particular message will reach fewer readers. Now make it easy for them to jump over your ads and follow the text without being interrupted, and you have today's situation of advertising on television.

Generally speaking, television has become an inconsistent and discontinuous plasma. Worse still, we magnify this haphazard programming by the way we consume it. We do not watch television programs; we sample, taste, choose, reject, and consume in bits and pieces. A never-ending flow crosses the screen, and we dip from one rivulet to another, often watching two or three different programs at once. The English call television "the two-minute culture"—the usual time they spend changing channels. The golden section of our attention span is now measured in seconds, not minutes. Young watchers even have a "nesting channel" from which they start their diurnal migration. Programmers even refer to this activity as *video grazing,* or *video surfing,* whereas advertisers refer to it with more apocalyptic descriptions.

The reason? The bane of advertising is the clicker. Invented in the 1950s as a wired remote called Lazy Bones (which should have been renamed Broken Bones, as it resulted in hundreds of trips and falls), refined as the Flashmatic, which was cordless but could be set off by sunlight, further polished by the installation of little tuning forks that could be triggered by a dog shaking its metal tags or the kid shaking the piggy bank. The clicker is now almost perfected, using infrared and inexpensive microchips. More than one hundred million of these gizmos have created the couch potato and almost wrecked television advertising. The average American male hits the button every forty-seven seconds. Now with the voice-activated model, just a moan will render millions of dollars of creative advertising worthless. It comes as no surprise that some refer to the clicker by the nickname The Power.

Worse still, although the networks and the FCC deny it, television ads are acoustically different from programming. The agencies know this; it is called hot mixing and results in having all the sounds in the commercial equally loud. Watching ads, you hear the beer being poured and the potato chips crunched as if your ear was at their level. Magnavox even has a television set with a feature called Smart Sound that recognizes the difference and will keep volume even throughout. The next step is obvious. Once the set recognizes a uniformly loud sequence, it could mute it. Put this technology on the VCR, and it could record the program while entirely omitting all the ads.

As Rosser Reeves knew back in the 1950s, the soft sell on television is almost impossible. If you make your pitch so entertaining that it will inhibit the switching and muting, you make your ad too entertaining to work. They remember the ad but forget the product. Many people still think the cute bunny with the drum advertises Duracell. Most respondents are not even sure what that nice couple involved in the slice-of-life romance are drinking. They may even remember the names—Tony and Sharon—but forget the coffee—was it Folgers or Taster's Choice? And what cola was Ray Charles drinking? They remember "Uh-huh." Anyone who grew up in the clicker-free world and saw the Anacin or Wisk ads will never forget that damn hammer and that ring around the collar.

Watching television today is like listening to the radio while driving a car. In the early days it was necessary to turn the station selector knob, then in the 1960s to press a preset button. Now you hit Scan or Search and wait for "your" culture to come forward. "Hurry up and choose," the machine says, but many of us just let it continually search. The radio generation is a one-thing-at-a-time generation, a "you can't do two things at once" generation. The TV generation, by contrast, does multitasking: doing homework, talking on the phone, watching several TV programs, and listening to the radio all at once. As contrasted with reading, television almost requires us to do something else while we are choosing what to watch. You can eat—the TV dinner and the TV tray

showed almost from the first what the medium was for. You can recline; you can walk around. An entire generation has raised its children with the machine on. You are still in perfect contact with the medium, still changing channels. Most of us use peripheral vision to consume most television. Television reads us to sleep and reads us awake. Did I see that on television, or did I dream it? "Do I sleep or view?" asks the modern Keats.

The producers of television flow know this. That is why so much is made of being the sleepy viewer's comforting friend. Aware that nothing will overcome the channel-changing impulse, the machine almost whines, "Welcome to . . . ," "Good evening, folks," "We'll be right back," "See you next week," "Stay tuned," "Don't touch that dial," "You wouldn't turn your back on a friend, would you?" "Stay with me a bit longer. By the way, did you hear the story of . . . ?"

"Yep," we say, punching the key. "Already heard it." Formula and conformity are the hallmarks of television fare. As the television semiologists say, shows are homologues of each other and semilogues of those in the genre. Entertainments share diachronic and synchronic similarities; they refer to individual texts as well as to all precursors and successors. What the academics mean is that repetition and redundancy are what viewers want. We want choice among equals. Media reformers have found this out, to their dismay. The availability of three channels or thirty channels does not change the lack of product differentiation. All networks ultimately behave as one, as do all shows within a genre. This is also true of commercials.

The television generation is not overwhelmed by this charade of choice; rather, the absorption of superfluous choice is what we do best. A decade ago grocery stores carried about 9,000 items; they now stock about 24,000. M&Ms come in 70 different packages. Revlon makes 158 shades of lipstick. Crest toothpaste comes in 36 sizes and shapes and flavors. Sony produces more than 100 varieties of Walkman devices, Seiko makes more than 3,000 watches, and Philips has 800 models of color TVs. Don't even think about sneakers. We are even eager to be offered choice where there is none to speak of. AT&T offers "the right choice"; Wendy's, "There is no better choice"; Pepsi,

*Adult eats its young. Magnavox advertises an ad-smart television.

"The choice of a new generation"; Coke, "The real choice"; "Taster's Choice is the choice for taste." We'll settle for the promise of choice, even when we know it is a delusion. But why? Is it because we do not want choice or because so many of us want the same or nearly the same thing? Who knows? Even advertisers don't understand it. Is there a relationship between the number of soft drinks and television channels—about twenty-seven? If you think we absorb superfluous choice, understand we are pikers compared to Generation X, the MTV generation. By ignoring ads, Gen X'ers can handle a flood of choice often, to the distress of advertising agencies.

The purpose of television is to keep you watching television at least long enough to see the advertisements. The illusion of choice is the tribute the medium pays to the attention span. Programs are the scheduled interruptions of marketing bulletins, and marketing bulletins are successful only to the degree that people see them. "We break through the clutter," says the promotion campaign of a major network, wisely neglecting to mention not only where the clutter comes from but also that clutter is what we now watch television to see. Part of the attraction of the Super Bowl, television's most-watched sporting event, is the promise of a glut of clutter. There is almost as much written about the Super Bowl ads as about the Super Bore itself. The genius of MTV is that it is so cluttered that we do not need to change channels. The flow is endlessly shifted for us by a programmer with an itchy clicker finger. In the jungle of television we need not study individual entries to understand the species. Each episode condenses the whole show, as well as the entire genre, as well as the entire medium. In the television phylum ontogeny recapitulates phylogeny. So too does each commercial seek to sell its own product while acting out principles formulated over generations of other commercials. It is like a language made up entirely of idioms: we never need pay attention to the phonemes. Television is an eternal void that must be refilled each day from beginning to end. Watch it once, you've watched it a hundred times. And that is precisely its attraction. And its current problem as an advertising conduit.

Every programmer's worst fear is that we might change the channel. Especially fearsome are the edges of shows where, after 22 or 55 minutes of sequences, we are moved through the boundary rituals of changing shows. Viewers tend to go off on their own when pods of commercials are broadcast. These commercials are built on a 10-second scale (10, 30, 60, 120 seconds) inherited from radio days when they were split around station identification. The 64 to 94 seconds of the traditional break between shows are the most terrifying moments in Adcult. Each show is under stress to keep audiences, not only from drifting to other shows but especially away from the set. Television shows are chosen in part for how well they deliver an audience across these half-hour breaks—called flowthrough.

Because this hiatus is the riskiest time for programmers, we often find the "newsbreak," a conflation of a break in programming with the breaking of an urgent story. We hear the news music and see the newscaster at the news-

➤ CBS buys its own broadcast time to sell trinkets for its own show: synergy in Adcult.

desk telling us to stay there for the news—complete story at eleven. So too the opening credits of each show are punchy with the promise of pleasure to come and are contrived to hold us through the next commercial pod. The networks are now testing cold openings—that is, no title credits or theme songs that alert the viewer that a commercial is coming up. The commercial pod itself is being disbursed in what is called seamless programming. Ads will appear at random. When programmers are convinced that a show is never going to build audience quickly enough, it will be bonged, or shown twice, during the same week at different times. Because no one knows what is playing when, the assumption is that watchers will never know when they saw it but will stay with it if they see it again. Often wishful thinking is all that is left to programmers.

As the nets have seen their audience share dwindle to less than half what it was a decade ago, they have started to behave like commodities sold by advertising agencies. They have started to brand themselves, hoping that if viewers don't know what they are watching because everything seems the same, at least they'll be loyal to CBS. When you see those little network logos in the corner of your set, known in the trade as bugs, or boogers, when you see your favorite NBC television personality on your Kellogg product, when you see CBS and Sears offering a sweepstakes in which you win something at the store by watching not some program but some network, when CBS pays millions to rent the services of David Letterman and then millions more to advertise that fact, when NBC advertises the power of its television advertising on its affiliate CNBC, when the networks (not the local stations) now thank viewers at the end of each broadcast day for watching, you know that the battle for shelf space on the spectrum is truly intense. And then when you see that in the commercial pod following the MCA-produced *Northern Exposure* CBS is running ads for sweatshirts with the show's logo, baseball hats, and a stuffed toy moose, and all you have to do is call an 800 number, you know something is up in Adcult. You are just on the edge of what television is going to be about. It is striving to be clicker proof.

Advertising executives used to say that television shows were the meat in the commercial sandwich. Say good-bye to the meat. Thanks to cable, the battle for audience share has intensified, sparing no one. Witness the state of the nationally subsidized network, the Public Broadcasting System. PBS did two things well. It imported shows from the BBC like *Masterpiece Theater*, and it aped commercial television with such shows as *Sesame Street*. Too much of its audience pretended to watch and then pretended to donate, all the time decrying the sorry state of commercial television. Thanks to cable, PBS now has to compete with Disney, A&E, and the Discovery Channel for BBCesque programming. Cable stations, chronically hungry for product, can pay well in excess of the $125,000 to $150,000 per hour that Mobil pays for *Masterpiece Theater*. With its own productions like *American Playhouse* PBS loses audience. When PBS wants money, it knows where the audience is. During beg-a-thon pledge weeks, *Masterpiece Theater* and *American Playhouse* are banished to the cellar, along with any series on American poetry and Bill Moyers. Up from the archives of popular-culture schlock come classic movies, specials on Bing Crosby, Lerner and Loewe, Grace Kelly and Marilyn Monroe, as well as retrospectives on the Beatles, Elvis, and rock 'n' roll tributes like *Shake, Rattle, and Roll*. Then people watch. Although Ken Burns's *Civil War* and *Baseball* series received massive media attention and the highest ratings of any PBS series, their actual audience share was that of a mediocre sitcom.

To survive PBS became a commercial network. Once cable was strung up, highcult television started down the slippery slope to Adcult. PBS carries commercials. Of course, it does not call these intrusions advertisements. They are enhanced underwriting or corporate endowments. What started with a five-second display of sloshing gasoline in the red *o* of the Mobil logo has expanded so that now we hear "Rhapsody in Blue" along with a soaring United Airlines plane, or "True Colors," the theme song of Kodak, along with a full half-minute of the photographic "Memories of your life." A billboard spot for *TV Guide* puts this sentence on the screen: "The magazine that makes the good things on TV better," and Coca-Cola intones that it is "The people who keep you refreshed with the crisp clean taste of Sprite." Look at the beginning of the *MacNeil/Lehrer Newshour* and you see Fritos, Pepsi, and Pizza Hut all coming out of a hinged-open globe. Any doubt of the message? Who brings you the world and its news? Or better yet, check *Wall Street Week with Louis Rukeyser*, brought to you by some brokerage firms. During the show Rukeyser actually touts his book on the public airwaves, complete with the ubiquitous 800 number.

PBS is a great advertising medium. The network even has its own ad agency, Public Broadcast Marketing, Inc., to make the pitch. Not only are the shows relatively clutter free with great cost per million, but the IRS even allows such underwritings to be considered a charitable contribution. The only no-nos are saying how great the product is and mentioning price. Notice how close these restrictions are to the initial taboos placed on commercial radio. Needless to say, the original PBS charter forbade any commercialism whatsoever.

PBS is only being sideswiped by Adcult. The real effect on television occurred in 1981 when Marc Fowler, a Reagan campaign stalwart, was appointed to head the FCC. Fowler's most important statement was his definition of television as "just another appliance—a toaster with pictures," but his most important rulings had to do with what happened if two stations on cable were showing the same program. What if some superstation like WTBS in Atlanta and your local independent station were both showing *Gilligan's Island* for the umpteenth time? The FCC essentially said that the local station could do anything it wanted. It could show all ads if it wanted. The twelve-minute-per-hour commercial limit was lifted. For those in the "find a niche and fill it" school of capitalism Fowler had provided just such a niche. If you were to program your local station precisely to be in conflict with another station, you could be guaranteed safe passage around the FCC restrictions on advertising. Of course, no infomercial programming was available . . . yet. No one had envisioned what a full half-hour ad even looked like.

The acts of Fowler notwithstanding, the great divide between advertising and programming was falling anyway. In the 1970s the afternoon airwaves were overrun with toy-based shows like *He-Man, GI Joe, Thundarr the Barbarian, Blackstar,* and *Mr. T,* in which plasticine vigilantes literally pounded good sense and manners into evil villains. The progenitor of the modern bash-'em-up storm troopers was Prince Adam, aka He-Man, who, together with the Masters of the Universe, was continually at war protecting his natal Castle Grayskull from the evil Skeletor. However, his real job was to sell toys. In a merchandising coup Filmation Associates, a subsidiary of Westinghouse, animated a fantasy around this 5.5-inch warrior and tried to sell it to the networks. *He-Man and the Masters of the Universe* was a crude, poorly crafted cartoon, but it was full of screen-bursting violence. The networks, still cautious about the relationship between advertising and entertainment, were timid.

However, hundreds of independent stations on cable were desperate for "filler" shows to put into the local-access air before the profitable prime time begins at 8 P.M. The number of independents had tripled between 1972 and 1980, and most of them were unable to afford the prices of afternoon syndicated reruns, which the majors ran primarily to cover these midafternoon doldrums. The independent stations bought *He-Man* and in so doing essentially allowed the toy companies to create their own temporary networks. These independents, through the prototype of what is now called barter syndication, were paid by exchanging air time for programming. The station receives the programming gratis and then sells part or all the commercial time and pockets the proceeds. By the time *Thundercats* came to the market in the mid-1980s, Lorimar Telepictures had cut a deal whereby it paid a percentage return to the station based on how well the toys were selling in the broadcast area. In order to maximize its return the television station saturated its audience with specific toy-driven cartoons. The more toys sold, the larger the station's cut. This carved a direct path from airwaves to shopping aisles. Others would follow.

About the same time that kidvid was moving across the afternoon programming horizon, Warner Amex Satellite Entertainment Company (now owned by a consortium of conglomerates—the usual suspects) was starting a nonstop, twenty-four-hour commercial channel beamed via satellite across the United States. Musicians had made performance films of their acts since the 1940s, so why not show them along with advertising? The effect of these videos was immediate, transforming not only the recording industry but show business as well. Quick cutting, slow dissolves, computer-generated images, animation, wild angles, multiple-image montages, hallucinatory special effects, Chromakey, magnified close-ups, masked screens—everything that is implied in that portmanteau term *state of the art* was involved.

For a while even the advertisers, who had introduced the music video, were the adapters of their own frantic styles. Coke, Levi's, and Ford spots were almost interchangeable with what was on MTV, except that these clips were in thirty-second segments. In fact, the advertisement and the music video occasionally interpenetrated. Michael Jackson promoted Pepsi in his videos and made Pepsi commercials that were knock-offs of the videos. Even mainline advertisements have been affected. Just one case in point: a recent American Express commercial for travelers' checks opens with a burglar breaking into a hotel room while the occupant is in the shower. As the thief rummages, a newscast playing on the TV shifts to a commercial. It is last year's commercial, with Karl Malden warning, "Don't leave home without it!" As the burglar absconds with wallet, the camera zooms in on Malden repeating his caveat. On MTV and the toy-based cartoons the entertainment is the advertisement and the advertisement is the show.

If romantic art struggles for the condition of opera, and if Newtonian science aspires to pure mathematics, television—all modern free-market commercial television—seeks the state of pure advertisement. Ideally, the entertainment and the advertisement would melt into a seamless "advertainment." Put that in the past tense. It's already happened. The infomercial and the Home Shopping Network have removed the last membrane separating entertainment content from advertising commercial. Both Adcult genres depend on a number of propitious developments. First, the removal of legal restrictions on advertising load. Second, the excess supply of both time and transmission capacity (today's coaxial cable can easily carry fifty channels). Third, the viewer needs a way to crudely interact with this programming if a sale is to be made. The 800 numbers were the beginning of interactive media, for they allow consumers to place orders and enable the sponsor to collect customer data within hours, not days. "Call now! Operators are standing by. . . . "

The ad agency is also standing by. Ad agencies can test a spiel over the weekend in an isolated market and know by Tuesday whether they can roll it out nationwide during the next weekend. That would be suicide in print, where the timeframe is months, not days. But because most of the televised products can only be bought by phone, the sponsor has one of the very few chances in Adcult to know exactly how well the ad draws. And finally, the method of payment is the credit card. Quick, efficient, and ripe with yet more information (this time for the bank), the sixteen-digit number completes the circuit—the information superhighway as dirt road.

The infomercials look so much like real programs that it is often only in the last few minutes that you realize that the film noir you have been watching, and is making you feel afraid to go out on the street, is really trying to sell you a stun gun. Or the instructional exercise show is trying to sell you a home gymnasium in easy payments. Or those pleasant celebrities chatting in the living room are really hawking vitamin supplements. For a while the infomercial shown most often was the Soloflex ad in which godlike youngsters worked themselves into an almost sexual lather as the voice-over suggested reverently that such bodies are possible for us couch potatoes at home. We potatoes, if we watch television long enough, can now also learn how to inhibit baldness, become rich in real estate, cut rocks with Ginzu knives, cook in woks, become thin with body cream, quit smoking without using willpower, wax our cars so that they can resist a flame thrower, and learn to dance so that we'll never be dateless again.

Usually, nothing is particularly objectionable about these infomercials, other than that they are being passed off as documentaries or spontaneous talk shows. If you are willing to sell time to Oral Roberts or to *He-Man and the Masters of the Universe,* whom can you deny? Anyone with a fistful of dollars can get on the public airwaves. Not only do stations get rid of excess time, they are also currently not liable as transmitters of deceptive ads. Best yet, in the Adcult tradition of what transformed newspapers, they get paid up front. No wonder that in 1992–1993 the Lifetime Channel aired forty-three hours of infomercials each week (more than six a day) for almost 25 percent of its schedule; the Nashville Network aired forty-two hours a week, the Family Channel twenty-eight hours, USA Network nineteen hours, and so forth. The industry counters that, after all, it may be entertaining to have Cher answer the question "Did you ever look at your hair and want to cry?"; Barbi Benton assure you that you can "Play the piano overnight"; Dick Clark answer the question "Is there love after marriage?"; Morgan Fairchild tell "How to raise drug-free kids"; Fran Tarkenton help with "Personal power, thirty days to unlimited success," and, of course, Brenda Vacarro tell us how to "Light his fire." But each case is shilling a study-in-the-privacy-of-your-home (and pay a lot of money) course.

Now that infomercials have stopped growing like algae at the edges of the programming pond, they are about to edge into prime time. To make the transition they are being called long-form marketing and direct-response television and are sponsored by companies like Volvo, Cuisinart, Sears, MCI, Saturn, Corning, and Philips. This genre is no longer a "withhold and thrust" kind of selling but a way for companies to make an extended point much the way the famous "hands" ads for Kraft introduced new products like Cheese Whiz to the market. You can show your audience how to use your product. This illusion of depth was not lost on Ross Perot with his flip-cards of doom.

By far the most interesting mutation of advertainment was "The Ringers," an infomercial created by Jordan McGrath, Case & Taylor for Bell Atlantic. In this half-hour show we see a sitcom family with plumber dad, working mom, teenage kids, and various in-laws dealing with life's problems in the Al Bundy–Bart Simpson manner. As the show progresses, the dad occasionally turns to the audience and demonstrates how call waiting, call forwarding, and return calling all work to help his mildly outrageous family. It's corny. "America's funniest PHONE-IEST family" we are told in the typically dim-witted theme song. "If you want to meet the Ringers, just pick up the phone / Cause no one in this family can leave the phone alone." But it is effective, especially cost effective. To broadcast "The Ringers" in the Baltimore area for eight hours after midnight cost $8,000. The press exposure about the ad was worth that much. "The Ringers" is also pure Adcult—the ad as entertainment.

The influence of the infomercial should not be minimized. It only looks like the Rodney Dangerfield of television. Not only has the infomercial spawned print relatives, the advertorial (the exploded advertising section that acts as a roadblock to reading yet looks like surrounding text) and the outsert (the advertising section that is bagged with the magazine, often prepared in the same editorial manner as the parent text), and not only are there the cable channels just for infomercials (ATV, or advertising television, and the National Advertising Channel—twenty-four hours of commercials), but the infomercial is the philosophical basis of the shop-at-home networks.

One key to direct selling on television is *not* to kid the customer into thinking you are *not* selling direct on television. Most selling on television is like door-to-door selling. The foot must be placed carefully, and the commercial interruption is that foot. The shop-at-home networks, however, are like selling inside the store. The customer's foot is already at your counter. You have to close the sale. Advertising is not so important. Getting the money is. So, in a sense the shop-at-home phenomenon is outside the pale of Adcult, as are most catalogs and much direct mail. The quid pro quo of exchanging entertainment for pitch is lessened as pure information (object, color, size, price) increases. But because the entire medium is clearly moving in this direction, let's have a quick look.

As has usually been the case in Adcult, technology is driving this shift. As digital replaces analog signals, video compression will make some five hundred channels possible on the same cable. This circuit is already crudely interactive, because you have to use your phone to complete the loop. When fiber-optic cable is used, the electronic highway will allow two-way communication. You use your receiver as transmitter. You will move a cursor on the television screen to indicate choice. But what goes inside these information pipes is going to be a problem analogous to deciding what you print with a high-speed printing press. The answer is . . . everything, including the store.

Shopping from home started when Roy Speer, stuck with a surplus of electric can openers he received when one of his radio station's advertisers went bankrupt, realized he could make more money selling the gadgets to listeners than selling air time to advertisers. He was right. And when he moved media from radio to television, the market exploded. His Home Shopping Network (HSN) now has twenty-three thousand incoming telephone lines that use an automated system to field as many as twenty thousand calls a minute. Most purchases are made by keying in various numbers with the touch-tone phone, but there are two thousand operators for those who need the personal touch. Better yet, all sales information is immediately available and displayable on a computer screen: how much inventory left, which pitches are working best, the price at which they bite. . . .

Supposedly, when Barry Diller (who used to make movies for Paramount and television shows for Fox) saw his friend Diane Von Furstenberg sell $1.2 million-worth of clothing in ninety minutes, he too was hooked. He anted up $25 million for a stake in QVC (Quality Value Convenience), a competitor of HSN's. The days of ersatz gold chains, zirconium diamonds, radio earmuffs, spray-on vitamins, music-box-cum-toilet-paper dispensers, and autographed Bibles were over. Now here come Donna Karan, Calvin Klein, Saks Fifth Avenue, Macy's, and Nordstrom's with suitcases full of stuff, as well as the usual valets—Time Warner, Viacom, Philips, Blockbuster, Turner, Tele-Communications, Inc., and the Baby Bells—eager to lend a hand.

What this portends is not clear. Will it be goodbye mall, hello video wall? Who knows? One thing is certain: if shop-at-home behaves like other innovations in selling or delivering the goods, the ramifications for advertising will be considerable. As Don Logan, a top executive at Time Warner, said when addressing the National Association of Advertisers, "Stop thinking about it as the 'information superhighway' and start thinking about it as the 'marketing superhighway'" (Elliott, "Advertisers Gather," 1994:D22). As we have seen, in Adcult little information is transmitted without marketing. Unless advertising can be made an important part of the superhighway, many lanes will turn to mud.

3 ✦ STRONG ENOUGH FOR A MAN BUT MADE FOR A WOMAN

THE WORK OF ADCULT

The near-total utilization of television for corporate marketing represents at the same time the daily ideological instruction of the viewer.

• HERBERT I. SCHILLER, *CULTURE INC.*

Learning about the world is increasingly a by-product of mass marketing. Most of the stories about life and values are told not by parents, grandparents, teachers, clergy and others with stories to tell, but by a handful of distant conglomerates with something to sell.

• GEORGE GERBNER, "TELEVISION VIOLENCE"

☞ *WHAT* "work" does advertising do and how well does it do it? Aside from comforting purchasers by assuring them they made the right choice, aside from comforting CEOs and employees that their work is important, and aside from certain unpredictable short-term increases in consumption, most advertising does not perform as advertised. Take away the tax deductions that corporations get for advertising, and most expenditures would dry up overnight.

Although elaborate proofs of advertising's impotence are available, the simple fact is that you cannot put a meter on the relationship between increased advertising and increased sales. If you could, agencies would charge clients by how much they have increased sales, not by how much media space they have purchased.

Neil H. Borden of the Harvard Business School first demonstrated the inconclusiveness of most advertising in his definitive work, *The Economic Effects of Advertising* (1942), and Michael Schudson reconfirmed Borden's thesis in 1984 in *Advertising: The Uneasy Profession*. Even advertisers know how iffy most advertising is, as Leo Bogart makes clear in *Strategy in Advertising* (1990) and as one-time ad critic for the *New York Times* Randall Rothenberg relates with reference to a specific product in *Where the Suckers Moon* (1994).

What advertising does, and how it does it, has little to do with the movement of specific goods. Like religion, which has little to do with the actual delivery of salvation in the next world but everything to do with the ordering of life in this one, commercial speech has little to do with material objects per se but everything to do with how we perceive them. What is ultimately branded in advertising is not objects but consumers. If religion serves to justify the ways of God to man, advertising serves to justify the ways of things to people.

Modern consumerism is not a replacement of religion but a continuation, a secularizing, of a struggle for order. Salvation through consumption is not a contradiction but a necessity. For although capitalism requires people to be pious in the workplace, to believe to work is to pray, to "lay not up for yourselves treasures on earth," to be Calvinistic in the assembly line, it survives by encouraging us to be raving maniacs at the cash register, to be pagans at saturnalian events like Christmas, and to be woefully insecure about ourselves, especially about our body size, our odors, our face, and even about our gender. The other side of work, work, work is spend, spend, spend, and *here* advertising is king.

I never want to imply that, in creating order in our lives, advertising is "doing" something to us for which we are not covertly responsible. We are not victims of advertising. We make our media. Our media makes us. Commercialism is not making us behave against our better judgment. Commercialism is our better judgment. Not only are we willing to consume, and not only does consuming make us happy, "getting and spending" is what gives our lives order and purpose. We have a tendency to consider advertising in the way we consider many other cultural events, like politics, law, and religion, as somehow "out there" beyond our control. Our desire to individualize experience causes us to forget that people and their leaders, males and females, readers and writers, young and old, and even producers and consumers are continually interacting, that the struggle is not for dominance but for expansion. In the language of William Blake the endeavor is not to separate the Prolific and the Devourers, not to blame one for the condition of the other, but to understand that the excitement and the danger of cultural change lie in the shifting of forces. In this sense advertising is yet another site at which the sometimes opposing forces of a culture are brought to bear on each other.

I make this point now because advertising—commercial speech—has become a primary hot spot of modern culture. Advertising has been blamed for the rise of eating disorders, the eruption of violence in the streets, our epidemic of depression, the despoiling of cultural icons, the corruption of politics, the carnivalization of holy times like Christmas, and the gnatlike attention span of our youth. All of this is true. Advertising contributes. But it is by no means the whole truth. Advertising is more a mirror than a lamp. That we demonize it, that we see ourselves as helpless and innocent victims of its overpowering force, that it has become scapegoat du jour, says far more about our eagerness to be passive in the face of complexity than about our understanding of how it does its work.

'WHERE'S THE BEEF? THE SUBLIMINAL EXPLANATION OF ADVERTISING

If you ask the ordinary man on the street (a character created by advertising in the 1940s, incidentally, along with Brand X) to tell you how advertising works, you will probably hear the actual word, or at least the concept of, *subliminal*. Most people believe that advertising sneaks some foreign matter under the surface, slides some message under the margin of consciousness, that stimulates us to feel some anxiety that we can relieve only by consuming a product we would ordinarily not buy. This is utter nonsense but utterly powerful nonsense.

This paranoia began with the invention of the Tachistoscope by the Eastman Kodak Company in the early 1950s. This super-fast strobe light—it could flash at 1/60,000th of a second—was the reason we saw all those photographs of bullets in mid air and open-winged hummingbirds in the pages of *National Geographic* and *Life*. It was also the reason that an unemployed market researcher named James M. Vicary made a lot of money and mischief. In the spirit of his predecessor, P. T. Barnum, Vicary contacted marketing directors and advertising managers in New York, offering to instruct them (on plump retainers) in a new selling technique based on the Tachistoscope. He called his technique "subliminal advertising." Just as the flash would catch the image on thin-emulsion photographic film, so too could you project an image so fast that the brain would record what the eye did not see. The strobe analogy was compelling. The viewer might have a vague sensation of déjà vu, unaware of what caused it. All the better for advertising, because the viewer could not expunge it with conscious criticism.

America of the 1950s was a fecund pasture into which to cast this seed. The communist menace was working in exactly this way, spreading red spores throughout our adolescents, making them grow into juvenile delinquents, and pseudoscientists like Dr. Ernest Dichter were explaining the eerie MR (motivational research) to Madison Avenue for hundreds of dollars an hour. Foul contagion was loose in the land. Thank goodness for Vance Packard's *The Hidden Persuaders*, which told us what people with foreign names were doing on our shores. The book was a best-seller for months. Dichter was no more a doctor than Sanders was a colonel, but who cared? Dichter had a German accent, a mansion high above the Hudson River that housed his Institute for Motivational Research, and a repertoire of quotable statements like "a sedan is a wife but a convertible is a mistress."

◆ Why fight it?
Join in. If consumers
believe you use
subliminal
seduction, use it.

PEOPLE HAVE BEEN TRYING TO FIND THE BREASTS IN THESE ICE CUBES SINCE 1957.

The advertising industry is sometimes charged with sneaking seductive little pictures into ads. Supposedly, these pictures can get you to buy a product without your even seeing them.

Consider the photograph above. According to some people, there's a pair of female breasts

hidden in the patterns of light refracted by the ice cubes.

Well, if you really searched you probably could see the breasts. For that matter, you could also see Millard Fillmore, a stuffed pork chop and a 1946 Dodge.

The point is that so-called "subliminal advertising" simply

doesn't exist. Overactive imaginations, however, most certainly do.

So if anyone claims to see breasts in that drink up there, they aren't in the ice cubes.

They're in the eye of the beholder.

ADVERTISING
ANOTHER WORD FOR FREEDOM OF CHOICE.
American Association of Advertising Agencies.

Like Dichter, Vicary was the right man at the right time. He didn't have a phony title, an institute, a German accent, or any proof of what he was peddling, but no matter. In the manner of Barnum, the grand poobah of Adcult, Vicary made it up. He claimed that experiments had been done at an unidentified motion picture theater on 45,699 unidentified persons at some unspecified but recent time. While watching a movie, the audience had been subliminally exposed to two messages. One said "Eat popcorn," the other "Drink Coke." Did they ever! Vicary swore that the invisible advertising had increased sales of popcorn an average of 57.5 percent and increased the sales of Coca-Cola an average of 18.1 percent (Rogers 1992:4). No explanation was offered for the difference in size of the percentages, no allowance was made for variations in attendance, and no other details were provided as to how or under what conditions the purported tests had been conducted. Vicary claimed he could not discuss these inconsistencies, nor would he divulge the place of study or detail the actual technique used, because it was part of his patent application for his own version of the Tachistoscope. This was top-secret stuff in a time when we believed in top-secret stuff.

For paranoids Vicary's claims were manna from heaven. He leavened the loaf by continually asserting he would always use his subliminal technique for the good. In fact, subliminal advertising might immediately improve the electronic media, because the ads could be removed from their pods and embedded in the programs so no one would be annoyed by "There is no spit in a Cremo." On the surface at least Vicary promised ad-free entertainment. The FCC was not so sure. After WTWO in Bangor, Maine, conducted a publicity stunt experimenting with on-air suggestion, the FCC ordered Vicary's firm, the Subliminal Projection Company, to conduct a closed-circuit demonstration in Washington, D.C. During January 1958, before an audience of members of Congress, bureaucrats from appropriate agencies, reporters, and broadcasters, Vicary flashed his "Eat popcorn." *Printers' Ink*, the advertising

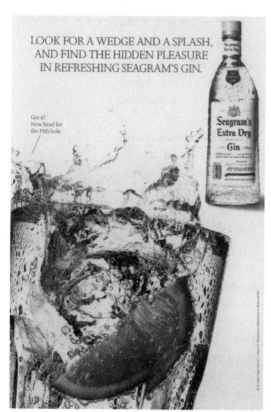

◆ An entire campaign dedicated to the subliminal.

trade journal, commented, "Having gone to see something that is not supposed to be seen, and having not seen it, as forecast, the FCC and Congressmen seemed satisfied." After the show Senator Charles E. Potter waggishly said, "I think I want a hot dog" (Rogers 1992:6).

Vicary tempered his claims. His retainers were growing smaller. OK, OK, his patent claim had never been filed, he admitted. No longer did he call it subliminal advertising. Now he referred to it as *reminder advertising* and likened it to what you see out of the corner of your eye. Vicary's time was over. He had earned millions of dollars in retainers and consulting fees from Madison Avenue firms, and it was time for a rest. In 1958 he disappeared, leaving no bank accounts, no clothes in his closet, and no forwarding address. Vicary has dubious immortality, however, as a chapter in American popular culture. His scam, along with such immortal tales as the vanishing hitchhikers, sewer alligators, eyelids Superglued shut, rat tails in soft drinks, and microwaved pets are parts of what Jan Harold Brunvand (*The Choking Doberman, The Vanishing Hitchhiker*) calls "urban legends." If they are not true, they ought to be.

Vicary's lucrative franchise for selling Americans' paranoia back to them was picked up by a Canadian sociologist, Wilson Bryan Key. What separates

THE PLEASURE OF SEAGRAM'S GIN.
IS IT HIDDEN OR REFRESHINGLY OBVIOUS?

ONE PART SUNSET. ONE PART SEAGRAM'S GIN.
YES, YOU'LL FIND THE HIDDEN PLEASURE.

Key from Vicary is that Key, a one-time professor, is sincere. He looks at ads and sees *fuck* written all over crackers, vaginas on the forearms of little children, and penises in pictures of ice cubes. He really believes that every day we are bombarded with a flood of images (not just words, as Vicary believed) to make us drink, smoke, and party in ways we never would normally.

Q. CAN YOU FIND THE HIDDEN PLEASURE
IN REFRESHING SEAGRAM'S GIN?

Starting with *Subliminal Seduction* in the early 1970s, Key has churned out five books, all with the same thesis: advertising agencies secretly embed "sublims" in images in such a way as to make us so insecure that we will buy their product to find surcease. How do you spell *relief*? According to Key: p-u-r-c-h-a-s-e. I don't want to belabor his argument, but suffice it to say that any object longer than it is wide is a penis. Everything else is a vagina. Although Key has lost his tenure at a Canadian university, in part for his scholarly craziness, it makes no difference. He has earned more than Vicary plying his trade.

Two matters are important. First, Madison Avenue would howl at the Vicary-Key thesis were it not so preposterous. Remember, ad execs don't want you to buy crackers or beer or cars. They want you to buy Ritz, Schlitz, and Studebakers. What they sell is brands, not products. It is not that they wouldn't love to sneak selling messages under the surface; it is just that the process has not proved effective. They've tried it. Advertisers love to mock subliminal selling, because they know it will be looked at, especially by the disaffected young. So Miller Lite recycled *Saturday Night Live*'s Subliminal Man in a spot, and Toyota has a commercial for its Paseo in which the car is sitting in front of a motel as the voiceover proclaims, "We think you'll like the new Paseo so much, we don't have to use cheap advertising tricks to play on your emotions. So you won't see any young models in bikinis. There is no pressure." Between each sentence flash the words EXCITING, SEXY, and ACT NOW. In 1994 Del Monte ran a commercial in which the words *Del Monte* and *fresh* were intercut with photographs of succulent fruits and vegetables. The word flashes were hardly subliminal, lasting almost a second, but you got the point: this was a playful way of resolving the problems of selling canned food.

Before Ogilvy & Mather did the long-running campaign for Seagrams, the agency found that 62 percent of the public believed that subliminal ads do exist and that 56 percent believed that such ads worked in motivating other people (not themselves, of course) to buy unwanted things. O&M also found that 54 percent liked the idea of the subliminal spoof, presumably because they could see how others were suckered (Savan 1991:51). Clearly, the notion of outwitting Svengali is pleasurable even if the reality means falling for his pitch.

Having said that subliminal seduction is tripe, Vicary and Key do have it right. The real work of advertising *is* subliminal. But not in the sense of messages slid below the surface, but subliminal in the sense that we aren't aware of what commercial speech is saying.

A Little Dab'll Do Ya: The Weight of Advertising

Advertising's most obvious cultural influence is on the media that carry it. As a general rule the greater the advertising load, the greater the sponsor's control of content. Self-serving and sententious rationalizations about the First Amendment and a free press aside, why shouldn't advertisers have a say in content? He who pays the piper calls the tune. What needs inspection is not why the media favors advertising interests, but why we are so shocked at collusion.

The Chinese wall separating editorial content from advertising is a peculiarly American concoction. The English were ready to admit there was no free lunch a century ago. The hoary bromide that "freedom of the press in Britain is freedom to print such of the proprietor's prejudices as the advertisers don't object to" was well known to the founders of the BBC. This is why British broadcasting developed free of advertiser constraint. We knew it too until the rise of the weekly newsmagazine in the 1940s. Part of the reaction to the demise of American muckraking was a call for a new medium to present the news free of all pressures but the Truth. Henry Luce expressed the radical view that became central: the church of editorial integrity is eternally separate

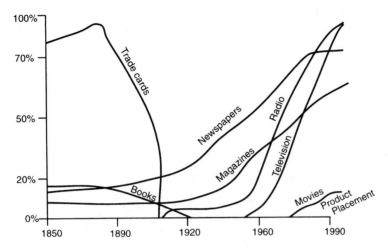

♦ Advertising Load—Percentage of Revenue Generated from Advertising.

from the state of advertising business. *Time* culture became the goal of journalism schools, and, had it not been for the rapidly encroaching world of electronic culture now embodied by Time *Warner* culture, the myth might well have survived.

A more precise moment when the China wall disintegrated might be in the 1960s when *Reader's Digest* went commercial. Even before the *Digest* accepted ads, it had experienced the censoring powers of advertising. After the magazine warned its readers of the dangers of cigarette smoking in 1957, BBDO suddenly dropped the *Digest*'s $1.6 million account at the behest of its client, the American Tobacco Company. Ironically, the magazine never accepted cigarette advertising. But in 1986 the *Digest* turned down an advertising supplement on heart disease and cigarette smoking prepared by the American Heart Association. Why? The RJR Nabisco and Philip Morris companies not only make cigarettes, they also package food stuffs through their Del Monte, Nabisco, General Foods, and Kraft subsidiaries. Those foodstuffs are a major source of the *Digest*'s advertising revenue. As Larry White makes clear in *Merchants of Death*, such occurrences are not the exception but the rule.

Adcult rule number one: Speech is never free. Here are a few examples of the rule at work:

    🙦 General Motors refused to advertise in *Automobile* magazine for three months because editor David E. Davis attacked GM for sloppy business practices. Toyota Motor Corporation withheld ads from *Road and Track* when one of its cars did not make the "Best 10" list. "Enthusiast magazines" are always advertiser friendly, none more so than the automotive genre.

🍃 The *Harvard Business Review* killed an already-accepted story, "Why IBM Failed," because of pressure from a long-standing and big contributor.

🍃 ABC gave kindest treatment to Ross Perot during the 1992 presidential campaign. It was the softest network on Perot's remarkable imitation of a dolt on *60 Minutes*. Was there any connection between this and ABC's receipt of $11.3 million for running Perot's infomercials, whereas CBS ran $4 million-worth and NBC ran $4.5 million-worth?

🍃 Because they were threatened by their main sponsors, bridal magazines refuse to take ads from, or even mention the existence of, companies selling used bridal gowns.

🍃 In 1989 the Portland *Oregonian* destroyed tens of thousands of Sunday papers when an advertising salesperson objected to an article in the real estate section on how to buy a home without using a broker.

🍃 Tobacco companies have always exerted editorial clout. The industry has spent about $4 for every person in the United States on advertising, or about $1,000 per year for every cigarette-related death since 1954. In 1959, when Arthur Godfrey said smoking made him feel bad, Lorillard said too bad, good-bye as a sponsor. In the early days of television NBC had a news show called *The Camel News Caravan*. Camel barred any news filmed with No Smoking signs in the background. Cigarette companies have pressured magazines not to run ads for Bantron and other antismoking medication. They even have been able to pressure *Cosmopolitan* and *Psychology Today* into refusing ads for stop-smoking clinics. In October 1985 *Time* magazine deleted all references to the hazards of smoking in a special section dedicated to health issues. In the same year the *New Republic*, in financial straits and under new ownership, canned an article on the dangerous effects of smoking. The piece was later published in the *Washington Monthly*, complete with an explanation of why the sister journal found it so dangerous to its financial health. A few years later (1988) it was *Newsweek*'s turn. A cover article, "What You Should Know About Heart Attacks," made no mention of the contribution of smoking. The back cover carried the usual full-page ad for Malibu cigarettes. As I write this, Philip Morris has launched a massive billion-dollar suit against ABC News for reporting that the tobacco industry withheld important studies linking nicotine with addiction.

🍃 DuPont pressured the Reader's Digest Company not to have its book subsidiary publish *DuPont: Behind the Nylon Curtain* by withdrawing its ads. Never one to quit, DuPont also forced the cancellation of this book as a selection in the Fortune Book Club by threatening to remove ads from all the Time, Inc., magazines.

🍃 Here's my recent favorite: Mercedes Benz, through its ad agency Scali, McCabe, Sloves, sent a letter to magazine publishers insisting that they run Mercedes ads "only in a proper editorial environment." This meant no anti-German stories. "Any issue containing editorials denigrating to

Mercedes-Benz . . . or containing material that may lead to a negative bias toward German products, should not carry a Mercedes-Benz advertisement." Failure to comply would result in nonpayment. The agency asked publishers to return a signed copy of the letter to indicate agreement. According to the *Wall Street Journal*, an M-B spokesman said, "We don't think there will be any reluctance to sign this letter. The magazines don't have to do anything, except not run our ads" (Goldman 1993:B4). When you spend almost $15 million on magazine ads, you expect to get "an appropriate context."

Admittedly, direct advertiser pressure is the exception, not the rule. No one should be upset when Ronald Perelman, who controls Revlon, pulls his ads from all Hearst magazines because one, *Esquire*, published an unflattering article on Perelman's girlfriend. That's business as usual. However, much more energy is expended in the gray area of implied censorship and still more in self-censorship. A call from a car manufacturer noting that a lot of television news time is spent on acid rain, or an offhand but contrived comment to an advertising rep to the effect that an editorial bias has been noted by a sponsor, is probably more effective and certainly more common than any out-in-the-open action. But even this covert control pales in comparison with the powers implicit in the unarticulated relationship between the conglomerated media empire and the conglomerated production empire. How can CBS News cover what happens at K-mart when the two companies have a "relationship marketing" agreement to "cross-promote" products? And what of NBC and Sears with the same back-scratching agreements? The question is not how Time Warner's *Entertainment Weekly* can ever review Warner Bros. movies fairly. The question really is how can the *Washington Post*, for which cigarette ads are a minor source of advertising revenue, objectively cover their danger when over at its sister publication, *Newsweek*, tobacco is bringing in almost $17 million a year? Perhaps it can. But let earnings per share fall, and see what happens.

Ironically, the First Amendment, which protects speech from governmental "abridgement," makes no provision against external corporate forces and certainly not even a hint of protection against internal forces. Nor should it. The framers of the Constitution could never have realized that, once advertising was loaded into a medium, the danger to free speech is more likely to come from within than from without. For every time the government attempts to suppress its Pentagon Papers, industry attempts to do the same a hundredfold, and the media do it to themselves a thousandfold. "Advertisers, not governments, are the primary censors of media content in the United States today," writes C. Edwin Baker, the foremost authority on the First Amendment, in the *Pennsylvania Law Review*. And he continues, "Or maybe it should be said that advertisers are second after the media itself, which engages in self-censorship for both good and bad reasons" (1992:2200).

Need proof of self-censorship? Here are some stories you will rarely, if ever, see in your local newspaper: how to bargain in buying a new and/or used car, how to buy a house without a Realtor, what the relation of "suggested retail price" is to the listed price, and nasty reviews of chain-owned eateries. Here's why: 30 to 40 percent of all classified ads are for cars, real estate accounts for 18.5 percent of all classified ads, and department stores accounted for $17 billion of local newspaper buys in 1989. And as television time has become more expensive, restaurant chains have gone to couponing in newspapers. In a survey done by the *Washington Journalism Review* of forty-two real estate editors, almost half had been told by senior editors not to offend advertisers, and some 80 percent of the advertisers had threatened to pull ads if the environment became less friendly (Collins 1992:25).

Once again cigarette companies are the major force in hushing media noise. Joe Camel rarely slides on his brass knuckles. The media know the drill. University of Michigan researchers found that, in a study of one hundred magazines over twenty-five years, magazines carrying tobacco ads were 38 percent less likely to discuss the risks of smoking than those magazines without tobacco ads. Women's magazines were the worst offenders. They were 50 percent less likely to cover the dangers. What is especially ironic is that good health is a primary concern of these magazines. When Helen Gurley Brown, impresaria of *Cosmopolitan*, was asked by the *Washington Post* to explain why a magazine so concerned with the well-being of young women should neglect such a large danger, she candidly said, "Having come from the advertising world myself, I think, 'Who needs somebody you're paying millions of dollars a year to come back and bite you on the ankle?' " (Lipman 1992:B5).

This is not the place, and I am not the person, to express indignation about how the "right" to the truth has been abridged by covert and overt advertiser pressure. Let others, like Roland Collins (*Dictating Content*, 1992) James E. Squires (*Read All About It!*, 1993), Ben Bagdikian (*The Media Monopoly*, 1983), and the monthly exposés in the *Columbia Journalism Review* and the *American Journalism Review* (formerly the *Washington Journalism Review*) sound the alarm. Still, the irony is too massive to resist: the two largest advertisers in Adcult are liquor and cigarettes. They are also the two chief causes of premature death and loss of work. Together they control 65 percent of newspaper space and 22 percent of television time. This is one of the few places where greedy lawyers with class-action lawsuits will do more than hundreds of wailing critics and hundreds of thousands of wheezing "innocent victims."

You're in Good Hands with . . . : *Advertising and the Politics of the Moment*

Of course, the taint of advertiser control colors such matters as television and radio programming, genres of entertainment, and even what passes as news coverage. In fact, I could argue that the concept of news is itself an advertising construct developed in the eighteenth century as a way to attract readership to print-based gossip.

Now that advertising itself has become news, companies often supply footage of how ads were made (Frito-Lay reported that 1,724 independent television stations aired a company-produced promo of its Super Bowl ads), or package an ad as news (L.A. Gear produced a spot about how a missing child was located with the reflectors on her L.A. Gear Twilight Sneakers). Sometimes they even insert the ad in what looks to be a news program, called "blurmercials," which conflate the newsperson with the ad. So, for instance, we see the CBS weatherman talking to the video image of Jaclyn Smith about K-mart as matters slowly segue to an ad, or see Simon Prebble, former BBC anchor, chatting with an executive of AT&T, Kodak, GTE, or Holiday Inn. We do not realize that these are paid spots until we are already into the commercial.

On the *Today* show the Disney company sponsors "Movie News Special Report," which many viewers assume is an NBC news segment because of the news-anchor type who introduces vignettes just like a regular reviewer. Naturally, he has only good things to say and naturally we are only shown a small "Paid for by Buena Vista" note at the end of his spiel. However, the most obvious interpenetration of advertising and the news is in political campaigns. If war is an extension of politics, modern politics is an extension of successful advertising. A political campaign, as Albert Lasker, the guiding genius of Lord & Thomas, observed in the 1930s, is just another advertising campaign.

Although political marketing dates back to Andrew Jackson's 1828 campaign against John Quincy Adams, the defining event of political maneuvering in Adcult would surely be the 1952 election campaign of Dwight Eisenhower. Rossier Reeves of Ted Bates & Company offered to help the general. Reeves was the master of the relentless hard sell. From his rudimentary research with the subscription lists of *Reader's Digest*, he compiled a series of questions that he had the proverbial man in the street ask the camera. Later the studio-bound general read his answers off huge cue cards, as best he could without his glasses. (Reeves thought the eyeglasses did not look presidential.) To concocted questions about such matters as inflation, Ike would respond that Mamie had been reminding him of this the other day at the grocery store. The campaign, called "Eisenhower Answers America," was only on television, totally canned, and a stunning success. Let Stevenson take chances; Ike was well fortified. "To think an old soldier should come to this," Ike huffed. He was not alone. Marya Mannes, writing in the liberal *Reporter*, mocked the marriage of Madison Avenue and Washington:

> Eisenhower hits the spot
> One full General, that's a lot
> Feeling sluggish, feeling sick?

Take a dose of Ike and Dick.
Philip Morris, Lucky Strike,
Alka Seltzer, I like Ike.

　　　• (Halberstam 1993:27)

As is typical of Adcult, the same people who sell you the candidate also sell you the send-up. So on one hand, Madison Avenue has produced such masterpieces as the Willy Horton ad, LBJ's "daisy" ad, and the "Morning in America" campaign. On the other hand, advertisers use the same hoopla to wrap red and blue bunting around their products, as when Anheuser-Busch calls Budweiser "our can-to-date," Nabisco presents shopping lists of cookies and crackers in the form of make-believe ballots, Crown Royal features a picture of a donkey, an elephant, and a bottle of Seagram's liquor with the caption "Democratic Party, Republican Party, Cocktail Party," and UPS runs a picture of an overnight mailing pack with the line "How any Democrat can make it to the White House overnight." Is it any wonder that in a context like this, we should debate such matters as health care, not in Congress but in Harry and Louise advertisements?

As one argument goes, advertising has corrupted democracy by its eagerness to compress, reduce, and even distort in order to sell; the counterargument is that in the modern world a politician who cannot do exactly that is going to be ineffective. When Richard Nixon picked H. R. Haldeman to be his chief of staff, he was not unmindful of what he was doing. Haldeman was the manager of the Los Angeles office of J. Walter Thompson. As Ed McCabe, CEO of Scalli, McCabe, Sloves, said of Michael Dukakis's presidential campaign, "Privately, I wondered how a man who couldn't mount an effective ad campaign would be able to manage a country" (Leiss et al. 1990:389). Ronald Reagan's ability to advertise his edges made him an effective leader. Reagan did exactly what Rosser Reeves was attempting to do for Eisenhower. He traded intellectual content for emotional appeal.

Advertising's mania to be associated with whatever cause is current (as a way of borrowing credibility for its own agenda)

Dan Quayle

"Don't forget to vot."
　　　–Kenneth Cole

"Come by our Pre-Election Sale going on now."
253 Columbus Ave. at 73b　　　95 Fifth Ave. at 15th

◆ Adcult and the
politics of the
nanosecond.

may be cynical but not always blameworthy. For instance, the environmental movement owes much of its potency to having been used by advertising as yet another way to borrow value. When products are essentially interchangeable, one that appears to be concerned with the environment has a selling point. So Chevrolet loves ducks, Mobil's Hefty bags are friendly to landfills, and Tampax has an applicator that is earth friendly. Often the entire claim is made on the basis of environmental correctness, as with Ben & Jerry's, Esprit, Timberland, or the Body Shop.

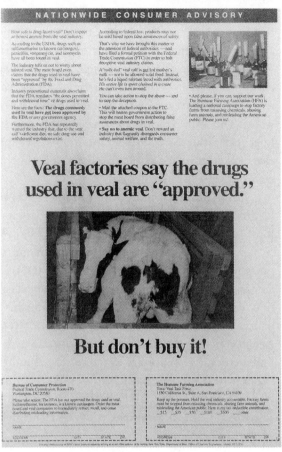

• Ever wonder where all those teenage vegetarians came from? This ad was more powerful than salmonella.

In an interesting turn the English, always first to subvert subversion before it does them in, have even recycled old detergent commercials from Procter & Gamble and Unilever. In one ad a talking head babbles about getting dirt you can't see, while the superimposed script claims that the soap company is so keen on recycling that it is even reusing its old commercials.

Is there an inverse relationship in Adcult between the nastier a company has been and the likelihood that it will claim the high ground? StarKist, which once made its living killing dolphins, now presents itself with pictures of poster-children dolphins nuzzling their momma. DuPont runs ads of applauding sea animals while an oil tanker (owned by Conoco, a DuPont subsidiary) steams by on the horizon to the strains of Beethoven's "Ode to Joy." P&G touts its "disposable diapers," but they won't compost; L'Eggs makes a big deal about changing its egg-shaped container but neglects to explain why it used such a wasteful package in the first place. And Exxon has the gall to proclaim its oil-spill cleanup efforts, without mentioning that its Captain Hazelwood helped make the mess.

What suffers most in the battle for the environmental high ground is the language. According to the *New York Times*, more than 10 percent of packaged goods now carry some kind of environmental claim (Specter 1991:B1). Such claims, often balderdash, make advertising sense. The Roper Organization found that "true-blue green" consumers are willing to pay almost 20 percent more if an environmental claim can be made that sticks. But what sticks? What do *all natural, kind to animals, environmentally friendly,* and *safe for the environment* mean? What about *recyclable, recycled, biodegradable,* and *organically grown*? *Biodegradable* is nonsense, as most everything is, and *recyclable* is worse. The term *recycled paper* means only that some minuscule part of the huge paper roll was made of scraps. Almost all paper can be legally called recycled. Any idea what nuclear-free light bulbs, botanically correct shampoo, or environmentally safe nails are?

Advertising is far more powerful and intrusive than any comments about its influence on media content and current affairs can demonstrate. The real force of Adcult is felt where we least expect it: in our nervous system, in our shared myths, in our concepts of self, and in our marking of time. It is here in our senses, in our stories, in our mirrors, and in our calendric rhythms that we feel the true *subliminal* force of commercialism. Let me reiterate. This is not a one-sided process. "They" are not doing this to "us." You cannot tell the dancer from this dance. Nor can you tell the advertiser from the audience in Adcult. We are actively creating and organizing a context for value and purpose every bit as important as the world around the medieval peasant. What may separate modern participants is that they may have some dim understanding of how advertising justifies to human beings their habits of consumption—the relationship of commercial language, the exchange of objects, and the ordering of life.

Be All That You Can Be: What You Be to Advertisers

Before looking at the degree to which our relationship with advertising colonizes and configures our perceptions of culture, self, and time, we might pause to see how advertisers see us. For although we may find comfort in the well-advertised myth of individualism and free will, to ad agencies we are tribes of consumers wandering through aisles of objects, hopelessly confused and eternally willing—nay, eager—to be instructed, even intimidated. Mass production means mass marketing, and mass marketing means the creation of mass stereotypes. Like objects on shelves we too cluster in groups. We find meaning together. As we mature, we move from shelf to shelf, from aisle to aisle, between what the historian Daniel Boorstin calls "consumption communities." Finally, as full-grown consumers we stabilize in our buying, and hence meaning-making, patterns. Advertisers soon lose interest in us, not just because we stop buying but because we have stopped changing brands.

The object of advertising is not only to brand similar objects but also to brand consumers. Just as readers make different meanings for texts, buyers make different meanings for products. To explain his job Rosser Reeves used to hold up two quarters and claim his job was to make you believe they were different and, more important, that one was better than the other. Hence at the macro level the task of advertising is to convince different sets of consumers—target groups—that the quarter they observe is somehow different in meaning and value from the same quarter their across-the-tracks neighbors are seeing. If Anheuser-Busch wants to maximize its sales, the woman driving the BMW believes she drinks a different Budweiser than the man in the Chevy pickup.

Cigarette companies were the first to figure out the vagaries of affiliation in the 1930s. Most blindfolded smokers couldn't tell what brand they were smoking, including their own. It was easier to make different advertising claims to different audiences than to make cigarettes with different tastes. Cigarettes are hardly unique. Ask beer drinkers why they prefer a particular brand, and invariably they tell you, "It's the taste," "This goes down well," "This is light and refreshing," "This is rich and smooth." And they will say this about a beer that has been described as their brand but is not. Serve the eight or so most popular domestic brands of beer to your friends, and ask them to isolate the brand they think they recognize. You will soon see that the taste of beer is in the advertising, not in the palate.

Anheuser-Busch spent $3 per barrel in 1980 to market a barrel of beer; today it spends $9. Because the cost of reaching a thousand television households has doubled while the audience has segmented because of cable, why not concentrate on a particular market segment by tailoring ads that emphasize, in different degrees, the Clydesdales, Ed McMahon, Beechwood aging, the red-and-white can, the spotted dog, the Eagle, as well as "the crisp, clean taste"? Although you cannot be all things to all people, the object is to be as many things to as many segments as possible. The ultimate goal is to convince as many segments as possible that "This Bud's for you" is a sincere statement, albeit outrageous.

The study of audiences goes by any number of names: psychographics, ethnographics, macrosegmentation, but all are based on the principle that birds of a feather flock together. The object of much consumer research is not to try to twist our feathers so that we will flock to your product but to put your product in a place past which we will have to fly and perhaps stop to roost. After roosting, we will eventually think that this is a part of our flyway and return to it again and again. From the early sociological speculations of scholars like David Reisman, who made the distinction between inner- and outer-directed communities, and Abraham Maslow, who posited a five-tier stair of "needs growth," the advertising industry has embraced the concept of positioning as a way to take advantage of the indwelling styles and aspirations of consumers.

Distinguishing this descriptive approach from the behaviorism of earlier advertising "science" is important. The behaviorists saw consumers as lab mice struggling in the maze. From the 1930s, when John Watson left Johns Hopkins to work at J. Walter Thompson, to the 1950s when Dr. Ernest Dichter was demonized in Vance Packard's paranoid *The Hidden Persuaders*, this view of the consumer as irrepressible moron held sway. After billions of wasted dollars and a failure rate higher than 80 percent for new products, few advertisers today would have such confidence to predict behavior or even have the temerity to say what objects mean. What modern psychographic systems do is far less hubristic.

Almost every large agency has its own research department with its own proprietary system of audience inspection. As a general rule the larger the agency, the more it loves to test. Agencies will test anything: brand and product segmentation, copy evaluation, location testing, recall; if it can be observed by otherwise-unemployed Ph.D.s, it will be evaluated for something. Agencies spend hundreds of thousands of clients' dollars testing and testing and testing. To a considerable degree this is because it is less expensive for an agency to test and be wrong than just to be wrong.

Here's why. Agencies have two selling jobs. The easy one is to produce and place the ad. The hard one is to convince the client to spend millions of dollars to run it. The agency makes money only if the second job is done. So there is a continual tension not just between the agency's research and the client's research but between the agency's creative types and the agency's scientific types. As the English ad man John Ward observes, "Advertising is a craft executed by people who aspire to be artists, but assessed by those who aspire to be scientists. I cannot imagine any human relationship more perfectly designed to produce total mayhem" (Mayer 1991:157). Undeniably, much advertising research is like a lamppost to a drunk. In tight times sponsors drop advertising and agencies drop research.

Because different products have different meanings to different audiences, segmentation studies are crucial. Although agencies have their own systems of naming these groups, they are really jazzed-up versions of the old-fashioned terms *upper class, middle class, lower-middle class,* or the English "not in our class, dear," or *U* or *non-U.* The current supplier of much information and jargon about these segments is a nonprofit organization in Palo Alto, California, which in a proper Adcult manner has taken advantage of its proximity to a prestigious institution by calling itself the Stanford Research Institute (SRI).

The psychographic system of SRI is called acronymically VALS (now VALS2+), short for Values and Lifestyle System. Essentially this schematic, shown in figure 3.2, is based on the commonsense view that consumers are motivated "to acquire products, services, and experiences that provide satisfaction and give shape, substance, and character to their identities" in bundles. The more "resources" (namely, money, but health, self-confidence, and energy also figure) each group of consumers has, the more likely they are to buy the "products, services, and experiences" of the group with which they associate. But resources are not the only determinant. We are also motivated by such ineffables as principles, status, and action. When SRI describes these various audiences, they peel apart like this (I have provided them with an appropriate car to show their differences):

• Actualizers. These people at the top of the pyramid are the ideal of everyone *except* advertisers. They have "it" already or will soon. They are sophisticated take-charge people interested in independence and character. They don't need new things; in fact, they already have their things. If not, they already know what the finer things are and refuse to be told. They don't need a new car, but if they do, they'll read *Consumer Reports*. They do not need a hood ornament on their car.

• Fulfilled. Here are mature, satisfied, comfortable souls who support the status quo. Often they are literally or figuratively retired. They value functionality, durability, and practicality. They drive something called a town car, which is made by all the big auto makers.

• Believers. As the word expresses, these people support traditional codes of family, church, and community, wearing good Republican cloth

• The VALS2 Paradigm: A Taxonomy of Taste (and Disposable Income) in Adcult.

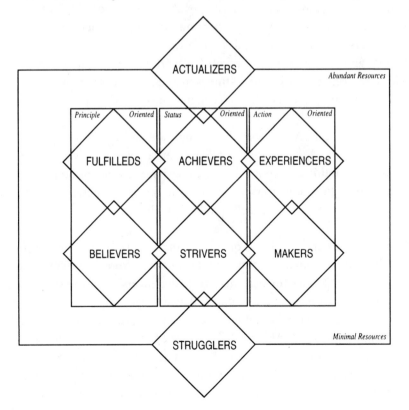

coats. As consumers they are predictable, favoring American products and recognizable brands. They regularly attend church and Wal-Mart, and they are transported there in a mid-range automobile like an Oldsmobile. Whether Oldsmobile likes it or not, they do indeed drive "your father's Oldsmobile."

    Achievers. If consumerism has an ideal, it is achievers. Cha-ching, goes the cash register. Wedded to job as a source of duty, reward, and prestige, these are the people who not only favor the establishment, they *are* the establishment. They like the concept of prestige. They demonstrate their success by buying such objects as prestigious cars. They like hood ornaments.

    Strivers. Young strivers are fine; they may mature into achievers. But old strivers can be nasty; they may well be bitter. Because they are unsure of themselves, young strivers are eager to be branded so long as the brand is elevating. Money defines success and they don't have enough of it. Being a yuppie is fine as long as the prospect of upward mobility looms. Strivers like foreign cars even if it means only leasing one.

    Experiencers. Here is life on the edge—enthusiastic, impulsive, and even reckless. Their energy finds expression in sports, social events, and "doing something." Politically and personally uncommitted, experiencers are an advertising dream come true, because they see consumption as fulfillment and are willing to spend a high percentage of their disposable income to attain it. When you wonder who could possibly care how quickly a car will accelerate from zero to sixty miles per hour, it is the experiencers.

    Makers. Here is the practical side of Experiencers; makers like to build things and they experience the world by working on it. Conservative, suspicious, respectful, they like to do things in and to their homes, like adding a room, canning vegetables, or changing the oil in their pickup trucks.

    Strugglers. Like Actualizers, these people are outside the pale of Adcult, not by choice but by economics. Strugglers are chronically poor. Their repertoire of things is limited because they have so little. Although they clip coupons like Actualizers, theirs are from the newspaper, not from bonds. Their transportation is usually public, if at all.

    The categories are very fluid, of course, and we may move through as many as three of them in our lifetimes. So, for instance, from ages eighteen to twenty-four most people (61 percent) are Experiencers in desire or deed, whereas fewer than 1 percent are Fulfilled. Between ages fifty-five and sixty-four, however, the Actualizers, Fulfilled, and Strugglers claim about 15 percent of the population each, whereas the Believers have settled out at about a fifth. The Achievers, Strivers, and Makers fill about 10 percent apiece, with the remaining 2 percent Experiencers. The numbers can be broken down at every stage, allowing for marital status, education, household size, dependent children, home ownership, household income, and occupation. More interesting still is the ability to accurately predict the appearance of certain goods in each grouping. SRI sells data on precisely who buys single-lens reflex cameras, who owns a laptop computer, who drinks herbal tea, who phones before 5 P.M., who reads *Reader's Digest*, and who watches *Beavis and Butthead*.

Given the fabulous expense of communicating "meaning" for a product, the simplemindedness of a system like VALS2+ becomes less risible. When you spend millions of dollars for a few points of market share for your otherwise indistinguishable product, the idea that you might be able to attract the owners of socket wrenches by shifting ad content around a bit makes sense. Once you realize that in taste tests consumers cannot tell their brand of cigarette from others, including their own—nor can they distinguish such products as soap, gasoline, cola, beer, water, or what-have-you—it is clear that the product is unimportant; the audience must be isolated and sold.

You Can't Fool Mother Nature: Advertising and Myth Making

In a sense advertisers try to spread the mythology of their object horizontally, placing their product on the map of other similar products. They stake out and "own" certain emotional territory of target audiences. Or at least they try to. This used to be commonly called the USP, or Unique Selling Proposition. Every agency has a different name for this activity and pretends that it just discovered it.

Lately, the USP has been modestly called "finding the soul of a brand." No matter what it's called, it works the same. Truth is not important, staking the claim is. Although all brewers steam-cleaned their bottles, the claim by Schlitz in the 1930s that all their bottles were steam-cleaned established the notion that purity-of-product was unique to this brewer. Often the claim has nothing to do with the product but with the brand. So, for instance, Pepsi owns the concept of a new generation; Kodak owns the special moment of maturation, like the first haircut or first day at school; for a while Chevrolet attempted to own Americana, as in "Hot dogs, apple pie, and Chevrolet"; Miller Beer attempts to own early evening with Millertime; "The night belongs to Michelob."

From the point of view of cultural history, advertising also provides a vertical sense of how an object (and its consumers) have emerged from the past. The consumable object and its attendant advertising are our shared memories. Often the object travels with an endorser, who takes on the role of mythic analogy.

When a campaign is successful, the character with whom the audience is supposed to identify and the object coalesce, not just with each other but with a tradition as deep and powerful as any myth. So Betty Crocker draws some of her power from the archetype of the great mother. The Breck Girl, Coca-Cola girl, and Cover Girl are what we have for archetypical maidens. The White

Rock girl is clearly drawn from the image of the ancient nymph. The sexy superwomen of Sharp Products and Noxzema shaving cream are the dim analog of the woman in boots, the She Who Must Be Obeyed, Juno. For men we find the Ancient Father in the Quaker Oats man. The factotum is Mr. Goodwrench or the Maytag repairman. The lone warrior is the Marlboro Man; the magician is Mr. Clean; Father Nature is the Jolly Green Giant and . . . you get the point. Even mystical places, those far-off locales to which we must journey like Hercules in order to find the consumable objects of quest, have been provided by every fast-food franchise that beckons you into McDonaldland, South of the Border Land (Taco Bell), or Lake Edna (Kentucky Fried Chicken).

Putting aside for the moment the rather unheroic prospect of making the modern copywriter into Joseph Campbell, the stories generated by advertising are indeed what we have for mythic culture. Margaret Mead once mourned the loss of adaptive myths in modern culture, claiming that coming of age in the West meant coming to maturity devoid of role models and heroes. Admittedly, it is rather demoralizing to think that the Man from Glad and the Frito Bandito are what we have for Ulysses and Achilles. Yet the sure sign that a character has become part of the culture is not merely that it is recognizable but that it has been memorialized.

Typical of such memorializing is the grandly named Museum of Modern Mythology in San Francisco. In its pantheon are about three thousand advertising characters in their various incarnations as dolls, pillows, banks, and salt shakers. All the usual suspects are here: Poppin' Fresh, Colonel Sanders, Cap'n Crunch, Mr. Peanut, Mr. Bubble, and the Jolly Green Giant. Ronald McDonald, Shoney's Big Boy, Joe Isuzu, Bartles & Jaymes, and the Energizer Bunny are waiting to be inducted. People separate out by age as they move through the museum's rooms to cluster around the campaigns they experienced in their youth. Surely, this is more than nostalgia. It is an awareness of an important, if hardly numinous, common experience.

◆ The changing face of Betty: from Mrs. Crocker to Ms. Crocker.

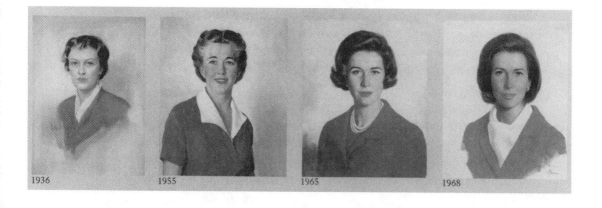

1936   1955   1965   1968

Do You Know Me? The Role of Celebrity

Long ago the gods were imaged in human forms but resided in far-away places. Today we confer deity on actual people in the here and now. Celebrity is a point-of-sale phenomenon. As Clive James has pointed out in his juicy book *Fame in the Twentieth Century*, people used to be famous for what they did. Then, he argues, in the modern world they became famous for what they were doing while they did what made them famous. In Adcult, I contend, you are not known for what you did or what you were doing when you did it. You are famous for what you endorse while doing what you did that used to be what made you famous.

The condition of being celebrated is ancient, doubtless one of our most central socializing devices, because it separates leaders from the tribe. In all cultures certain people are capable of *celebratus,* or the condition of being honored, not just for what they have done but for what they can continue to do for us. This recognition is not always a function of the individuals' specific acts but of the roles they play. In fact, the elevation of certain people—celebrities—is often dependent on their being able to perform certain rites. In the church we still honor the role of the priest in celebrating certain events like baptism, the Eucharist, marriage, and the rites of death. Celebrities are those leaders; they are the priests.

Celebrities/priests are central characters of Adcult. They have one foot in our world and one foot in adtopia. They must be recognized as "one of us" and "one of them." More important still, they have to be able to make us believe that they are sincere when they "endorse" a product that we know full well they are paid to use. This phenomenon is hardly new. Look at the walls of Renaissance churches, and you will see an endless procession of martyrs and saints who are invariably undergoing the most exciting experiences in the ser-

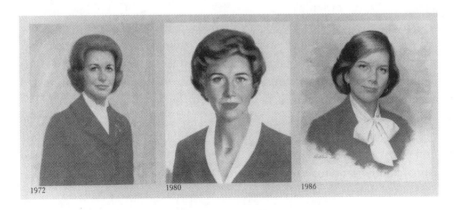

1972   1980   1986

vice of what we are being invited to join. They are not supernumeraries on the stage but foils for those of us in the audience. In their heroic deeds and sufferings they are endorsing a product, renting their glory, if you will, for the corporation. We see them rewarded with salvation, the same salvation proffered to us.

Although the process of contrived reward is hardly new, nor the conflating of fame and celebrity, the linking of it to a manufactured object certainly is. In a universe of interchangeable products the celebrity endorsement becomes a central part of the brand magic. "Be like Mike," the Gatorade slogan promises. If you replenish your lost bodily fluids with their greenish slime, you will not only be drinking Michael Jordan's brand but will be participating in his majesty. This is what we have for the Eucharist.

Creating fame, and then applying it to a purchasable object, starts in the industrial revolution. Lord Byron was acutely, at times painfully, aware that he was selling books of poetry in direct proportion to the selling of Byronism. He was the first modern man to find the sacred intersection of notoriety and merchandising. John Murry, his publisher, knew it too and encouraged the nascent tabloids to "cover" his client.

Michael Ovitz at CAA, the Hollywood talent agency, carries on this tradition, except that he rents his talent—aka stars—to the other companies. Celebrity is a commodity—sellebrity. What is unique to Adcult is that the confecting and merchandising of fame is often far more important than the product. Who among us does not know that Tina Turner drives a Plymouth, Michael J. Fox drinks Pepsi, Bill Cosby eats Jello, and that Tip O'Neill carried the American Express card? But who among us can figure out what the relationship is between these celebrities and these products?

The ability to quickly generate celebrity and then link that value to a product is a hallmark of Adcult. The holy grail is to find a celebrity, rent the star's glory to endorse some product, thereby increasing its value, and in so doing make the celebrity better known. Apocalypse in Adcult occurs when the celebrity, the product, and the consuming audience are branded together as one. Consumable object, identification character, and consumer can't be separated. Not only can you drink Michael Jordan, you can even wear him as a shoe (Nike's Air Jordan).

In the pretelevision world the medium defined the aspect of celebrity to be bound to the product. So in radio it was the voice and in magazines it was the face. The effect of hearing the voice of legendary radio host Arthur Godfrey seeming spontaneously to rhapsodize Lipton Tea revolutionized advertising. And when Jack Benny used to begin his show with "Jell-O again," instead of "hello again," the results were immediate at the A&P. The celebrity voice is still important, not in the radio sense but in the application of a voice over certain images. We may not even recognize the voice of Donald Sutherland for Volvo, Michael Douglas for Infiniti, Gene Hackman for United, James Stewart for Campbell's Soup, or Jason Robards for Xerox, but we respond, perhaps subconsciously, to the voice we somehow know is from above.

In print, thanks to photography and the airbrush, this synecdochic mixup led to the creation of the professional face. It was not enough to have some beautiful body display your clothes; the body had to be a somebody with that "face." You get to be that face by commodifying it with certain products. When everything fits, you get . . . Voilà! the model. The word *model* is not a haphazard coinage. It means a physical shape worthy of copy, as with an artist's model or, more appropriately, an image assignable to mass production (and obsolescence) like Chevrolet's new model of the Camaro.

Many young women in Adcult long to be models. When Noxzema wanted to introduce its skin-care products for women in the 1960s, it decided to show women using its products as if they were appearing on the covers of magazines. The product line was called Cover Girl. In the background of the ad you see the woman as she literally appeared on such a cover. The image had a kind of fun-house mirror attraction—you were seeing the cover girl as Cover Girl on the cover. The barely veiled promise of the advertising was that

◆ Cover Girl girl: the model model.

you too could become such a creature. Certain magazines soon objected, because they were being used to give free ad space to other magazines, but the concept of the cover-girl face available to all stuck.

The Breck Girl (now enshrined in the Breck Girl Hall of Fame at the headquarters of the Dial Corporation) attempted to do the same by celebritizing an aspect of the head, namely, hair. Clairol also made hair an accessory, changeable at will ("Does she or doesn't she?"). Although the most famous Cover Girl was Cheryl Tiegs (now immortalized with the requisite exercise video, doll, and long-term contract with Sears), the concept of face-as-celebrity complete with that hair on top of a long body continues in Claudia Schiffer, Cindy Crawford, Nikki Taylor, Linda Evangelista, and Fiona Campbell-Walter. Sometimes the model breaks loose from advertising life and becomes a television or movie star, as in the case of Candice Bergen, Kim Basinger, Cybill Shepherd, Brooke Shields, Christie Brinkley, Lauren Hutton, and Ali McGraw. Adcult is nothing if not democratic with celebrity, always willing to share, especially if it increases value on both sides of the equation.

With television the process became more complicated still, because the celebritized metonomy of voice or face was replaced by the entire celebritized persona. Perhaps another solecism—*telebrity*—is in order to separate the tiny screen actor from the movie star. The movie star *may* be typecast; the television celebrity has to be. The nature of weekly revivals of the same show means that a series must be coherent. The first such advertising telebrity was Gertrude Berg who, in the 1960s, sold S.O.S. pads in the Yiddish-inflected language of her television character Molly Goldberg. "With soap, it's loaded," came from Molly, not Gertrude. Better known were commercials in which Chris Robinson and Peter Bergman, actors who portrayed doctors on soap operas, sold cold medicine by acknowledging, "I am not a doctor, but I play one on TV." Better yet was Robert Young. A film star who played various roles to an earlier generation, to us he was a telebrity father—first as father-father on *Life with Father*, then as father-doctor on *Marcus Welby, M.D.* When he later prescribed decaffeinated coffee for upset nerves, we got the patriarchal double whammy. Sometimes the mix is so powerful that the ad creates its own reality. By the 1980s James Garner and Mariette Hartley were so successful in a Polaroid campaign that many believed they were indeed husband and wife. And by the late 1980s matters were so thoroughly confused that we had a political leader who most of us knew not as an actor in B movies but as a telebrity employed by General Electric. What better qualification for the presidential host of Adcult?

We now accept the intermingling of fact and fiction almost without hesitation. If life imitates art, advertising imitates both. Magical thinking is not an occupational hazard, it is the *only* way to understand much in Adcult. For instance, when Alan Alda and the cordial gang of misfits from *M*A*S*H* rented their telebrity to IBM in order to sell a product hardly available during the Korean War—the personal computer—they even pretended to be behaving just as they did in countless medical emergencies. Sometimes a "star" will so cover the product in the persona of the role she plays that the telebrity takes over. It is not Candice Bergen but Murphy Brown who has the take-charge persona necessary to plug the business efficiencies of Sprint, even though the ad tells us differently. It is not Tim Allen who is touting the values of Builders Square, but Tim Taylor—the macho character on *Home Improvement.* When Jerry Seinfeld extols the American Express Card it is his sitcom self doing the plugging. Ditto Angela Lansbury doing her impression of the *Murder, She Wrote* sleuth, finding the hidden value in Bufferin. Sometimes this interpenetration can be downright confusing, as when Craig T. Nelson and Shelley Fabares banter about Kraft products while calling each other by their names from the show *Coach.* The confusion is purposeful. It catches our attention. It also catches the attention of the networks. ABC rejected ads with Jerry Seinfeld and Bart Simpson (for Butterfinger), saying they were too promotional for their respective non-ABC shows, and CBS has not let Sprint run its Candice Bergen ads during *Murphy Brown.*

Sometimes a character straight from Adcult jumps loose from the advertising persona and becomes an independent character. This usually happens with models. But as Clara Peller of Wendy's "Where's the Beef?" fame showed, sometimes it takes more than a beautiful face. The prize for the most unusual trip out of Adcult, however, has to go to Jim Davis, who used to be the Beef Butcher for the Winn Dixie grocery chain. He was so good that he was hired to be the patriarch of the Ewing clan on *Dallas.* When he died, the patriarch of Southfork died. But there was Davis, aka Jock Ewing, still on the tube selling beef from beyond the grave. He was not alone in cheating death. Michael Landon was doing his infomercial for improving your kid's grades long after he had passed into the next world. And what are we to make of the fact that on the Video Storyboard Tests Delta Burke (zaftig star then of *Designing Women*) scored high in "celebrity endorsement recall" although she appeared in no commercials? She is so much an Adcult telebrity that she doesn't have to endorse anything to be known as an endorser. [1]

What Madison Avenue often learns to its distress is that celebrity is like Jello. What looks so solid can all too often melt away. Witness the debacle of Michael Jackson: the poles of charismatic attraction can be immediately reversed. The enemy of Adcult is always real life. Reality bites. Bruce Willis pitched Seagram's Golden Wine Cooler until it was rumored in tabloids that

---

1. Seven times a year a company called Marketing Evaluations polls a sample audience to find out how viewers perceive certain performers, politicians, sports figures, products, and even shows. Then they calibrate recognition by value. Their pollsters ask if this is someone you like a lot, somewhat, or not at all. Although they have tried to test for believability, this is too elusive a trait. Networks pay almost $100,000 per year to find out how their casting is going and choose accordingly. So do advertising agencies. Although she is instantly recognized by 93 percent of the sample, you don't see Roseanne in commercials because only 15 percent consider her likeable.

"Who said it's good to be the Queen?"

My ads tell you I'm the Queen of the Helmsley Palace, which suggests that all I have to do is march through the elegant lobby or down the grand staircase... I wish it were that simple... but it's not.

In order to make the Helmsley Hotels the most respected hotels in New York, I have to work harder than Cinderella (before the ball).

Because I care so much about the Helmsley reputation, I personally select the finest linens, hangers that do come out of the closet, the highest quality TVs, clock-radios, lamps, and furnishings. (Is that any way for a Queen to spend her day?)

Most importantly I have to be diligent about the people we hire. It is crucial that every one of my staff provides the kind of sincere, caring service my guests have come to expect.

When I'm not working with my staff, I'm answering letters from people all over the world. Most of them are letters of praise for the service at my hotels. Many are suggestions (I'm always open to good suggestions) This is a job I can't delegate. These letters were written to me, and they'll be answered by me.

And, just when I think I have a few minutes to sit down and polish the 5 diamonds awarded by the AAA to the Helmsley Palace and never to any other hotel in New York), the phone rings.

Making sure that every guest receives royal treatment at every Helmsley Hotel takes a lot of work.

It's not easy being the Queen... but don't worry, I'm not abdicating.

*Leona M. Helmsley, President
Helmsley-Harley Hotels*

The Helmsley Hotels of New York

| THE HELMSLEY PALACE | PARK LANE | HARLEY OF NEW YORK | ST. MORITZ ON THE PARK | MIDDLETOWNE HARLEY | WINDSOR HARLEY |

The Helmsley Palace is the only Hotel in New York ever to receive the ● Five Diamond Award ●●●●●

For reservations call Toll-free: 800/221-4982 or in New York, 212/888-1624. TELEX: 640-543. Or call your travel agent.

he had "a drinking problem." Ringo Starr had the same problem with Sun Country wine coolers. Once Mike Tyson and Robin Givens stopped cooing and started punching, Diet Pepsi headed for the showers. When Macaulay Culkin, star of the *Home Alone*s, said of Sprite, "I'm not crazy about the stuff. But money is money," ad execs reached for the bourbon. James Garner underwent heart surgery; the beef industry bled. When Cybill Shepherd, spokeswoman for L'Oréal, admitted she didn't dye her hair, many ad execs pulled theirs. Hertz fell over itself running away from O. J. Simpson. But this is a two-way street. Sometimes being a celebrity in Adcult is injurious to the celebrity's health. When fame is in remission, the results can be harsh. So reviled was Leona Helmsley, self-cast as the rich bitch and queen of her hotels, that her sentencing for tax evasion may well have been harsher for all her well-advertised crowing.

Working around the problem of celebrity crash is possible. There is safety in art (as we will see next chapter) and in numbers, as in the sequential celebrity motif. The serial campaign was first used by Black Glama with famous women draped in fur and can now be seen in ads for the Gap, Barneys, Oldsmobile, and the milk producers. The technique can be captivating, as with Annie Leibovitz's images for American Express. Her shots of Tom Clancy buried in a foxhole, Rob Reiner dressed à la Erich von Stroheim, Sammy Davis Jr. doing a soft shoe in the desert, and James Earl Jones petting a bunny get it both ways. The photographs are as interesting as the celebrities, and there are so many celebrities that no one will remember if one of them goes over the wall. Cartoon characters make excellent endorsers, because the agency can pretty well control even Bart Simpson's behavior. Why we should listen to what a drawing on celluloid tells us is another question entirely.

The safest human celebrity is certainly a dead one. Because most of what a celebrity does in Adcult is attract attention, no one questions the inappropriateness of an impossible endorsement. Humphrey Bogart, Marilyn Monroe, and even James Dean magically appearing to tout Diet Coke are shocking enough; no one cares that the product was introduced long after their demise.

And when the Gap runs a campaign in which Babe Ruth, Ernest Hemingway, and the same James Dean are endorsing khaki, who is disturbed by the fact that the Gap was not even incorporated until the 1960s? Indeed, as ads for *Rolling Stone* claim, perception is reality.

Life Is Short, Play Hard: The Athletic Life in Adcult

One central role of sports in American culture is to produce a never ending entourage of celebrities who appeal to one of the most difficult audiences to reach—adolescent males. In the VALS topology these males cross the most consumption-prone segments, but they respond to relatively few advertising-based entertainments. Although women do most of the purchasing of FMCGs, these men can be counted on for certain big-ticket items like cars and big-profit items like electronics and beer. But they are hard to round up and keep still.

The athlete as pitchman is in many ways more efficient than the movie star or the telebrity because he is not playing anyone other than himself. In fact, he does not play anyone. He plays a game. The audience need not deconstruct the icon. He appears as he is, a physical embodiment of an audience goal. Michael Jordan made not only professional basketball in the 1980s but also Gatorade and Nike. He was recompensed accordingly. The salary he earned on the court was nothing compared to the millions (about twenty) of dollars he made endorsing everything from Chevrolet to Wheaties.

Attracting sports celebrities requires sporting events, not just any sporting events but demographically distinct sporting events. Fans don't determine these events, advertising agencies do. *USA Today*, which knows this kind of stuff, estimates that sponsors contribute five times as much to sporting events as do fans. The *Sporting News*, which knows even more, compiled a list of the one hundred most important people in sports. The people from the consumer marketing giants and ad agencies outnumber players four to one. In fact, the *only* active athlete was Jack Nicklaus. The true commissioners of sports are the marketing people at Anheuser-Busch and the media buyers at Leo Burnett.

Little wonder, then, that the finish-line tape of the Boston Marathon was moved from the Prudential to the John Hancock Building as sponsors changed or that Jose Cuervo Tequila made beach volleyball so important a sport that ESPN found it worthwhile to feature it (although liquor advertising is forbidden on television). How else to explain the Blockbuster Bowl (football), the Rolaids Reliever (baseball), the Alamo International Diving competition, and the Snickers Millrose Games (track)? Sometimes having your name tied to some esoteric event can be positively prestigious, if only to a niche audience. Why do you think Rolex sponsors polo and Cadillac supports dressage? The phenomenon of borrowed interest has even caught up with croquet—brought to you by Jaguar Motor Cars, who else?

The phenomenon of sponsorship also answers a curious question. Why is there so much golf on television and why so little soccer? The answer has less to do with the visuals than the financials: golf can be commercialized and soccer can't. Take golf. You can attach your corporate name to a golf tournament for $500,000 to $1.5 million. You are then obligated to buy about half the commercial time—another $1.5 million for thirty-two commercial spots that you can use or resell. If you are clever, you can dress the players in all kinds of billboards to reinforce your corporate presence. On the PGA Senior Tour, for instance, the individual members of Team Cadillac wear the heroic crest on their golf shirts. They are not alone; every professional golfer carries a veritable backpack of endorsements. Every week Joyce Julius & Associates dutifully watch the week's tournament in slow motion. The company provides the sponsors with a weekly evaluation of their investment. So, for instance, during the Masters Tournament a few years ago (which severely limits the number of commercial interruptions), Lynx golf equipment logos were seen on players (especially on Freddie Couples's visor) for six minutes and twenty-seven seconds for $1,096,500; Dunlop Maxfli logos were observed for 3:17, valued at $558,165; Southern Bell logos clocked in at 2:39, for $450,500; and the Lexus automobile insignia appeared for 1:59, at $337,000. Someone should study how much extra value is achieved by sponsoring an especially slow putter like Bernard Langer, whose visor is before our eyes as he hunches over every interminable putt.

So what about soccer? Alas, although the French love advertising, they love soccer even more, and they control the commercial aspects of the game. The 1994 World Cup, the Super Bowl of soccer, was held in the United States. Twenty-four nations playing fifty-two games in nine major cities. What an advertising bonanza! Everyone will be watching! All over the world! Alas, what they saw was soccer. That's the problem. Not only is the game low scoring, which is not the fault of the French, but there is no stop in play—no infamous "TV Timeouts" so important to basketball. Nonstop forty-five-minute halves are anathema to Adcult. The best that can be hoped for in sponsoring soccer is to own the billboards surrounding the field or surrounding the clock in the upper corner of the television screen.

Sometimes the penetration of advertising into a sporting event is so complete that the event shrivels up and the advertising takes over. As we will see later in this chapter, when this happens the event becomes more a way to mark time than to conduct an athletic rivalry. We gather at these events not so much to watch as to mingle. Two of the most important of these feel-good events is one that happens every four years—the Olympics—and one that we celebrate annually—the Super Bowl. What they may lack in athletic sport, they make up in advertising virtuosity. They both serve to introduce the important ad campaigns we will be seeing for months.

Commercial time on the Super Bowl is the most expensive in the world—more than $40,000 a second, $1 million a spot. Everything expands during the Super Bowl; even the usual advertising load is doubled. A few years ago a record of sorts was set when 44 percent of a forty-five-minute stretch was dedicated to commercials and promos. This is not a game. It is a carnival of commercialism. Admittedly, commercialism is at the heart of all professional games. Recall that the National Football League and National Basketball Association developed from industrial leagues and that often the old team names carry the vestige of sponsorship. The Green Bay Packers were named after a local packing plant, and the Philadelphia 66ers were named for Phillips 66 gasoline. There is now talk that companies like Federal Express, Kodak, and Anheuser-Busch will team up with CBS to constitute a third league based on company teams. But the Super Bowl has always been unique. This event is a huge sweat lodge for men. Almost every male aged eighteen to forty-five is there.

The most important play in the Super Bowl is the launching of new campaigns. We know that Gillette and the cola companies will be showcasing new products. There will be the Bud Bowl, a loony cartoon for Nike, and the blow-the-budget ad from MasterLock. We even know that the game will end when the Most Valuable Player says, "I'm going to Walt Disney World!" (for which he pockets $50,000 to $75,000). The next day the MVP often appears on a box of Wheaties. We know all this because, to paraphrase Yogi Berra, the Super Bowl is déjà vu all over again. See it once, you've seen it a thousand times. Only the ads change. If you read the newspapers before and after the game, you will find almost as much ad coverage as football. The upstart *USA Today* goes all out, with sixty-eight volunteers wired to the "admeter" to record second-by-second reactions to commercials. Even the gray aunt, the *New York Times*, and the grumpy uncle, the *Wall Street Journal*, dedicate tons of newsprint to stories about the Super Bowl ads. Who knows (or cares) what teams played in the 1984 Super Bowl, but many people saw (or wish they had seen) the shown-only-once Chiat/Day anti-Orwellian commercial "1984," introducing Apple Computer's Macintosh. Now that was an event worth remembering.

Thank goodness the Olympics come only every four years. What was at one time a minor competition between amateur athletes was transformed in the mid-twentieth century into a political struggle and then in the 1980s into a commercial circus. The Olympic name and the interlocking rings are trademarked possessions of the International Olympic Committee, but almost everything else is up for grabs.

For the sixteen days of the Olympics we are treated to a maelstrom of mercenary merchandising. Until 1980 no advertising was allowed on the playing fields, and that meant no advertising whatsoever—no endorsements, no named equipment, no writing on any clothing, no nothing. Of course, this didn't mean that skiers, for instance, could not be photographed with their skis (brand names now in large letters on the ski bottoms turned out to camera), wearing RayBans, and clutching Evian bottles. It just meant that the illusion of amateur status had to be maintained. But the illusion was proving expensive. Professional sports appeared to be eating away the Olympic franchise, and so the muck-a-mucks in Greece allowed public endorsements so long as the money was used only for training purposes (which really meant it was put into trust until the amateur turned pro).

To make sure there was no subterfuge certain equipment manufacturers could not be sponsors, because no sponsor may provide equipment to a team. This is a special problem with shoes because shoes are necessary in so many events, and shoes are a worldwide branded commodity. So what did the shoe companies do? Observe Reebok in 1992. Reebok attempted to lay claim to an entire event, the decathlon, with its "Dan and Dave" campaign. Safely skirting the problem of sponsoring a team, the company essentially bet $30 million that either Dan O'Brien or Dave Johnson would first qualify for the team and then win the event. Reebok covered all possibilities by preparing ads in which each man won the gold with the loser congratulating him. What they didn't count on was that Dan wouldn't even make the team.

Undismayed, Reebok also paid a fee to supply ornamental uniforms with a small corporate logo to be worn by the athletes in public. These were not athletic uniforms, mind you; that would have been illegal. When the professional American basketball players ("America's Dream Team") stood in the hot glare of the television lights to collect their gold medals, the logos would be there for all the world to see. Unfortunately, Michael Jordan, paid millions of dollars to wear only Nike logos, balked. He threatened not to appear if he had to sport the foul Reebok insignia. Under the advice of his Nike lawyers he had earlier crossed out Rule 14 of the Olympic Code stipulating that he would wear the ornamental uniform for medal appearances. How to resolve the dilemma of conflicting loyalties? One of the first rules of Adcult was invoked: bid the stakes high enough and resolution can be found. Jordan was allowed to fold back the front flap of his jacket during the ceremony, thereby obscuring the offending blot.

The real excitement of the Olympics is not the sporting events. Whining fans claim it is, but when NBC provided an ad-free, pay-per-view version, the network found out the truth. The luge, badminton, canoe racing, biathlon, lots of swimming, speed walking, and the rest are not riveting television fare to an audience accustomed to professional wrestling and kick boxing. But the ads are. And some of the biggest competitions are between those corporations who pay to be sponsors and those who sneak in without paying their share. Called ambush or parasite marketing, this happens when a competitor attempts to use your venue against you.

The ambush of Olympian proportions is between American Express and Visa. Visa buys the sponsorship and says "Don't take American Express," but then AmEx buys television time and says, "You don't need Visa." They are not the only ones to dance this pas de deux. If Bristol-Myers Squibb's Clairol is

AND THE WINNER IS...

Major Credit Cards Accepted   FREE PARKING

7.31.92 THE PHILADELPHIA INQUIRER.
UNIVERSAL PRESS SYNDICATE.

♦ Tony Auth, "And the winner is . . ." *Philadelphia Inquirer*, 1992, Universal Press Syndicate.

the "official hair care sponsor," Procter & Gamble's Pert buys ad time. Coke is a sponsor, so Pepsi runs "a commercial salute" to Michael Jordan decked out in all his Olympic regalia (logos turned). The deep-pocket sponsor may not like this, but the law mandates that commercial speech cannot be prohibited if it meets network standards. Sometimes the ambush can work without buying television time. McDonald's forked over millions to be the exclusive fast-food sponsor for the 1988 Winter Games. Meanwhile, Wendy's ran a campaign claiming it was a " Proud sponsor of ABC's television coverage of the 1988 Winter Olympics," using the ABC logo like the Olympic rings. Wendy's splattered this all over print ads as well as in the restaurants, along with ski posters proclaiming "We'll be there!" One of the first acts of the Olympic committee of Atlanta was to buy up all the available billboard space for the summer 1996 Olympics. After all, if you are charging some dozen sponsors about $40 million, at least you can assure them the trip to the events will not prove embarrassing. Next the committee hired a full-time attorney with the daunting title of director of sponsor protection.

Aside from the Center for the Study of Commercialism (a nonprofit organization in Washington, D.C., that "exposes and opposes commercialism"), a few academics, and a handful of grumpy sports fans who actually remember when the term *amateur* was a reality, no one takes the commercialization of sports seriously. Certainly, no one puts forward the hoary argument that commercialism actually lowers ticket prices, because there used to be no ticket prices. Sports were free. That was the whole point. Besides, the quality of play has vastly improved as sports—even amateur sports—have become a venue for advertising.

To find any battle against Adcult's intrusion into popular culture, we must go to the women's movement. During the last generation a steady parade of Cassandras, from Betty Friedan to Naomi Wolf, has contended that the commodification of gender is not just a nuisance but a handicap. I must say that I do not find the feminist critique of advertising entirely fair-minded, but I give it because it is the only coherent indictment of Adcult that has ever had a political following, and it has produced real changes in the industry.

The feminist criticism starts with the relatively simple proposition from eighteenth-century empiricism: *esse est percepti*, to be is to be perceived. What we take ourselves to be is how we perceive ourselves to be perceived. And we see ourselves in the media. Before the argument cleaves into gender-based concerns, let's have a look at something both sexes share that is literally at the edge of self and other—our epidermis. For our skin is literally what we show to the world of our selves. And what we put on our skin is what we see on the skins of others and how we want ourselves to be seen.

Having clean skin is a modern concern—instilled, aided, and abetted by companies in the nineteenth century that were producing surpluses of an everyday product, namely, soap. At the beginning of this century most people cleaned the skin of their entire body only once a week. On Saturday night, both

◆ The Cleanliness Institute (1929) sees to it that cleanliness is not just next to godliness but crucial to employment as well. Lysol follows.

HE THOUGHT: "How absolutely lovely she is tonight!"

SHE THOUGHT: "How glad I am I washed my hair and changed to this fresh dress!"

Real cleanliness is the greatest beauty secret!

WHICH *two would you hire?*

experienced and intelligent | experienced and intelligent | experienced intelligent *and* CLEAN | experienced | experienced intelligent *and* CLEAN | experienced and intelligent

in anticipation of the sabbath and as a result of the organization necessary to supply sufficient hot water, the family bathed. The soap people used was made from animal fats leached through ashes. Such soap was labor intensive to produce, unwieldy to use, and smelly. Hair was washed once a month as the soap tended to add oil, not remove it. The toothbrush was unknown. The mouth, like the armpit, certainly produced odors, but they had not yet been labeled offensive. In fact, because they were the norm, they may well have not been "smelly" at all.

The mass production of soap made from vegetable oils rather than from organic materials, and the serendipitous discovery by James Gamble that overbeating the mixture would aerate it sufficiently so that it would float, and that this floating

could be associated in consumers' minds with purity ("Ninety-nine and forty-four one hundredths percent pure"), allowed Ivory to separate itself from other soaps like Pears' and Sapolio and advertise its "ownership" of purity. The importance of Palmolive as a soap name is lost to us, but it announced to early users that no animal fats were used.

The other matter that should not be forgotten, and which was known to the upper classes, is that human skin feels better when clean. The most important reason factory-made soap succeeded was that it was useful. By 1938, when the Scripps-Howard newspaper chain polled a cross section of its readers in sixteen cities, soap ranked second only to bread as an essential. As the same time soap was becoming second to food in advertising volume (Vinikas 1992:93). The cultural ramifications were considerable. A new term, *hygiene*, was coined, the cosmetics industry began, and the concept of gender was profoundly changed.

Skin was not alone. Soon those other uncharted territories of the body became colonized. No crevasse, cave, or gully would go uncharted. Consider Listerine, which started as a hospital disinfectant. You would have been considered vile had you swirled it around in your mouth at the turn of the century. It should be used on the walls of operating rooms. Looking for a way to extend product application, Gerard Lambert, the mildly dissolute heir of the family business (at Princeton in the 1920s he had been chauffeured from building to building), came across the term *halitosis* in a medical journal. Lambert never cared much for the chemical business, but he loved to write ads and now he did. In his reminiscential essay "How I Sold Listerine," he tells of how in the early ads he told the story of how "a young lassie lost the lad of her dreams" for reasons that we learn only by checking an asterisk. There, separated from the copy, is the offending condition that has caused so much modern love to go sour—halitosis. With a dedication worthy of an obsessive compulsive, young Lambert steadily increased his advertising until he had saturated magazine and newspaper culture. By 1928 he was the third-largest advertiser in magazines. By the 1930s, although he had to give up the claim of Listerine as aftershave lotion, the mouth was his.

In Adcult all the senses are up for grabs. Sight, of course, is self-evident. But take touch. From "the skin you love to touch" (thought by Albert Lasker to be the introduction of sex into advertising) to "reach out and touch someone" (to sell telephone use), the exploitation of "being in touch" is omnipresent. Shaving the underarms and legs to make them touchable is recent. Kissing on the lips is far more popular in a culture that sells special lip colors than in those with natural skin. Although no one has applied a kissometer, we probably kiss more in the 1990s than in the 1890s, in large part because of the concept of "kissable lips." To some Freudians the painting of lips in shades of red, the act of French kissing with plunging tongues, and even the injecting of silicone to make them appear chubbier, is a far more sophisticated translation of nether labia than advertisers may ever have

• How to sell a wall disinfectant: Have a heart, Listerine.

Maybelline invents
ColorFresh® Lipstick
Imagine color so rich, so bold.
With shine this outrageous.

Set a shining example. Show them what lip color was meant to be.
Devastating. Now you've got it. 10 scintillating shades with
plenty of polish. Brimming with lavish moisturizers.
New ColorFresh Lipstick. Leaps and bounds beyond the ordinary.

ColorFresh Lipstick only from **Maybelline**®

FORMULA 2

✦ Lips as labia: Freud amok on Madison Avenue.

intended. But if you look at lipstick ads in women's magazines, you may not be so sure.

But the really powerful sense in Adcult is smell. How else to explain the underarm deodorant Odorono? And what of the long-dormant but still linguistically resonant campaign of Lifebuoy soap, based on just the initials of what we all know so well as B.O. The business of deodorization could not have been successful without the germ theory of illness. The concept of bad germs hiding on the body ready to charge out and ambush the forces of good health was more than a powerful trope. It was the selling tool of an entire industry. Being able to link the smell of rot with the appearance of such bad germs was the trigger of ersatz hygiene.

The programming of the senses, the social bells and whistles of bad odor, was not created in Adcult but exploited by it. The Cleanliness Institute, founded by the Association of American Soap and Glycerine Producers, inundated not just the media but the school system with expert advice on hygiene. It lobbied for special classes in hygiene and got them. That the rise of modern scientific medicine, directed by principles of observation and experimentation, should have been hijacked by the descendants of the patent medicine industry is no surprise. That it remains so powerful is a surprise, how-ever. Much of the revenue flow of the major pharmaceutical companies in modern America, companies like Warner-Lambert, Bristol-Myers Squibb, Schering-Plough, American Home Products, Merck, and Upjohn, is not from proprietary drugs but from the over-the-counter concoctions to correct some natural deficiency or defend some body part from the attack of germs.

To some degree the germ theory is the basis of gender differentiation in the West. For once you remove dirt from the skin, pyorrhea from the mouth, and sweat from the armpit, the next step is clear: replenish, restore, replace, recreate. Cascading forth from the cosmetological cornucopia come all man-ner of deodorant sprays, antiperspirants, mouth washes, breath fresheners, foot powders, depilatories, scented shampoos, douches, clothes fresheners, and especially facial paint. To market many of these products, gender needs to be separated from sex. Sex is biological. Gender is cultural.

Arguably the most lasting contribution of Adcult is the ongoing creation and maintenance of gender. Until the 1920s men and women generally shared the same ideas and tools of cleanliness. Get rid of grime. The Gillette safety razor allowed men to more easily remove the natural growth of facial hair in a daily morning ritual. Women's ritual also centered on the face. Face paint-ing, once reserved for prostitutes ("painted ladies") became an accepted rou-tine in presenting the self for the day. It became required display for evening. Once the natural oils and dirt had been removed, the concept of cover-up became essential. Put on a face. Change the self. Look female. And be pre-pared to do this repeatedly during the day. Lacquering the soma with lipstick, eyestick, eyelash stick, fingernail stick became commonplace. Cosmetology became a science. Ideals like Miss America were spun out as examples of the perfectibility of this science when properly applied. Dressing and undressing became fetishized, because taking off and putting on was fundamental to femalehood. Gender was being branded.

Were women in the early twentieth century duped by the onslaught of cosmetics? Were they cajoled against their better judgment to wash off their natural selves and paint themselves anew? And for whom did they do this? Recall Helen Resor's line for Woodbury soap, which revolutionized Adcult: "For the skin you love to touch." Who is the "you" who touches your skin? You or he? Just who was your face for? Recall Shirley Perkoff's line, "The closer he gets, the better you look." Why wasn't it "The closer you get the bet-ter he looks?" Did the faceless corporations of "the beauty industry" use the various new media of women's magazines to promulgate a culture of the sub-jection of the female self to the male other? (It need not be mentioned that most cosmetic advertising is written by women to appear in magazines edited by women—admittedly in parts of corporations run by men, the majority of stock in which is owned by women. Big deal.)

◆ Adcult at work: the creation of B.O., acid mouth, and comedones (blackheads).

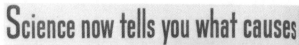

In one of the few dispassionate treatments of modern cultural cosmetology Vincent Vinikas writes in *Soft Soap, Hard Sell: American Hygiene in an Age of Advertisement*:

> Advertising certainly stimulated demand for lipsticks, powders, rouge, eye makeup and the rest. But the phenomenal surge in the sale of cosmetics cannot be credited to the new vehicles of mass persuasion that appeared in the early twentieth century. Instead, we must look to structural realignments in gender relations, as women assumed a more public identity than had been accorded them in the past. This reinterpretation of the meaning of female in America was signaled by Suffrage, the birth control movement, new conception of motherhood, and the development of new frameworks of opportunity for women beyond the confines of the home. It is only within the context of this fundamental change in the apperception of the woman's place—the conditional acceptance of the "New Woman"—that the cult of feminine beauty becomes comprehensible. • (1992:xv)

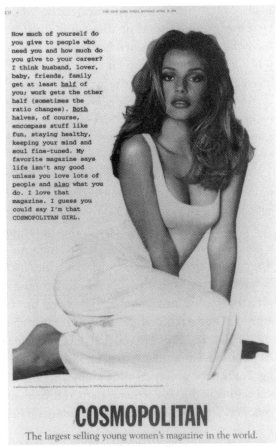

How much of yourself do you give to people who need you and how much do you give to your career? I think husband, lover, baby, friends, family get at least half of you; work gets the other half (sometimes the ratio changes). Both halves, of course, encompass stuff like fun, staying healthy, keeping your mind and soul fine-tuned. My favorite magazine says life isn't any good unless you love lots of people and also what you do. I love that magazine. I guess you could say I'm that COSMOPOLITAN GIRL.

COSMOPOLITAN
The largest selling young women's magazine in the world.

◆ The Cosmopolitan Girl: aspirations of the girl-next-door to be anything but. . . .

Certainly, we can see this transformation to New Womanhood if we leave the powder room for a moment and look sideways into the workplace. As the demand for clerical workers increased with industrialization, it was met with the increasing supply of well-educated women. The job of secretary, which until modern times had been the role of confidant or deputy to an important personage (secretary = someone who could keep a secret), became not just gender but machine linked. The telephone and the typewriter became the tools of the receptionist-secretary. In 1890 women did 60 percent of the typing jobs in the United States, in 1900 it was 77 percent, and by 1920 it was 90 percent. To be sure these jobs now carry a sense of belittlement, as in the term *Girl Friday*. Today's feminist wouldn't be caught dead operating in such a job. In Adcult the working woman is now pictured as jauntily swinging her Louis Vuitton briefcase as she enters the boardroom. Or she pats a male rump en route to Somewhere Important as in the infamous Charlie perfume ad of the 1970s. But the next generation of women may well find this Enjoli woman ("Bring home the bacon, fry it up in a pan") just as ridiculous as we find the image of the secretary in the 1950s, mooning over her new IBM Selectric. However, at the time women were moving into the workforce, they remarked upon no such degradation. Quite the opposite. The "new woman" was the woman at last independent of the stultifying confines of the family and at last earning an independent wage.

How we look back in the brief history of Adcult is always determined by what we see today. In a museum show as revealing of current sensitivities as knowledge of the past, the Cooper-Hewitt recently displayed the tools of the mid-century American secretary. The informing premise of "Mechanical Brides: Women and Machines from Home to Office" was that somehow "they" were "gendering" the work space for "us," and vice versa. The manufacturers of typewriters, telephones, and ironing boards were concocting and advertising a life for women devoid of real promise and excitement, to keep women if not servile then at least uncomfortable. You could not enter that marketplace as you were. You had to be re*fashioned*.

This view of woman-as-victim was especially true in the descriptive catalog. There is, however, a world of difference between shaping wants and needs and getting in the way of them. Herbert Muschamp, culture critic for the *New York Times*, made a central point about Adcult in his review of the show:

> So why has Cooper-Hewitt tried to tell its story as a narrative of deception? Because deception requires that someone is fooled, and someone else is doing the fooling. It sets up a plot of victims and oppressors. And what "Mechanical Brides" wants to illustrate is not simply that appliances are designed for women, but that they are also designed to keep women in their place. The secretary smiling at her desk has been duped into accepting a better typewriter instead of a better life. The curves and colors of her new Royal remind her that she is valued chiefly for being pretty.
>
> The case is not airtight. The advertisements do show women in subservient positions: washing their husbands' pants or taking their bosses' dictation. But it is far from clear that the sexy new typewriter is what dragged the woman into the typing pool or discourages her from climbing out of it. In fact, since consumers mostly are women, the warped case could also be made that they're the ones responsible for trapping men into roles of insufferably rigid masculinity. How do we know that some husbands in the 1950s didn't secretly long to drop their lawn mowers, pull on satin gloves and flash their wives the "Sheer Look?"
>
> The point is that the objects presented in this show invite more complex reading than the show itself allows. For instance, the secretary's smile may simply register that her new typewriter is a better piece of equipment. (When

I worked as a secretary, I may not have grinned from 9 to 5, but the I.B.M. Selectric III was a joy to use.) Then, too, the transformation of industrial appliances into highly styled objects reflected something more than the entrance of women into lower echelons of the work force. It also reflected the broader shift in the nation's economy from manufacturing to service industries that set a higher store on image.   • (1993:C1)

I pause on Muschamp's point because the same consciousness that informs "Mechanical Brides" (even the show's title distorts McLuhan's thesis in his book of the same title) is at the heart of the feminist indictment of Adcult. To a degree this view comes from the academy's love affair with Marxism. In its macrocosmic form everything is cultural politics. In its microcosmic form individuals are invariably victims. The so-called Frankfurt theorists of the 1950s and 1960s essentially argued that what we see in popular culture is the result of manipulation of the many for the profit of the few. The manipulators, aka "the culture industry," attempt to enlarge their "hegemony" by establishing their "ideological base" in the hearts and pocketbooks of the mindless. The masters of the media strive to "infantilize" the audience, to make it both docile and anxious and consumptive with "reified desire." The lords of Adcult are predators, and what they do in no way reflects or resolves genuine audience concerns.

We may think advertising is "just selling a product," but this is not so. It is selling the oppression of consumption. The weak and marginalized, especially the female and the black, are trapped into a commodifying system, a "false consciousness" and a "fetishism" that only the enlightened can correct. Not to worry, however. It just happens that the fully tenured, university-based critic who is making this argument is one of the enlightened.

Indeed, much of modern feminism indicates that many young women were paying too much attention in college. Certainly one of the most articulate recovered victims of Adcult's suffocating oppression is Naomi Wolf. The subtitle of her best-selling 1991 book—*The Beauty Myth: How Images of Beauty Are Used Against Women*—begs the question and gives the lie to much hope of objectivity. Had she spent less time in Women's Studies and more time reading history, she might have been less willing to contend that quite suddenly, just when she was entering her teenage years, the world completely changed. Essentially her thesis is that just when feminism was finally liberating women from "the men who hold them back" by providing economic independence, sexual freedom, career opportunities, and reproductive control, male-dominated culture fought back through its manipulation of the cosmetic, medical, media, and especially advertising worlds to enforce the draconian "beauty myth."

"We are in the midst of a violent backlash against feminism that uses images of female beauty as a political weapon against women's advancement: the beauty myth," is Wolf's point. This oppressive beauty myth is inflicted on millions of innocent women thousands of seconds each day by the incessant unreeling of unreal images of beauty. Advertising has become sexual harassment. Want to know why there are so many anorexics, so much cosmetic surgery, so many ad-fat womens' magazines touting fat-free diets? Ask Madison Avenue; it knows. Want to know why those string-bean images are omnipresent? Ask the men in the $300 billion cosmetic surgery industry, in the $33 billion diet industry, and in the $20 billion cosmetics industry; they know.

It is not the male bashing that I find upsetting (well, okay, a little), it is her ahistorical economy of mind. Please don't misunderstand. Why some women purge themselves, have breast implants, apply acid to their faces to peel off the wrinkles, go on innumerable, often dangerous, diets (according to one study, 90 percent of women say they have been on a diet and 20 percent of "normal" women binge once a month), and why fashion magazines have come to favor photo spreads of women wearing dog collars and chains and penciled-on bruises in order to advertise some colored grease to cover the lips, are parts of important cultural matters. It is self-evident that advertising plays a reflecting (and shaping) role in this process.

But the concept of doing something to your body to make it "beautiful" is no more new to girls than that adolescent boys are often sent out in a rite of passage to do some kind of group violence. If you stand in the right place and adjust your blinders just so, it will seem that the antisocial and often frightful behavior of young men in college fraternities is unique to our "troubled times." But it's not. It is our current expression of something far more deeply infused with culture *and* biology. Like all other myths, these bracketing events are up for grabs. They are never imposed on an unwilling culture. Advertising is the folklore of a commodity culture. As such it articulates and redirects, but it does not invent behavior. If it did we would all be wearing Corfam shoes, drinking Tab, New Coke, and Schlitz, lathering with Sapolio, brushing with Pepsodent, painkilling with Lydia Pinkham elixirs, listening to music on our eight-track stereos, watching video on our Beta machines, and tooling around in Edsels.

What happens to adolescent girls in Adcult is different from what happened two generations ago, in part because the products are so different. But the cult of feminine beauty is as old as the cult of the male warrior. (And, who knows, maybe just as obsolete.) Look at the ugly hags and sexy wenches in Chaucer or Shakespeare. Look at fairy tales, for goodness' sake. What is Cinderella all about? Revlon did not make this nonsense up, although it merchandises it. And it merchandises it because the myth still has resonance. The face of a woman has been a commodity for some time. How else to explain the mythopoetic powers of Cleopatra and Helen of Troy? A FACE THAT LAUNCHES SHIPS—a copywriter's dream headline. Her idealized shape expands and contracts. Breasts in particular come and go: relatively big in the 1950s when housewifery was central; small in the 1920s and the 1960s when suffrage and liberation were central. No one said that Twiggy made women anorexic. But flat-as-a-pancake Kate Moss is now offered as a sign of the manipulations of a male-dominated culture out to render the female helpless.

◆ Kate Moss, anorexic-looking and proud of it. The Gap is never far behind: "just the right shape" of what?

Far from being victims of a new deception, female anorexics stand in a long tradition of women who have internalized cultural imperatives to obliterate their sexuality for any number of reasons. It may be as appropriate to blame the inchoate ideals of feminism for the youthful confusions about power and control as it is to blame the hopelessly perfect images in the media.

In a howler of massive proportions Wolf claims some 150,000 deaths each year from anorexia, and she blames this "holocaust" (her word, please) on the industries of oppression. "How," she asks, "would America react to the mass self-immolation by hunger of its favorite sons?" A good question made all the more provocative by the fact that the statistic is utter nonsense. The National Center for Health Statistics reports that the annual toll from anorexia is fewer than 100—usually around 50, although in 1983 it spiked up to 101. To her credit Wolf has promised to correct the error in future editions. However, the distortion is as purposeful as it is powerful, for it allows her to invoke the most powerful analogy of the twentieth century. The image has already been picked up by textbooks used in Women's Studies. Modern life for young women in Adcult is like living next to a death camp.

To be sure, men have always been involved in matters of feminine beauty. This didn't start yesterday or even the day before. Remember the Judgment of Paris? As long ago as the third century A.D. Tertullian devoted a whole treatise to the subject of female dress, forbidding women to wear certain clothes or decorate their hair. All women, he wrote, should dress "as Eve mourning and repentant." Who can deny that his purpose was to control female sexuality and consolidate male power? And what of Thomas Aquinas, who implicitly acknowledged the bargain offered to compliant women when he wrote that nuns by renouncing sexuality "are promoted to the dignity of men whereby they are liberated from the subjection of men." Rascals have been around for awhile. And what of cultures different from ours, like present-day Iran, where the chador is used to protect otherwise oh-so-powerful men from the temptations of female flesh? And, for that matter, what was the Holy Roman Catholic Church doing with the cult of the virgin Mary?

Dark forces ("male institutions," "the economy," "Madison Avenue," "the power structure," "the cosmetics industry"), alarmed by the onward march of women, are not on the offensive, all due respect to the conspiracy and victim crowd: Catherine MacKinnon (feminist law), Andrea Dworkin (rape theory), Susan Faludi (backlash conspiracy), and Naomi Wolf (beauty myth). Women are not being systematically enervated by men just as the sisterhood struggles to be powerful. The idea that women are so utterly victimized by the way they are portrayed in their magazines that they starve themselves and become sick has a certain alluring simplicity. If only human nature were so simple. But anorexia and bulimia are multifactoral disorders more attributable to biology, environment, and personality than to the appearance of scrawny models in Diet Coke ads. This is not to deny the sexist nature of much of the media, or the reflective *and* aspirational nature of images cast in that media, but only to deny that conspiracy is the explanation.

Wolf tells an interesting story that she herself might ponder. Once, just before she was to deliver a lecture at a university, she was summoned to meet a group of women's studies majors to be sure she was right thinking. "Isn't the act of writing a book," asked a young woman accusingly, "in itself exclusionary to women who cannot read?" There are many answers to this transcendentally dumb question, short of howling in disbelief. One is that while it may be comforting to feel like a victim, it is usually counterproductive to act like one. This is not a gender-based problem. Listen to the bleats of full-grown white men in Detroit contending that the Japanese and Germans have stolen the American car market. By building better cars perhaps?

Having said that, it is of more than passing interest to see how much ads have changed, not so much because of feminist observations but from market pressure, a market that has changed because of feminism. If you watch early afternoon television, which used to be the entertainment ghetto for women, you will see few of the "two consumers in a kitchen"—type of advertising made standard by Procter & Gamble. If women today are house prisoners, their concerns are for personal injury lawyers, schooling programs like Hooked on Phonics, mortgage companies, Conway Twitty records, relief from vaginal itch, and a lot of kids' paraphernalia like diapers and toys. If you watch television ads for kitchen products, you are likely to see not frustrated housewives pleading for Mr. Clean or The Man from Glad, but Elayne Boozler controlling kitchen odor with Fantastik and wisecracks.

Television is filled with ads portraying women as being in control. What of the Maidenform ads (made at Ogilvy & Mather entirely by women) sym-

✦ A view of women in mid-century Adcult: part one.

Perfume and Parabolics

SPRINGMAID
FABRICS

SPRINGS MILLS

NO SEAMS TO WORRY ABOUT!

I'VE FALLEN FOR SEAMLESS STOCKINGS BY *Hanes*

bolically depicting the diversity of women with a rapid succession of thirty women's clothed torsos, each sporting different pins, with slogans ranging from "Right to Life" and "My Body, My Choice" to "No Pain, No Gain" and "Support Recycling." What of the Blockbuster ad in which the working heroine forgoes a date with a handsome man in order to watch a movie alone. Or the feisty woman at a gas pump telling us how she bought this Subaru, and how the '69 Mets choked. As I write this, two prime-time ads are poking fun at gender roles in advertising. In a Diet Coke commercial women office workers leer at a construction worker who takes off his shirt and opens the soft drink. The spot closes with their agreement to meet again tomorrow. And in a Hyundai ad women make suggestive comments about men who confuse flashy automobiles with virility. A hunk drives by in the economical Hyundai. Voyeurism? Certainly. Reverse sexism? Hardly. How come? Women are the target audience of both products.

In magazine ads Bamboo lingerie ridicules men for using words like *headlights, door knockers,* and *melons* and ends with the tag line, "Bamboo Lingerie, a company owned by two women. Put that in your pipe and smoke it." Liz Claiborne shoes flaunts the line, "Aren't there enough heels in your life?" while her fragrance ads use the theme "Reality is the best fantasy of all" and depict real-looking women in everyday situations. A new Maidenform "still-life" magazine ad shows a lacy bra lying on a table next to a stack of best-

◆ A more modern view in Adcult: part two.

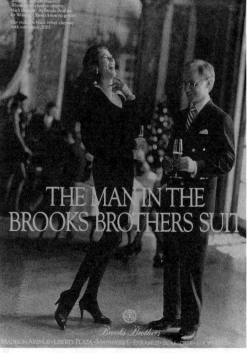

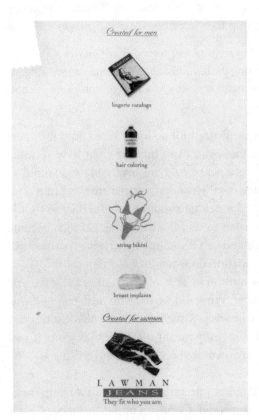

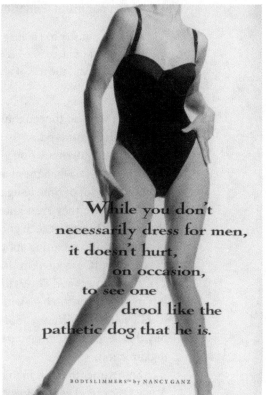

selling books by women. How about Nike's "You are not a goddess and you are never going to be a goddess" and its "You'll never be perfect" print ads? And Nike's three new black-and-white TV spots—its first TV campaign aimed at women—include one that says a woman's life should be as much of an announcement as her "selfish and shattering" scream at birth. Another advises, "Don't rush. The world rushes enough as it is."

⊷ A still-more modern view: part three.

In no way do I mean to overlook the "You've come a long way, baby" or the "I dreamed I was . . . in my Maidenform Bra" genre, or the use of pubescent eroticism in selling jeans, or the uniformly over-the-top cosmetic ads of women's magazines. Whether she is the Breck Girl, the Cover Girl, or the Cosmo Girl, the one girl she is *not* is the girl next door. Nor do I want to pretend that the Johnnie Walker, Calvin Klein, Virginia Slims et al. campaigns don't exist. But I do want to argue that this aspect of advertising is neither new nor oppressive. Would that it were so, many an advertiser might hope. Sex doesn't sell, but it certainly captures attention. The Springmaid Sheet ads of the 1930s, the busty women on the Coke calendars, the endless use of sex to focus concentration on cigarettes, automobiles, beer, and what-have-you were the steady diet of the generation of women who produced the generation of women who now find themselves helpless before the onslaught of Adcult.

Ann Simonton, onetime beauty contestant and now director of Media-Watch—a nonprofit feminist group that "monitors sexism," makes the case:

> The ad industry has managed to mainstream pornographic images and desensitize the populace into accepting the humiliation of women in advertising. By porno I mean the use of a woman's sexuality as if it were some kind of commodity for sale.　　　　　　　　　　　　　　• (Strnad 1993:S6)

If women were so thoroughly desensitized for so long, how could they perceive their plight? And what of men who can't buy the right kind of toilet paper, leave watermarks on the glassware, and are invariably too stupid to know what to do when they have a cold? How desensitized are they? In Adcult men spend a lot of time lying abed moaning about how awful they feel. Only occasionally do they even know what to do for a headache. Let men become the primary buyers of such goods and you'll see the roles change. Women will be lying around moaning about what to do when they feel punk.

This shift is evident in slow motion in beer ads. Men used to be the primary consumers and *buyers* of beer. What did we have for ads? Endless bimbos in steamy pickup bars with voiceovers assuring us the "The night belongs to Michelob," which any fool knew really meant the "chick" is yours if you buy this beer. Now women are buying more beer and the advertising is shifting direction.

Sometimes the shift in mythography gets stuck and we can see it up close. A few years ago Hal Riney & Partners did a send-up of the "get a beer, get a chick, celebrate the beer" tradition with its now infamous Swedish Bikini Team campaign for Stroh's Old Milwaukee brand. To understand the parody you needed to know that for years the Old Milwaukee commercials had featured young males out fishing, hiking, and generally bonding and, come sundown, drinking that beer and sighing in unison, "It doesn't get any better than this." In the send-up the fellows are all set to deliver the tag line when the Swedish Bikini Team arrives by raft or parachute or whatever. The joke is that the buxom beer bimbos (who are all wearing outrageous blond wigs) are clearly aware of the ridiculousness of the situation. The boys were quite wrong to think that "it doesn't get any better than this." It does. The punch line was missed in an avalanche of complaints, including some from women who worked in the brewery and thought they were being ridiculed, even harassed. As often happens in Adcult, the bikini team went on the cover of *Playboy*. The campaign was pulled, but it did show, if only for a second, the same shifting mythology of beer that has forever changed beer ads and literally shrunken the bosom of the St. Pauli Girl.

Gender differences are often confused with purchasing differences. When was the last time you saw a woman used in an automobile ad as an ornament? Forget it. In fact, some cars, like the Ford Probe, have so cornered the female market that no men even appear in the advertising. About half of all car-buying decisions are now made by women, compared with less than a third before the 1980s. Men buy most of the shaving cream, which is why the Gunilla Knutson "Take it off, men, take it all off " ad for Noxzema was such a success. And still is. Men also buy most of the small office products (fax machines, copiers), which is why Sharp Office Products runs the campaign with the sharply angular and steely technodominatrix who makes a point of repeating, "When I say Sharp, I mean business."

However, women buy most of the fragrances for men, which is why so many brands are keyed to perfume. Eternity for Men, Giorgio for Men, Passion for Men are all sold at the women's counter. So when Chanel does a television ad for Égoïste cologne for men (to be bought by women), it is an arty spot of thirty-two women screaming in French from their apartment windows. Dressed in ball gowns and long gloves, they yell such insults as "Miserable one" and "How could I have lived so long and been so disgraced?" all in French. Then they slam their shutters in unison against this cad. In focus groups the men had trouble understanding the message. They thought the French was important to translate. But women understood: this is how she wants her man to be. In such cases males are a "nice to" have, not a "have to" have audience. However, men still buy Old Spice. So the ad for them is the sailor home from the sea with the chick on his arm, tossing his Old Spice to young dweebs who so desperately need it.

Another example: young men buy their own pants. Their ads resemble the Bugle Boy campaign in which lots of sexy women are shown trying on men's jeans. But 60 percent of jeans for men older than twenty-five are bought by women. Hence the Dockers casual pants ads, in which the camera pans the butts and crotches as a bunch of guys have a chucklefest, are for women. So too is the send-up of the traditional male-bonding scene in which we see three golf buddies pitying a fourth for not being able to escape the clutches of his wife for a little weekend play. The scene shifts to the bedroom of the fourth as he is in the arms of his wife, having a far better time than he ever could have had on the links.

What we hear when we listen to the racket of Adcult is often deafening. It often seems as though a New Year's noisemaker is wailing the pitches of Calvin Klein, Benetton, or any of the in-your-ear campaigns designed to be fingernails on the chalkboard. But in truth, advertising is one of the most conservative forces in culture. It is more metronome than trumpet. Although individual ads do indeed claim the outer edge of acceptability, and their memorability often depends on this outrageousness, the accumulated force of commercial selling is more like a slow and continuous drumbeat of social norms. Again what commercial language does here with gender is exactly what all organizing systems do: it externalizes deep, culture-specific, occasionally even biologic, concerns and ties them to spe-

◆ Adcult at work:
testing, testing,
testing . . .

cific physical goods. In so doing Adcult behaves far more like a religion, gaining power as it colonizes distant aspects of life, making them part of a coherent pattern, than like an oppressive dictatorship forcing innocent and helpless consumers to give up their better judgment in order to aggrandize some evil mercantile power.

'When You Care Enough to Send the Very Best:
Festivals of Consumption in Adcult

We move through an invisible gel of time. In ancient days we knew where we were in the time flow by the amount of light and dark that occurred each day. And the rhythms of the seasons showed us where we were in our life*time* as we became aware of the cycles of vegetation. To mark these limits we have the light delineations of days, months, and years, as well as the growth delineations of furrowing, planting, tending, and harvesting. To mark these time blocks, we often celebrate some rite of passage.

The rise of the worlds' great religions saw the co-opting of these demarcations as they became tied to some mythic paradigm, no longer just of light and growth, but of human purpose. This syncretism is nowhere better seen than in the colonizing of ancient time markers by nascent Christianity. Not by happenstance does the birth of Jesus occur at the winter solstice; not by happenstance does the Resurrection happen in the springtime (on the Sunday following the first full moon after the vernal equinox). Nor do the attendant ceremonies of these time marks, in which we gather together to ask the Lord's blessing, exchange gifts, eat special foods, and sometimes exchange still more gifts have anything to do with whimsy. These ceremonies tell us where we are in time. The power of Christianity (and of any other enduring organizing system) is that it never does away with the old pattern but continually adapts it to changing needs.

So it is with Adcult. The ancient rhythms of the day, the artificial separation of the week, the solar mandates of the year are remembered in Adcult, as they are in Christianity, with specific services in which we are led from one time zone to another. From morning devotion to evening vespers to night-time prayer, from Sunday service to Sunday service, through a year punctuated with festivals of thanksgiving and grieving, Christians keep time with their church. The clock is on the church steeple and the church bells ring out these changes. From breakfast and morning news through coffee break to late-afternoon cocktail time to sign-off, from Saturday shopping to Saturday shopping, through a year punctuated by festivals of consumption and sales, modern Adcultists keep time with their advertising. Our clock is no longer on the church but inside the television set. We move in half-hour blocks from morning chat through midday soap operas to late afternoon reruns to the newshour to early prime to prime time to late fringe and finally into late night. During the teleyear we move from the introduction of the new shows in the fall through the sweeps weeks of winter to the reruns of summer. (Or at least we used to, until the chaos of cable.)

We begin our circadian rhythm with a meal called breakfast. Before Messrs. Post and Kellogg this meal consisted of breaking fast by finishing last night's dinner. In fact, if you go to Western Europe where break-fast traditions are still in force, you find the same meat courses of generations ago. Often table scraps were reheated—rashers and bangers and blood pudding. (What we didn't eat then went to the floor as dog food. There was no "dog food" until Ralston Purina's ad agency created it.) The abundant supply of grains, and the technology to treat and package them, led to the advertising claim that "Breakfast is the most important meal of the day." It is an important stop on "the road to Wellville." Cereal at breakfast is a uniquely American custom, embedded by the constant repetition of spurious claims of improved health (just like dog food) and energy (just like patent medicine). Breakfast stuck.

The coffee break, however, took more doing. Here we have a drug, caffeine, which stimulates the nervous system and provides a short-term increase in attentiveness. The producers of coffee, once they were able to grow and cure it in bulk, didn't know where to position their product. Was it a breakfast drink or a dinner drink? Initially it made sense to make coffee time near the end of the workday, and indeed many early ads show coffee being consumed near quitting time.

So too the cocktail hour, a celebration of yet another addictive drug, comes after quitting time in the industrial age. However, drinking alcohol comes during the day in agrarian cultures. In the eighteenth century the rise of first cheap gin, then rum, posed a hazard for the machine age. Although

◆ Adcult and the calendar: note the clock on the wall in the 1922 coffee time ad. Whoops, wrong time, change campaign. Alas, Sunday never became Puffed Grain Day.

such drinks were not only a triumph of technology but also a sign of agricultural proficiency (because they depend on producing a surplus of rye, corn, wheat, barley, sugar cane, apples, and potatoes), their consumption during the day was a hindrance to orderly production. "Blue Monday," for instance, came about because the culture was unable to separate drunkenness from the workweek. It was resolved, as Witold Rybczynski has argued in *Waiting for the Weekend* (1991), with the separation of Saturday, not Monday, from the week into the weekend. So too the cocktail hour is the way to separate work and play. Coffee went to the morning, alcohol to early evening.

Although the stars and the planets make the years, months, and days, people make the workweek and the workweek depends on the weekend. Who knows why we separate work from leisure—do we work to have leisure or is leisure a preparation for work?—but we separate it in almost every culture. No one knows how the seven-day cycle developed, but somehow it stuck. Across cultures and through history, dividing time into seven-day chunks is the habit of humans. Some years ago the Ford Foundation calculated that nine days would make more economic sense, as we would work in three shifts of three days with a three-day rest, but as much as machines would profit, humans wouldn't. We like seven days—that's all there is to it. Perhaps this has to do with digestion and food spoilage, or perhaps it is simply that enough work is simply enough; no one knows. But this much is clear. To separate workweeks from each other, cultures need an off-on switch with a day of transition. This rest day gets coded in early modern times with religious sanctions. So, to summarize, the "rest day" is demanded by workers, sanctified by a supernatural force, and reinforced by institutional events. Hence the universal appeal of what we call Sunday. But what about Saturday? Why don't we have six workdays and then rest day?

We did. Until the eighteenth century it was work, work, work, stop, work, work . . . in chunks of six and one. Then a number of interesting developments shifted the rhythm to five and two. These developments are at the heart of Adcult. First, efficient production meant surplus, and surplus means that market day was no longer a time where you *could* exchange stuff but a time when you *had* to exchange stuff. To capture the economies of mass production markets had to be expanded, and to do this the distribution systems had to be enlarged. Second, workers now needed time off to buy the excess goods. Third—and here the fun begins—just as the industrial revolution is providing buyers and sellers of surplus goods and labor, the brewers are making it possible to have not just a cocktail hour but a real bender. This bender occurs naturally enough on Sunday afternoon. It is paid for on Monday. "Keeping Saint Monday" was a common and thoroughly inefficient way of equilibrating work and leisure. It was prized by certain groups, like cobblers, barbers, and tailors who simply started work Monday afternoon. No one much cared about them, but when factory workers started to pay allegiance to

Saint Monday, something had to be done. When you fire up a steam engine, everyone should be sober and ready to work.

The Early Closing Society, started in the middle of the nineteenth century, was almost immediately successful in trading Monday for Saturday. It should have been, for almost every important interest group supported it, except, of course, for those cobblers, tailors, and barbers. (Many barbers still take Monday off but aren't sure why.) The church, the leaders of industry, and especially the retailers, all found the relocation of consumption, whether alcohol or piece goods, to Saturday much more to their liking. Some precedent for moving the time off from Monday to Saturday already existed. Printers and some home workers (usually weavers) had only half-Saturday work, either because there were no Sunday papers or because their work was picked up and paid for on Saturday—called reckoning day.

With the advent of trains and the ability to gather either at a country home (for the wealthy) or at a fair (for the working people), the idea of the "week-end" took hold. After World War I construction unions joined the movement to solidify the workweek by pushing for the eight-hour day ("eight hours for work, eight hours for rest, eight hours for what we will"), and the Saturday shutdown switch was installed. Some unions made up of predominantly Jewish workers, like the Amalgamated Clothing Workers of America, had already taken Saturday off. They got no argument from enlightened capitalists like Henry Ford. More time to shop meant more time to buy. Blue laws, those most peculiar edicts written on blue paper in the 1780s, were not repealed, partly because retailers lobbied for them. Close down Sunday, move Monday to Saturday, and open up Saturday for retail. The dance hall revelries and later the movie matinees reinforced the saturnalian quality of Saturday. Whatever Saturday may have been—a method to get rid of food before it spoiled, a way to increase work by organizing Monday, a placebo to counteract boredom, a way to get parishioners to church—we all know what it has become. It has become shopping day at the mall.

To really observe and appreciate the effect of Adcult on our sense of time, however, we need to turn from the circadian and weekly rituals of consumption to the calendric festivals. For here, supplanting such religious and political events that crossed the Atlantic, like Shrove Tuesday, Twelfth Night, Ash Wednesday, Whitsuntide, and even Punkie Night, are a series of holiday events sustained by commercial interests. In the Darwinian struggle for attention these festivals of consumption have outdistanced the ancient festivals of church time. *Holiday*, which derives its meaning from *holy day*, is now more appropriately Consume-like-crazy Day. Festivals may begin in the woods, they may move into the apse, but they end up at Sears.

With the eager help of my students let me take you through the year of a young adult. This thoroughly unscientific study was accomplished with the "instrument" in figure 3.3 and class discussion. Let's start the year at the beginning. New Year's Eve, a festival of enthusiastic drinking eagerly attended by adolescents, is almost always celebrated with the accompaniment of a television set. Else how would they know to sing "Auld Lang Syne" at midnight? Television shows the party goers how to respond when the ball falls and the howling begins. It shows them Times Square, a veritable son et lumière of billboard art called spectaculars in the trade. Although most of my students have not been to Times Square, they know about the Sony Jumbotron video screen, some twenty-three feet wide and four stories high. They know about these signs and how to respond to them, because they are a fixture of modern sports and concert entertainment. They are what we have for the recitative reading of the church service. Watch the sign. But the real importance of New Year's is not that we have to go to Times Square to celebrate it in accordance with some signs we see on TV. The real importance is that it marks the end of the football bowl season and the preparation for Super Bowl Sunday.

◆ How Time Is Spent and Events Are Celebrated in Adcult. SOURCE: Adapted from Mihalay Csikszentmihalyi and Eugene Rochberg-Halton, *The Meaning of Things: Domestic Symbols and the Self,* p. 265.

The last time each of the following events occurred, what did you do? with whom? where? what special objects were involved?

	ACTIVITY						WHO			WHERE						SPECIAL OBJECTS		
	T.V. SPECIAL	SPECIAL FOOD	PARTY	GO OUT (VISIT, MOVIE, ETC.)	RELIGIOUS	ALCOHOL	ALONE	IMMEDIATE FAMILY	RELATIVES	FRIENDS	OWN HOME	RELATIVES OR FRIENDS HOME	RESTAURANT OR NIGHTCLUB	CHURCH/SYNAGOGUE	PUBLIC PLACES	NOTHING	CARD OR PHONE	DECORATIONS / GIFT(S)
NEW YEAR'S																		
VALENTINE'S DAY																		
MEMORIAL DAY																		
4TH OF JULY																		
LABOR DAY																		
BIRTHDAY (OWN)																		
MOTHER'S DAY																		
FATHER'S DAY																		
ANNIVERSARY																		
GRANDPARENT'S DAY																		
ELECTION NIGHT																		
SUPERBOWL																		
MISS AMERICA PAGEANT																		
PRO SPORTS																		
ACADEMY AWARDS																		
ST. PATRICK'S DAY																		
COLUMBUS DAY																		
HALLOWE'EN																		
THANKSGIVING																		
SPRING BREAK																		
CHRISTMAS/HANNUKKAH																		
LENT/ROSH HASHANAH																		
SECRETARIES DAY																		
SATURDAY																		
SUNDAY																		
FRIEND'S VISIT																		
FRIEND'S ILLNESS																		
FRIEND'S MOVING																		
DEATH																		
WEDDING																		
BIRTH																		
DIVORCE																		

While my students are at home with family for New Year's, they are all together at school for the Super Bowl. All the men and most of the women will watch this game, and although many will not care much for the combat, it is nothing short of amazing how much they care for the advertising. They know new campaigns will break and they know things will move fast, so they pay attention. I have actually observed a student distressed that he missed the Apple 1984 ad that was shown only once during the game. He now watches, hoping to see another such important cultural event. Needless to say, they all know about the Bud Bowl.

The next event in their lives will be Valentine's Day. Here we have an almost pure example of syncretism, as Christianity layered the celebration of the martyrdom of St. Valentine over the Roman Feast of Lupercalia, which in turn hijacked the Greek Feast of Pan. With the reduction of postal rates in the late nineteenth century, and the perfection of chromolithography, the day was taken over by card companies. Valentine's Day is second only to Christmas in the number of cards moved through the mails. The card companies have not been alone. To magnify a minor aspect of the pagan ceremony—the drawing of lots for sweethearts—into a central concern, candy makers have confected the day, supplying sweetheart candies for the kiddies. Champagne makers have attempted the same for grown-ups, and of course florists have not been far behind.

Their advertising notwithstanding, champagne can no longer make an Adcult festival. Only beer can. If New Year's Eve were entering the Adcult calendar now, it would be a beer holiday. Beer has clout. About a month after the Washington's Birthday sales comes St. Patrick's Day. In Ireland this day is not unlike what American Christmas used to be: morning in church, afternoon sport (usually Gaelic games like rugby and horse racing), and finally family dinner. Few bars are open. March 17 is a serious day to the Irish, commemorating Patrick, who was kidnapped by the English, converted to Christianity, and returned home to convert the heathens (metaphorically: drive out the snakes). There are parades, yes. But here is what there are not: no green beer, no rivers dyed green, no shamrocks, no leprechauns, no green lines down highways, no Lucky Charms for breakfast, no soaping in Irish Spring showers, no one singing "When Irish Eyes Are Smiling," and especially no massive communal beer drunks. Our brewers have not only made this a day to get drunk, but each has even provided a special beer with which to do it. Killian's Irish Red bills itself as "The O'fficial Beer of St. Patrick's Day," never mentioning that it is brewed by the fine Republican Protestants of Adolph Coors Company of Golden, Colorado. No matter that it far outsells the top Irish import, Guinness Stout (which is owned by the English, but then again so is Bailey's Irish Cream). For those who wish to be Irish without getting drunk, Anheuser-Busch brews O'Doul's, a nonalcoholic brew with the comforting slogan, "It's what the leprechauns drink when they're not drinking beer." Per usual, the card companies are not far behind. Hallmark has 150 kinds of St.

Patrick's Day cards, most of them tasteless. Little wonder the Irish have lodged countless complaints against the stereotyping done by the American companies.

At the end of March comes Adcult's golden ring—a celebration of the advertising of a commodity by advertising it again. The Academy Awards ceremony is brought to us by the Academy of Motion Picture Arts and Sciences to promote the motion pictures that created the academy to promote the pictures. Well, not quite right. Actually, the Oscars are brought to us by Revlon, Royal Caribbean Cruise Lines, and J. C. Penney under the watchful eye of the motion picture studios, which are themselves minor parts of worldwide entertainment conglomerates like Matsushita, News Corp., Disney, Sony, Time Warner, Viacom, and you know the rest. The Oscars have had such a success in promoting themselves that there are now a handful of such awards, like the Tonys, Grammys, Golden Globes, Ace Awards, and the MTV Music Video Awards, in which the group giving the award is essentially advertising itself.[2]

In the 1930s the studio bosses under Louis B. Mayer sought a way to advertise their wares and swell profits. They also wanted to prevent the newly formed unions from cutting into their profits. So Meyer invented the Academy of Motion Picture Arts and Sciences, invoking all the semiotics of high culture: the academy, the arts, the sciences. Had the word *cinema* been in vogue, he doubtless would have used it instead of *motion pictures*. For advertisers the Oscars are the demographic flip side of the Super Bowl, and the advertising rates reflect this. It is the highest rated show for twenty-five- to forty-nine-year-old women, watched by almost half the households that are watching television. Ad rates are a bit lower than for the football game. If men's products are launched in January campaigns on the Super Bowl, women have to wait a few months. Because no beer is involved, the Oscars are not a central holiday, but many of my students will dress up and pretend to attend, celebrating the kitschiness.

They don't have to pretend for the next calendric event; this one's for them. Around Easter time thousands of adolescents migrate to Florida's beach shrines around Daytona Beach, Panama City, South Padre Island, and California's Palm Springs. Those students with more disposable income, and less ability to pass for drinking age, are off to Mexico, especially Cancún.

---

2. Alas, the advertising industry, which should understand the commercial value of public self-congratulations, has only botched its own. The Clios became almost hopelessly corrupt in the early 1990s, and now a number of fledgling awards like the Effie and the Addie are trying to take its place but without much national acceptance. My favorite? The Cresta, short for "creative standards." The worst? The International Andy Awards, short for who knows what? Only one international award, the Cannes Lion, has any credibility. A radical idea: instead of advertising agencies' getting dressed up and giving each other hundreds of awards for doing what they are supposed to do, why not have consumers judge advertising? A more radical idea: an award for ads that can be shown to sell products.

About 40 percent of the college population will make a trek during spring break. No card companies, please; no florists, no champagne, just beer, more beer, and perhaps a little suntan lotion. As could be predicted when such a demographically pure audience so dedicated to consumption congregates, the sponsors are waiting for them to arrive. Not only does MTV change its programming to bring the events to the melancholy stay-at-homes and younger sibling understudies, but beer companies run continuous ads in campus newspapers alerting all comers to the proper etiquette of getting drunk. Sometimes they make a mistake, as when Miller Brewing ran an ad featuring "4 Surefire Ways to Scam Babes," which was so politically incorrect that Miller had to apologize. So much commercial promotion is now involved in spring break that during a thinly veiled beach entertainment sponsored by a car company, the audience became unruly and three thousand Generation X'ers chanted, "Promo, promo, promo," drowning out the spiel.

Easter barely survives for this generation. A candy holiday can never compete with a beer holiday. In the paper-rock-scissors game of festivals, beer trumps candy, which trumps flowers. The celebration of spring rebirth has so enthused candy manufacturers that they now spend millions to emphasize a minor aspect of a fertility cult, namely, the burdening of the fecund rabbit with tons of heavy eggs. Who cares what a rabbit is doing laying eggs? Who cares how the rabbit gets these eggs, or why he hides them, so long as they are filled with sugary goo and covered with chocolate? The celebration of new life, the sunrise service, the Resurrection, the promise of Eastering is really not germane to a culture that is hermetically sealed off from the rhythms of the seasons. Easter does, however, mark the beginning of Daylight Saving Time, which lengthens the shopping day.

Until Cromwell's mischief had passed, Easter was not really important to the English and was never important to the Puritans. The Puritans detested all ceremonies, which probably explains why they disappeared so quickly. The first industries to see the rebirth potential in Easter were the clothing manufacturers. Although we now buy most new clothing around the back-to-school sales of Labor Day, the English signified a new beginning by buying Easter clothing. In early Adcult it was considered good luck to wear three new articles of clothing on this day, which of course you wore to church. You were seen advertising your prosperity. This tradition moved across the Atlantic. After services at St. Thomas or St. Bartholomew the young sophisticates of Manhattan would parade down Broadway to Canal Street along to the Battery. This was also a time to dress up pets and bring them along. This Easter parade is, alas, almost a thing of the past, because no company wants to sponsor, à la Macy's Thanksgiving Day Parade, such a religion-specific event at the wrong time of the merchandising year.

Not to worry, the kings of candyland, Nestlé, Mars, and Hershey, keep Easter alive and humming. They have been able to own three holidays during which they sell special candy at full retail price. There is Christmas candy

(candy canes), Halloween candy (candy corn), and Easter candy (chocolate bunnies and eggs). Seasonal candy accounts for most of these companies' profits, with Easter far in the lead with sales of more than $500 million. The only vestige of Christianity in the modern Easter celebration is the rolling of eggs, which may be a dim analog to the rolling of the stone from Jesus's tomb.

The really interesting April holiday is a restaurant holiday: Professional Secretary's Day® (always with the registered trademark symbol, if you please, in all the desktop calendars). May 27 is the busiest lunch day in cities, with overcrowded restaurants often going to double shifts. The greeting card companies, candy makers, and florists are also pleased that April now promises yet another chance to peddle their wares. But the real support for ProSec Day comes from the overnight express deliverers and the airlines. Federal Express sends special greetings to 320,000 secretaries, UPS is not far behind, and the airlines often send trinkets of appreciation. Why? Secretaries make most of the shipping and reservation decisions. According to the *Wall Street Journal*, which cares enough to know about these kinds of things, most professional secretaries hate the day (Duff 1993:B1). They would prefer a pay raise.

May is also a month of wonderful holidays. The month begins with May Day, a day of such exuberance that youngsters used to "go a-maying" at the crack of dawn "to fetch the flowers fresh." The fairest maid was crowned with a wreath as queen of May. Every village had a maypole on the green that the villagers entwined with flowers and then danced around, celebrating the glory of life renewed. Aside from the Russians, who liked to rumble their rocket

SECRETARY'S WEEK SUGGESTION ONE:

Take your secretaries to Friday's.

SECRETARY'S WEEK SUGGESTION TWO:

Let your secretaries take someone they'd actually want to go with.

◆ A table card from a chain restaurant (T.G.I. Friday) reminding patrons that secretaries would prefer a gift certificate to dining with them, neglecting to mention that most secretaries would probably prefer cash.

launchers through Red Square, and Vassar students, who enjoyed modern dance, and Freudians who delighted in explaining the relationship of the maypole to springtime, no one else really cares about the first day of May. Even April First and its celebration of stupidity have outdistanced May Day.

Perhaps there are too many other holidays in May to be distracted. First, there is Cinco de Mayo, a holiday sponsored by the distillers of tequila and Mexican fast-food restaurants, which has as much to do with Mexican Independence as St. Patrick has to do with Irish Catholicism. Second is the most important holiday in May. It is the day to which all Adcult holidays aspire—Mother's Day. It is a day so filled with guilt that even the hardest heart pays full retail.

In the early years of the twentieth century Anna Jarvis lived with her aged mother outside Philadelphia. Her mother was not an easy person to live with and Jarvis's other siblings quickly left home. The responsibility of caring for Mother fell to Jarvis. After a few difficult years, the woman died, and Jarvis entered a period of what has been uncharitably called "prolonged pathological mourning" (Jones 1980:177). She fashioned a small altar of dried flowers that she tended faithfully. People paid attention to Jarvis. She was so tender and devoted in her never ending mourning, she was so daughterly; she would speak of little other than her mother to anyone who would listen.

Although her siblings found Anna Jarvis tedious, others found her downright inspirational. John Wanamaker, master merchandiser of his self and his store, was transfixed. He encouraged Jarvis to copyright the day to make sure the integrity of her feelings was not compromised. Meanwhile, he ran special full-page ads in the *Philadelphia Inquirer*, incorporating her message of filial thanksgiving, organized an annual program of music and recitations in the store, gave flowers away to customers, and reportedly said that he would rather have been the founder of Mother's Day than the king of England. Not everyone agreed, certainly not Congress, which was petitioned to com-

◆ Hold on to your sombrero: here comes another holiday.

memorate the day but demurred. Alas, Anna Jarvis never lived to see either herself as a mother or her Mother's Day enshrined in Adcult.

World War I changed that. What with the boys separated from their moms and all, it seemed the least the government could do was to encourage the lads to write a special May-time message to mom. They did. "The hand that rocks the cradle rules the world" was the rallying cry. Mother's Day cards, called Mother Letters, were expedited past censors in record time and soon became an annual event around May 10. More important, in the years after the war the cause of mom was taken up by the burgeoning Sunday School Movement. As a way to increase attendance the second Sunday of May was set aside as a time to commemorate in church what the state seemed too timid to admit: moms rule. There was some precedent for this, as "mothering Sunday" had a peculiar history in the early industrial revolution. On mothering Sunday apprentices returned home, attended the mother church for a service in which the biblical story of Hannah was usually related, ate a piece of mothering cake at home, and perhaps had enough momisms to last a year.

As is usual for spring ceremonies, flowers were involved. You wore a red flower if your mother was living, a white one if she was not. In 1934 Postmaster James Farley ordered a commemorative Mother's Day stamp showing Whistler's Mother whiling away the time waiting for Junior to come home. Farley had the engraver crop the painting and insert a vase of carnations in the lower lefthand corner. Persnickety art historians and their fellow travelers were outraged that such a work of art (Whistler's *Mother* was so important that it had been sold to the French in 1891 and was in the Louvre) had been used so crassly as a postage stamp. Farley apologized, but who cared? Mothers would have their day and indeed they did. By 1950 Mother's Day had become the second-largest retail sales holiday. Helped out by AT&T, MCI, and the other phone companies, as well as by the candy makers, florists (especially the carnation growers), and the U.S. Postal Service, we now spend billions of dollars each second Sunday in May to make sure that mom is acknowledged and appreciated—very often from a distance.

My students now enter a long refractory period, from late May to late October. It's summer vacation. To be sure, there is beer drinking on Memorial Day with the running of the Indianapolis 500, and there is Father's Day in early June in which we are supposed to give dad not much, and July 4 and beer, then Labor Day, and return to school. Pity poor Columbus Day. Not only did the day's "hero" inflict all kinds of hardship on the Native Americans, and not only do the Italians make lousy beer, but this is simply the wrong time of year to buy stuff, any stuff. The telephone companies make pathetic attempts to encourage us to "discover" new values by calling home, but we're too smart. We know what's coming up in a month or so.

If you want to see the powers of Budweiser, Miller, and Coors really let loose in Adcult, wait until the end of October. The night used to belong to the

Druid, not Michelob. Halloween was yet another pagan festival, this one having to do with the harvest and the coming on of cold weather. Bonfires were lit and chants sung for safe passage through dangerous winter. Bonfire Night was taken over by the church to become All Hallow's Eve, with perhaps a little of Guy Fawkes Day mixed in, accounting for the appearance of prankish games. All we now share with the Druids is the link with dying light, as this time marks our return to standard time and the end of Daylight Saving Time. That we get dressed up in the costumes of characters that may well have scared us, that we demand and get treats, and that mischief is just below the surface all reinforce Halloween as an empowering event for the underaged. To candy makers this kind of subversion is nirvana. After all, this is the nature of candy.

To their brewing brethren, however, this was a time for despair. A night is a terrible thing to waste. What had started as a most somber adult ceremony was been taken over by the kiddies but, thanks to the brewers, it is rapidly becoming an adult, albeit young adult, time again. About ten years ago Halloween became an Oktoberfest event. Go to your grocery store now, and what do you see surrounding the stacks of fully priced candy? Stacks of beer and tons of advertising. This is a holiday in the process of being colonized by Adcult.

So we have Coors Light, "the official beer of Halloween," changing its slogan so that the word *fright* is substituted for *right,* making "It's the fright beer now." Anheuser-Busch has a young woman dressed as a vampire telling celebrants, "I vant to drink your Bud," and Miller pictures the Frankenstein monster under the ambiguous line, "Keep a level head this Halloween." When the National Parent-Teacher Association, the National Council on Alcoholism and Drug Dependence, and the Center for Science in the Public Interest tattled on the beer companies and told the surgeon general what was going on, she scolded the brewers. Representatives of Miller, Anheuser-Busch, and Coors denied that their Halloween ads were aimed at underage consumers. The marketing approach, they said, had been driven by consumer research showing that Halloween had already become a popular occasion for adult parties. Say no more. Case closed.

All these festivals of consumption are just so many Groundhog Days compared to the festival to settle the score, the festival of festivals, the only festival to achieve transcendental status—Christmas. We need not be reminded of its central place in Adcult. Here is the make-it or break-it event, not only of parenthood but of family life for the whole year. Western capitalism depends on it. Uzi owners, cockfight enthusiasts, and militant vegetarians who complain of being marginalized have only an inkling of what Grinches feel during this season.

Christmas season starts during a wonderful holiday, Thanksgiving. Of course, Thanksgiving has nothing whatsoever to do with the Pilgrims and collegial times with Squanto, the affable Indian. It has everything to do with Sarah Josepha Hale's crusade in the 1820s to make a family time for remembering her ancestors who came over on the you-know-what. As editor of the

Boston-based *Ladies' Magazine* she had a bully pulpit. After the divisiveness of the Civil War President Lincoln thought it a good idea to celebrate our communal past. He proclaimed the last Thursday in November as a day to give national thanks. And so it continued until 1939, when an Ohio department store owner named Fred Lazarus Jr. proposed that Thanksgiving be moved one week earlier to provide a bit more shopping time. Tired of the depression, FDR agreed. The Republicans and right-thinking people were shocked, and

• Halloween modernized: Goodbye candy, hello beer.

a Joint Resolution of Congress restored the fourth Thursday in 1941. But too late. Macy's parade had already started and Santa was cropping up at stores. Christmas had begun.

Christmas is a great demonstration of the calendric dynamics of Adcult at work. What started as a pagan ceremony celebrating the winter solstice, became a Roman feast day, was pretty much ignored by all (especially by the Puritans, whose anticelebration regulations stood until the late eighteenth century, complete with fines for those who do work on "such days as Christmas"), was for a short time a religious day (the only one sanctioned by the U.S. government), was serendipitously discovered by the department stores as an efficient way of "working off" the end-of-year surplus, and now has been returned full cycle as a pagan ceremony.

The last turn of the Christmas screw was applied December 24, 1867, when R. H. Macy kept his store open until midnight. He set a one-day sales record of more than $6,000. A few years later he was decorating his windows with dolls and trinkets, and it was all over. By the 1870s Christmas sales were double the next best holiday, Mother's Day. In December 1891 F. W. Woolworth was on the bandwagon, exhorting his store managers:

> This is our harvest time. Make it pay. . . . Give your store a holiday appearance. Hang up Christmas ornaments. Perhaps have a tree in the window. Make the store look different. . . . This is also a good time to work off "stickers" or unsal-

able goods, for they will sell during the excitement when you **could not give** them away other times. Mend all broken toys and dolls every day.

• (Boorstin 1973:159)

By the end of the century Woolworth had done something else to stimulate sales. Quite by accident, to avert a Christmas strike, F. W. gave his workers a bonus. He presented $5 to each employee for each year of employment, not to exceed $25. The multiplier effect was soon felt as other companies followed suit. No good Christmas deed ever goes unpunished, regardless of motive, and by 1951 the National Labor Relations Board had ruled that the Christmas bonus was no bonus at all but an expected remuneration. To make economic matters still more explosive, banks joined the splurge by marketing Christmas Club savings (read, spending) accounts that matured just in time to pay full retail prices at the department stores. The juggernaut of Christmas, to a considerable degree fueled by Jewish merchants in New York, now couldn't be stopped. In 1946, after years of protesting the singing of Christian carols in the public schools, the Rabbinical Assembly of America realized it couldn't fight what it in part had started. The rabbis solved the problem by elevating a minor holiday of their own, Hanukkah, and slipstreamed it into the calendar. Soon Hanukkah became paganized with not one but eight days of giving. No power resists Adcult.

You can keep Christ out of Christmas but not Santa. This character, a weird conflation of St. Nicholas (a down-on-his-luck nobleman who helped young women turn away from prostitution), and Kriss Kringle (perhaps a German barbarism of *Christ-kintle,* a gift giver) is the apogee of magical thinking. He has become so powerful that when kids are told he doesn't exist, their parents become depressed. Santa Claus was a creation of Clement Clarke Moore and Thomas Nast. In 1822 Moore wrote a poem for his daughters that was reprinted in newspapers and found its way a decade later into the *New York Book of Poetry.* In his poem "A Visit from St. Nicholas" (not "The Night Before Christmas") an elflike creature runs about Christmas Eve delivering presents. He is tiny, small enough to come down the chimney.

> When what to my wondering eyes should appear,
> But a miniature sleigh, and eight tiny rein-deer;
> With a little old driver, so lively and quick,
> I knew in a moment it must be St. Nick.

St. Nick was plumped up into full-sized Santa by the editorial cartoonist Thomas Nast. In 1869 he collected these images from *Harper's Weekly* and published them in a book called *Santa Claus and His Works.* If we have Moore to thank for the reindeer (and all their great reindeer names), we have Nast to thank for fattening up Santa and sending him to the North Pole.

By the end of the nineteenth century Santa was everywhere. He was in newspapers, in magazines, a doll, on calendars, in children's books, and—

thanks to Louis Prang—on Christmas cards. He first appears in a suit sketched by Nast but now, with chromolithography, colored red. But Santa is not ready for prime time yet. He still needs a little tuck here, a little letting out there. He needs a big belt, he needs those buccaneer boots, he needs a beard trim, he needs shtick. He gets it. The jolly old St. Nick that we know from countless images did not come from Macy's department store, neither did he originate in the imaginations of Moore and Nast, nor did he come from Western European folklore. He came from the yearly advertisements of the Coca-Cola Company.

In the 1920s Coca-Cola was having difficulty selling its soft drink during the winter. The soda execs wanted to make it a cold weather beverage. "Thirst knows no season" was their initial winter campaign. At first they decided to show how a winter personage like Santa could enjoy a soft drink in December. They showed Santa chugalugging with the Sprite Boy (the addled young soda jerk with the Coke bottle cap jauntily stuck on his head). But then they got lucky. They started showing Santa relaxing from his travails by drinking a Coke, then showed how the kids might leave a Coke (not milk) for Santa, and then implied that the gifts coming in from Santa were in exchange for the Coke. Pay dirt. Santa's presents might not be in exchange for a Coke, but they were "worth" a Coke. Coke's Santa was elbowing aside other Santas. Coke's Santa was starting to own Christmas.

From the late 1930s until the mid-1950s Haddon H. Sundblom spent much of the year preparing his Santas for the D'Arcy Agency in St. Louis. He would do two or three Santas for mass-market magazines and then one for billboards and maybe another for point-of-sale items. They almost always showed Santa giving presents and receiving Coke, sharing his Coke with the kids surrounded by toys, playing with the toys and drinking the Coke, or reading a letter from a kid while drinking the Coke left like the glass of milk. The ad lines read "They knew what I wanted," "It's my gift for thirst," "And now the gift for thirst," or "Travel refreshed." Sundblom was quick to glom on to any passing motif. After Disney made *Bambi* and Gene Autry sang "Here Comes Santa Claus," the reindeer were often worked into the illustration. After all, the provenance of Rudolph the Red Nosed Reindeer was pure Adcult. Rudolph was created by Robert L. May, a copywriter for Montgomery Ward, and his story proved so popular that 2.3 million copies of "Rudolph" were sent out with the catalog in 1939.

It is an axiom of modern merchandising that what you make during Christmas is your profit for the year. One of the most accurate predictors of future spending is what Toys 'R' Us does in December. So important is the figure that the company now makes no public announcements of its Christmas sales until mid-January, lest it roil the markets. Giving—although it can hardly be called *giving* in any traditional sense of the word—is the essence of this festival of consumption. So the key is to make not-giving unspeakably

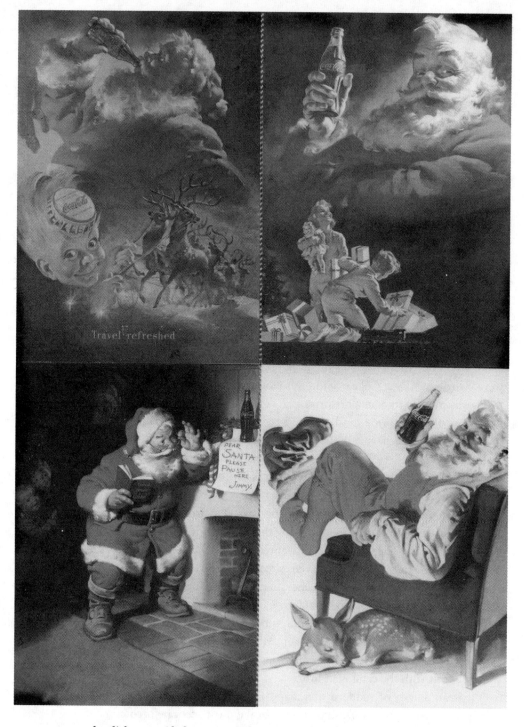

churlish even if, from a retail point of view, as F. W. Woolworth implied, most of what is given is junk.

Not-giving is the mythic responsibility of Scrooge. Whereas Santa is front and center, dispensing his subtle blackmail, his evil twin Scrooge is on hand to be ridiculed for his more sensible behavior. Scrooge says hoard, hoard, hoard; Santa says spend, spend, spend. Our almost totally subversive reading of Charles

Dickens's *A Christmas Carol* is a case study of how popular imagination, in consort with Walt Disney and the department store industry, renders meaning in Adcult. Dickens's tale is now everywhere. Hundreds of editions are in print—well over 225 adaptations for stage, screen, and radio; it is on records, tape, and CDs; it is a ballet, an opera, a musical, in hundreds of cartoons; its characters are omnipresent in advertising. Scrooge has jumped loose of his text, becoming such characters as Scrooge McDuck for Disney or the Grinch for

HE RUNS LIKE HE'S ON DURACELL.

DURACELL® BATTERIES NOTHING LASTS LONGER   DURACELL

• The Coca-Cola Santa is not just the Duracell Santa but the worldwide Santa.

Dr. Seuss. We willingly—nay, gleefully—have subverted the character of Scrooge and the moral of the story to serve the greater glory of Adcult.

Who cares that *A Christmas Carol* was a potboiler written because Dickens desperately needed to recoup the losses of *Martin Chuzzlewit*? Who cares that the story was not serialized, because Dickens reckoned he could make more by publishing it whole? And especially who cares that Scrooge's redemptive act was most assuredly not to give presents at all but to give succor to the poor? Dickens saw the story as a plea for compassion, a way to relieve the distress of the urban poor, an act of noblesse oblige, a redress of his own miserable childhood. What redeems Ebenezer Scrooge in print is definitely *not* that he gives presents, or a turkey, but that he takes fatherly responsibility for Tiny Tim, the crippled son of his clerk Bob Cratchit. This is what Scrooge means when he says, "I will love Christmas in my heart and try to keep it all the year." When *A Christmas Carol* was published in 1843, Christmas gifts were not exchanged and most companies did not even take the day off. What makes you a Scrooge today is that you refuse to heft your share of "deadweight" gifts.[3] No mention is made of caring for the less fortunate. The paradox is palpable, perhaps instructive.

---

3. Economists call junky objects "deadweight" gifts. Deadweight is short for "deadweight loss," which is the difference between what the gift giver has spent and the value the recipient places on it.

The *work* of commercial advertising, that it arrests attention long enough for an otherwise overlooked message to be delivered, has mightily altered the cultures it has entered. Not only has it commandeered the media in which it appears, but it has also affected content. That television shows, for instance, are filled with middle-class stories; that these stories often revolve around consumable objects, that they are told in discrete twelve-minute segments, and that they have uniformly happy endings is partially the result of the demands of advertisers.

More profound than the influence of advertising on the form and content of media, however, is its transformation of the audience's sense of time and self. An example is how weddings have been modified in the last half-century as they have become ritualized ceremonies of acquisition. Two generations ago no one had heard of such things as the bridal registry, nonrecyclable wedding garments, an industry of how-to manuals ("on the wedding day they give one another a piece of wedding jewelry—tiny diamond earrings or a pearl necklace for her, priced anywhere from $35 to $60,000, and cufflinks or a wrist watch for him" [Baldrige 1992:13A]), elaborate ring exchanges, and even now, as I write this, the development of wedding-day jewelry exchanges between the participants and their in-laws. Spend an hour reading a bride's magazine, or look at the ubiquitous newspaper supplements, and you will see Adcult hard at work making what was once a communal or civil or religious ceremony into a holiday of consumption.

But we now turn to yet another region colonized by advertising, a region long thought immune to the blandishments of the vulgar, the sacred preserve of Highcult and the inner sanctum of Victorian value, a world of value ripe for the plucking—the world of art.

Billions of dollars are "wasted" each Christmas as Uncle Louie receives a glow-in-the-dark necktie from his niece to whom he has sent Nerf golf clubs. Both parties would be better off exchanging cash. But they don't, and that is what makes the transaction so interesting to economists. In Adcult currency exchange would be unthinkable.

4 ✦ HALO EVERYBODY, HIGHLOW

ADCULT AND THE COLLAPSE
OF CULTURAL HIERARCHY

For some time I have been trying new themes far different from those around which you
have seen me entwine my verses up to now. I believe that I have found a source of inspiration in prospectuses . . . catalogues, posters, advertisements of all sorts. Believe me, they
contain the poetry of our epoch. I shall make it spring forth.

• GUILLIAUME APOLLINAIRE, *SOIRÉES*, 1912

When playing the opening bars of *Non Piu Andrai* to a class of school children the other
day I was surprised to find them all smiling their recognition and quietly joining in with
words which had no connection with Mozart's opera. One of the singers explained that this
tune, with the new words, is used in an advertisement on television. Such a travesty is surely
barbarous, dishonorable and mischievous. Who can undo the debasing effect of attempting
to wed noble music to the banal words of an advertisement? And what could be more
incongruous during a performance of *The Magic Flute* than to find oneself thinking irre-
sistibly of some advertised commodity?

• LETTER TO THE *MANCHESTER GUARDIAN*, FEBRUARY 3, 1958

☞ *WHY* was there so much art in Tuscan Italy in the late sixteenth century? Why is there so much advertising in the United States in the late
twentieth century? The answers, I think, are similar enough to be considered together. If we can forget for a moment what we have been
taught since grade school—namely, art = good and advertising = bad—
and concentrate instead on the degree of cultural use and saturation, we
may be able to see how organized speech, whether in the employ of an
ecclesiastical market or a commercial one, responds with exquisite sen-
sitivity to the concerns of its audience.

Although it will always *seem* that they, be they the Church of Rome
or the hucksters of Madison Avenue, are imposing their will on innocent us by bombarding us daily with images of a world view that we
really don't want (and certainly never asked for), what we will *see* is that
is that these two iconic systems are Richter scales forever measuring our
most intimate concerns. They are both parts of our nervous system,

externalized at different historical times but fundamentally doing the same job. They organize value.

To see low-culture advertising and high-culture art as one and the same is an academic sacrilege. After all, separating them has been the major goal of the modern educational enterprise. So for now let us concentrate only on whatever it was that filled, say, Florence during what we call the Renaissance, and then we'll take a look at what fills, say, Manhattan, during the late twentieth century.

Oh, Just Charge It, Leonardo

Renaissance stuff, which was only later called art, was everywhere. It covered churches both inside and out. New churches and chapels were being built continuously just to showcase these things. So much of this church stuff existed that soon it was appearing in peoples' homes, not just the homes of the rich but of the middle class as well. Sometimes even servants had these objects in their rooms. New kinds of furniture had to be constructed in which to keep them—elaborate chests, cabinets, credenzas, and armoires. At the end of the Renaissance it was not unheard of for a family to have hundreds of paintings and religious icons stored away like bric-a-brac, just as we might have stacks of old magazines and souvenirs in the attic today.

If you really wanted to see the glut of objects, however, you had to go inside the churches. Florentine churches were as cluttered with this iconic stuff as commercial television is with interruptions or as newspapers are with messages from Sears. The Holy Roman Catholic Church is quite possibly the most material-oriented religion ever developed, not because the church fathers wanted it but because the parishioners clearly did and could afford it.

The magic of transubstantiation almost demands an elaborate panoply of objects. Convincing a populace that this is not bread and wine but blood and flesh would tax even the most experienced juggler of signifiers. As with no other religion the Catholic service is filled with display items such as chalices, patens, caskets, chasubles, pyxes, tabernacles, plates, screens, candlesticks, bells, ewers, cruets, stoles, and ladles. Some objects even change form and color depending on the seasons. Furnishings such as altars, thrones, lecterns, scepters, croziers, umbrellas, fans, and, above all, the trappings and equipment needed for public processions and celebrations were all over the place. Liturgical apparatus of all kinds was used, then cast aside as newer models appeared— flashier models, ones more likely to arrest audience attention. During the sixteenth century certain Florentine churches celebrated more than a hundred masses a day. They needed more space. They devoured new media.

The saying of the mass, the major programming event of the day, was soon franchised as an early pay-per-view narrowcast. The commemorative mass was marketed like an indulgence to be sold to the highest bidder. In fact, the mass itself became a device traded about the way media space is bought and sold in the up-front and after-markets today. Florentine churches became mass factories, advertising and selling the surplus they were producing. When they needed more hardware for celebrating baptism, they added baptisteries with elaborate fonts and still more paraphernalia. They also had a lively business in merchandising the cult of saints, in the manufacture of relics and reliquaries, and, most important, in delivering the final ceremonies of Christian passage. The elaborate announcements and celebrations of celebrity death associated with specific churches were among the key signifiers of power. Churches fiercely competed for these internments, an early version of celebrity endorsement, even promising wall space and appropriate sculptural celebration.

The city-state-church became an ever expanding medium dedicated to the production and display of articles. These conglomerated media companies competed to amass more and more decoration. Florence went toe to toe with Siena, much as Los Angeles competes with San Francisco, Dallas with Houston, and Time Warner with Viacom. The main cathedral, the duomo, was corporate headquarters, fitted out with Ozymandian glee. It is hard to look at Brunelleschi's architecture for the Duomo of Florence and not know that it involved state-of-the-art technology and advertising. How can you look at Ghiberti's doors and not know that they open up more than a church? And what of the hundreds of convents, friaries, monasteries, and other church buildings that sprouted throughout the city? Surely, they were servicing a demand so prevalent and powerful that it was willing to countenance outrageous waste.

Those edifices that survive have one thing in common: intense decoration. They literally are covered top to bottom with ecclesiastical decoration like mosaics and murals, and artists painted frescoes inside, often one atop another, some lasting only a few years. We do not refer to this as conspicuous consumption; no mention is made of the ridiculousness of what might be considered Cadillac fins. We never compare the Italian Renaissance with the Dutch tulip bulb fiasco of the seventeenth century, and certainly no mention is ever made of massive waste. Please, shhhh, this is Art.

One reason the supply of this art-stuff is so abundant, as Johns Hopkins economic historian Richard Goldthwaite argues in *Wealth and the Demand for Art in Italy, 1300–1600*, was that demand was great. Competition in stuffing those spaces full of eye-catching objects was intense, because those spaces could be used to sell services. Art was advertising. The mendicant orders like the Franciscans, Dominicans, Carmelites, Servites, Augustinian (or Austin) Friars, all established by the mid-thirteenth century, were organizing massive fund-raising drives by providing memorial opportunities for large contributors. So successful were they that new orders like the Theatines, Barnabites, Jesuits, Oratorians of St. Philip, and Neri Somaschi joined the fray, all needing displays to attract attention. So-called second orders for nuns and third orders for laity (Tertiaries) joined other confraternities (of which **Florence** alone boasted more than one hundred) in needing their own apparatus, their own display, their own signage, their own drop-dead campaigns.

Soon merchant families were clamoring for inclusion. They wanted their banners hung, their corporate story told, their own monumental sculpture and their own stained glass, their names on the books, and they wanted this done inside the church proper. The privatization of liturgical space, called lai-cization, only increased the competition for media attention. Florentine churches essentially franchised space, renting walls along the aisles, in the transepts, and even along the chancel rails. Entire vestries, porches, oratories, altars, sacristies, chapter rooms, and, most lucratively, inner chapels were sold to the highest bidder. Corporate families like the Medici, the Strozzi, and the Riccardi usually had their own chapels inside the Duomo, space in smaller churches around Florence, and private chapels in their houses. The guilds too wanted a piece of this action.[1]

What makes Florence so important is that the real art of the Renaissance was not confined to objects. Donald Trump did not perfect the art of the deal. Little wonder that double-entry bookkeeping, the adoption of the florin as international currency, and the colonization of ecclesiastical space all occurred in the same place at the same time.

Meeting this kind of demand required factories. We know the names of a few of the foremen. In school we are taught that the Renaissance had a dis-proportionate number of master craftsmen called geniuses. Was there something in the water of the Arno? They are names to conjure with: Leonardo, Michelangelo, Botticelli, and the rest. We might understand history better if we moved the spotlight from the supply side to the demand side and recog-nized the bizarre confluence of demand (ecclesiastical and laity) that centered on the consumption of articles fabricated by thousands of hands, some more talented than others. Given the outrageous demand, that some of these hands would produce extraordinary works was predictable.

The artisans who succeeded did not labor in obscurity. But thousands of others did. The successful became rich men indeed, and if they could have worn three-piece suits and ridden in chauffeured limos, they would have. They did not make up their own ideas. They were told what to paint, what to carve, what to cast, and the criterion was clear: create a campaign, attract attention. Was any work of the Florence Renaissance produced independent of corporate underwriting—what the art historians call patronage—made just to glory in the joy of creation? Name it. Who labored unknown in the gar-ret, obsessed with his own genius? Name him. Sixteenth-century Giorgio

---

1. This ancient desire continues today, of course. The same laicization occurs in what we have for the modern church, namely, the university. When Penn State makes Pepsi its corporate sponsor, and Duke outfits all its basketball players in Nikes, they are allowing once sacred territory to become an extension of corporate interests.

Vasari certainly couldn't locate him. Even Masaccio, who died so young, was known, if not to the populace then to other artists. Toiling unknown is the stuff of romantic myth. Although the man in the piazza might never know who painted the fresco, those in the business certainly did. Florentine artists were not genetic mutants.

Much of what these artists produced was not what church fathers wanted so much as what the congregation demanded. If a crowd grew in front of a certain wall panel, the artists produced similar panels. If an altar proved popular, imitations soon appeared. "I need a fresco like Giotto's," says the Benedictine superior, as he watches the crowd thinning out in his church. "I need another Donatello but bigger," says the Brandon Tartikoff of earlier times. Perhaps he thinks congregants have been engaging in entirely too much "channel surfing" between churches. Cultural authority, which seems to us as descending from above, in truth radiated from below—from the pews, from the hands holding the remote controls. In the Renaissance they changed channels with their feet; in modern times we let our fingers do the walking.

The Renaissance concern—nay, obsession—with image design and construction ended not because of surfeit, not because there was no more space to fill, not because the baroque took clutter to the *n*th degree. Nor did the Renaissance end because the melancholy northerners were fed up with a church that was not holy, Roman, or Catholic. Nor did supply dry up because no new artists were coming along. Art is not a fluke. Renaissance art ended because the frantic demand ended. The weird confluence that had so overheated the market disappeared. Ecclesiastical images were no longer so important. The rise of print (the graphic revolution), the interest in the natural sciences, the market reward for producing objects of practical use, left nonutilitarian art to be produced by the few for the pleasure of the fewer. The myth of the artist as melancholy outcast, unknown, fiercely independent, obsessed by genius, working alone in obscurity, replaced the reality of artist as craftsman, as agency rep, responding to meet demand. Graven images, the stock-in-trade of thousands of guildsmen, would become progressively less important until in the nineteenth century they became anomalies, hoarded by very wealthy collectors or housed in special institutions called museums.

PRINCE ALBERT IN A CAN

The legacy of Renaissance decoration has not been lost in Adcult. The embourgeoisement of art, or the extending of the reach of art in Adcult, occurs in many modes (art in ads, art as ads, art of ads, commissioning artists to make ads, buying art to put ads . . .). For if advertising celebrates acquisition, and acquisition depends on perceived value, here in the high-culture world of art is a vast repository of value ready to be exploited. The two-way relationship between commercial culture and art culture, although promoting an arm's-length separation, is inching ever closer to closing the gap. As this gap closes, Adcult is resembling the Italian Renaissance.

To understand the role of art in Adcult we need go back not just to the Renaissance but to Victorianism. Of the many prejudices masquerading as distinctions bequeathed us by the Victorians none has proved more virulent than the myth of redemptive art. In a sense, the Renaissance was a Victorian creation and so too is our modern understanding of what art "means" and "does." The modernist view of art as sacralization, of canonization, of separation, of authentication was an extension of Victorianism. The new High Church of Art was in the ascendancy, the folkloric and popular ostracized. The struggle to establish aesthetic standards and then to pretend that these had been there all along, to separate true art from the philistine, to dole out serious art like the bread and wine of the Eucharist was taken seriously because the stakes were thought to be high. Art became the new religion. John Ruskin, Matthew Arnold, and Walter Pater were the new bishops. Did we want salvation?

In an age that took phrenology seriously, this highbrow-lowbrow dichotomy was no mere metaphor but a genuine cultural choice. Did we want to run the risk of deevolution, of rebarbarization? If we want to be pure and strong, we must excise the dross. Purification was not only for the individual soul; it was for the national spirit and perhaps even for the species. Entrance to the City on the Hill could not be gained by playing in the mud of this world, and we could not create the New Jerusalem by allowing the masses to determine the moral architecture. The *mobile vulgus,* popularized in Victorian times as the *mob,* must be immobilized. We must embed in cultural amber the "best that has been thought," not the most popular, or the most entertaining, or even the most interesting. Needless to say, making these distinctions stick was the triumph of middle-class authority. The university becomes the church. The professor soon wears the priest's robes and speaks in a special lingo. Matters turn serious. Salvation awaits.

Ironically, the achievement of cultural hierarchies is still one of the enduring legacies of the nineteenth century. Labeling something as art is still a powerful generator of value no matter how carelessly the label is applied. One lasting contribution of the National Endowment for the Arts is to show how easily trash can be passed off as important if you first label it as done by an artist. As well, we don't need Marxists to tell us that much of what constituted artistic taste was based on the separation of classes in a society. "I've got it" means so much more if you haven't. If the etiology of taste depends on the myth of an aristocracy keeping the vulgar at bay—in effect distancing them with the wedge of art, making them think they need high culture to be fulfilled—Adcult has performed a refreshing and democratic service in reversing the polarities. After all, Adcult asserts that "you've got it" if you consume the product.

In this context we can understand the shocking "degradation of culture" that occurred when the famous *Bubbles* chromolithograph appeared in 1887. This sacrilege, or miscegenation, depending on your favorite Victorian trope, had a curious history. Sir John E. Millais had painted his grandson watching a soap bubble he had just blown through a clay pipe. The painting was warmly received as *A Child's World* at the Royal Academy. Here was childhood personified.

• The beginning of the end: Adcult appropriates highcult as Pears' commandeers John Millais' *Bubbles* in the late 1880s.

Sir William Ingram bought the painting to use as a full-page illustration in the 1887 Christmas number of the *Illustrated London News*. Like other magazines of the time, the *ILN* was then engaged in the circulation-building endeavor of covering its pages with images suitable for framing. The painting gained a vast following, because it portrayed the maudlin sentimentality of childhood so popular with middle-class Victorians. Once he had used the image, Ingram sold the painting and all its rights to Thomas J. Barratt of Pears' Soap Company. Barratt's great claim to fame in the advertising world was his dedication to saturation campaigns. He is said to have painted "Good morning! Have you used your Pears' Soap?" on so many surfaces that genteel people were bashful about greeting each other with the salutation lest they be contaminated with commercial speech. Predictably, he had *A Child's World* engraved with a few minor changes, most important the *Pears'* on the soap.

Although Barratt had been able to wrangle a testimonial from Henry Ward Beecher, the eminent American minister (a variation on cleanliness being next to godliness), he was not so lucky when he presented his refashioned "chromo" to Sir John. The painter was furious about the exploitation of his work, and he was not alone. Marie Corelli, a popular novelist of the day, straightaway put these words in the mouth of a character in *The Sorrows of Satan* (1895):

> I am one of those who think the fame of Millais as an artist was marred when he degraded himself to the level of painting the little green boy blowing bubbles of Pears' soap. *That was an advertisement*, and that very incident in his

career, trifling as it seems, will prevent his ever standing on the dignified height of distinction with such masters in Art as Romney, Sir Peter Lely, Gainsborough and Reynolds. • (quoted in Turner 1953:153)

Although Millais was able to convince Corelli to remove this off-hand comment in future editions by explaining his plight, Barratt was steadfast. The painting was his to use as he deemed fit. The bright line between art and advertising was forevermore blurred. What the Victorians had rent asunder, namely, art and commerce, was now rejoined. The renaissance of art as a selling tool began anew. Only the sponsors had changed.

The number of artists who would lend their talents to Adcult are legion: W. P. Firth, Dudley Hardy, Aubrey Beardsley in England, Frederic Remington, Maxfield Parrish, Will Bradley, Edward Penfield in the United States, and, most important, the French poster painters like Jules Chéret, Pierre Bonnard, and Toulouse-Lautrec. Admittedly, there has always been traffic in what is essentially souvenir art: Landseer's painting of *Fido's Bath*, which becomes the dogs playing cards on velvet, W. P. Firth's *The Good Pastor*, which becomes the calendar Jesus, and the degradation of pre-Raphaelite sentimentality, which becomes commercialized in the saucer-eyed waifs mass-painted by the Keenes.

I Dreamed I Was Painted in My Maidenform Bra

But far more interesting than the renting of artistic talent to portray the manufactured object as an objet d'art, or the transformation of pets-Jesus-children into commercial treacle, is the invocation of highcult art to increase the value of the object of consumption. For just as the mendicant orders of Florence competed with each other by associating their decorative display of devotional images with their church, so do modern corporations align their products with the mystical value of art.

More persuasive, however, than the appropriation of objects is the lifting of the entire paradigm of value. Adcult is coming to own art. Art is becoming the unique selling proposition of advertising. Long before "the culture of . . ." became an academic cliché, "the art of . . ." was a standard flag of advertising value.

The inclusion of works of art, as well as the invocation of Art itself, is now assumed in Adcult in much the same way that religious iconography was the symbol system of Renaissance decoration. When you want to borrow value for an object, you insert it near objects already certified as valuable. Value leaks. Because religious objects have been pretty much bled of commercial worth (and are often too ambiguous to invoke anyway), art has become the source of trickle-down value. If you don't want to use the term *art*, just put a picture frame around your object.

The movement on both sides of the advertising = art equation was apparent as early as the 1920s. Artists and advertisers explored what each had

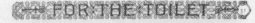

FOR THE TOILET

All the relics of antiquity, both in art and sculpture, prove the idea of the ancients to have been that

ADAM WAS CREATED WITHOUT A BEARD.

Shaggy, unkempt beards were common among fallen, barbarous nations, until the time of the EMPEROR JULIAN, who was the FIRST to denounce them.

For Half a Century WILLIAMS' SHAVING SOAPS have been the delight of Gentlemen who shave themselves. Eminent Physicians recommend their healing properties as preventive and curative of cutaneous diseases. Their extreme richness and creaminess of lather, rare delicacy, and exquisite fragrance have established them as the favorites of those who are MOST PARTICULAR in regard to toilet requisites.

WILLIAMS' SHAVING STICK.

THIS EXQUISITE TOILET ARTICLE contains all of those rich and lasting qualities which have made our "GENUINE YANKEE" SHAVING SOAP famous for fifty years. Delicately scented with finely selected Attar of Roses. Each Stick in a neat Wood Case, covered with Red Morocco Leatherette. VERY PORTABLE, INDISPENSABLE TO TRAVELERS.

A CONVENIENCE AND LUXURY FOR ALL WHO SHAVE.

If your Druggist does not keep Williams' Shaving Soaps, they will be sent, post-paid, to any address upon receipt of price in stamps or currency, as follows: WILLIAMS' SHAVING STICK, 25 cents; GENUINE YANKEE SOAP, 15 cents; WILLIAMS' CELEBRATED BARBERS' SOAP—for toilet use—a Pound Packa e—6 cakes—by mail, 40 cents. Registered Packages, 10 cents extra.

Address **THE J. B. WILLIAMS CO. Glastonbury, Connecticut, U. S. A.**

(Formerly Williams & Bros., Manchester.) Established 1840

For Half a Century Manufacturers of the "GENUINE YANKEE" SHAVING SOAP.

Comfort

In Every Position and Posture

"Our experience with Men's Underwear has taught us that the DROP SEAT Union Suit is the most comfortable form of Underwear a man can wear."

Statement from one of America's Largest Department Stores

Imperial TRADE MARK

"DROP SEAT" Union Suits

Made both in loose fitting Athletic styles—Nainsooks, Soisette, silk mixtures and other woven fabrics—and in light weight knitted fabrics— Lisles, Mercerized Lisles and summer weight worsteds.

The "DROP SEAT" construction does away with the necessity of closing the openings with double thicknesses or folds of cloth and eliminates all possibility of chafing.

Ask your dealer to show you IMPERIAL "DROP SEAT"

THE IMPERIAL UNDERWEAR COMPANY
Piqua, Ohio

THE PILLAGE OF PARIS

—and raw tobaccos have no place in cigarettes

They are not present in Luckies ... the mildest cigarette you ever smoked

WE buy the finest, the very finest tobaccos in all the world— but that does not explain why folks everywhere regard Lucky Strike as the mildest cigarette. The fact is, we never overlook the truth that "Nature in the Raw is Seldom Mild"—so these fine tobaccos, after proper aging and mellowing, are then given the benefit of that Lucky Strike purifying process, described by the words—"It's toasted". That's why folks in every city, town and hamlet say that Luckies are such mild cigarettes.

"It's toasted"

That package of mild Luckies

◆ The role of art in Adcult: value by association. Here are some examples from early Adcult.

White Shoulders
The best the world has to offer.

A Classic Fragrance. At fine department stores and Evyan Shops.

Ever wonder where we'd be if history had been herstory?

VIRGINIA SLIMS
YOU'VE COME A LONG WAY, BABY

SURGEON GENERAL'S WARNING: Smoking Causes Lung Cancer, Heart Disease, Emphysema, And May Complicate Pregnancy.

And some from modern Adcult.

Grande Odalisque, J.A.D. Ingres, Musee de Louvre, Paris

A SUBJECT YOU MAY NEVER HAVE DISCUSSED WITH ANYONE.

You may not have discussed it with anyone, but like so many women, you may be experiencing the annoyance and discomfort of vaginal dryness.

A lack of vaginal moisture.

Vaginal dryness occurs for women at many times in life. Feminine moisture may become insufficient just before menstruation, following childbirth or during menopause. It can cause a woman discomfort, particularly during intimacy.

Specially formulated Gyne-Moistrin.™

For a woman's comfort, new Gyne-Moistrin gel has been specially formulated to relieve her vaginal dryness. At last, a woman has moisture that feels so

much like her own. Now a woman doesn't have to use messy lubricants or lotions.

Delicate feminine moisture.

Light. Non-greasy. Natural feeling. Gyne-Moistrin isn't runny or messy. It isn't sticky like a lubricant. It won't stain. The moisture of Gyne-Moistrin is as delicate as a woman's delicate vaginal area.

Part of your femininity.

Gyne-Moistrin is simple to use, on your fingertip or with its applicator. It's pure, non-irritating, a gentle, safe, hormone-free formula. New Gyne-Moistrin gel is specially created for her comfort, for her feelings as a woman.

Relieves vaginal dryness

Gyne-Moistrin
Vaginal Moisturizing Gel

The moisture so important to a woman's body.

Schering-Plough® © 1991 Schering-Plough HealthCare Products Inc.

What if Rembrandt had run out of funds?

We could be missing out on a masterpiece. Support the arts.

Bell Atlantic
We're More Than Just Talk.

DETROIT GRAND PRIX XII

JUNE 11,12,13, 1993

ITT

If it's really a painting by Fragonard, it says Fragonard.
If it's really a Micro Blind by Levolor, it says Levolor.

LEVOLOR
FOREVER
NEVER WORRY
WARRANTY

Lift a Levolor

TABU
The Forbidden Fragrance by Dana
PARIS · NEW YORK · LONDON

Create Your Own Miracle At Home

The first time you sit down at the keyboard, you're probably going to be skeptical. But after an hour, two incredible things dawn on you. First, real music is actually coming from your fingertips. Second, you're having more fun learning than you've had since kindergarten. It must be a Miracle.

The Miracle Piano Teaching System is a revolutionary keyboard and software combination that can easily teach anyone how to play the piano.

You'll learn at your own individual pace with creative, artfully intelligent software that rewards your progress and guides you individually through your tough spots. Astoundingly, you will learn to play chords and two-handed pieces in the first few lessons.

Just like keyboards costing much more, the Miracle has velocity-sensitive keys, 128 instruments, MIDI technology and full-range stereo speakers built right in. It hooks up quickly and easily to your Nintendo Entertainment System®, Super NES®, Sega Genesis™, Amiga®, Macintosh® or IBM/PC or compatible.

For less than the price of 10 traditional piano lessons, you get the most patient music teacher in the world and a keyboard that everyone in the family can enjoy, any time of the day or night.

Create your own Miracle at home. Give the gift of music to your child or to yourself. With the Miracle — the most revolutionary piano teaching system in the world.

The Miracle Piano Teaching System
Call 1-800-843-8018 for a dealer near you

Centuries ago, their predecessors sculpted incredible shapes out of stone. Today they sculpt leather so it precisely fits your foot.

This is the kind of craftsmanship that exists in few parts of the world. And it involves, instead of a hammer and chisel, a technique of leather-shaping based in

heavy-load conditions on steep trails. What our craftsmen built is a trio of masterpieces, our new World Hikers. There's the Up Country Plus, for full-load use, featuring our exclusive Gore-Tex® leather linings. Next is the Up Country for moderate loads and the Front Country for heavy-duty day hiking.

ITALIAN CRAFTSMEN DID THIS WITH MARBLE. THINK WHAT THEY CAN DO WITH A TIMBERLAND® HIKING BOOT.

high-quality bench work which involves a special contoured last. This attention to detail helps make the boot feel as though it were carved exactly to the shape of your foot. Yours and no one else's.

Combine this level of craftsmanship with Timberland's legendary superiority in selecting boot materials, and the result is newsworthy hiking gear that elevates quality standards for the entire field.

To create this footwear Renaissance, we collaborated with the most talented bootmakers of Montebelluna, Italy. We supplied them with waterproof Pittards® leather, the best there is, and an exclusive carbon-rubber sole we developed with Vibram for 360° of traction under

Wear any of them with any waterproof, breathable hiking storm shell and your body will stay as dry and comfortable as your two feet. Not only are the sleeves articulated, but so is the lining — to give you total freedom of movement on the most challenging terrain.

The art of hiking. Now on exhibit at Timberland stores and selected dealers. For information call 1-800-445-5545.

BOOTS, SHOES, CLOTHING, WIND, WATER, EARTH AND SKY.

Softer. Thicker. Unusually Durable And Almost Unshrinkable.

Bassett-Walker Sturdy Sweats Can Make Anybody Look Like A Jock.

Body by Renoir.   **BODY BY MARIKA.**

► MORE SPANDEX ► TOTAL BODY CONTROL ► NEW **M CONTROL** BODYWEAR BY MARIKA ◄

Available at Belk/Leggett; Macy's

"Woman Dressing"

LEVI'S
JEANS FOR WOMEN

Levi's® 550® Relaxed Fit Jeans. Relaxed waist, relaxed thigh, tapered leg.

THE BOMBAY SAPPHIRE MARTINI. AS INTERPRETED BY ADAM TIHANY.

POUR SOMETHING PRICELESS.

HENNESSY
Martini

Discover this classic. Combine 2 oz. of Hennessy V.S and a squeeze of lemon over ice. Stir gently, don't shake. Strain into a chilled martini glass. Or ask your bartender.

DUTCH MASTERPIECE.

JOIN THE WORLD IN A HEINEKEN

GRAND FRESCO.

For gift delivery of Grand Marnier® Liqueur (except where prohibited by law) call 1-800-243-3787. Product of France. Made with fine cognac brandy 40% alc/vol (80 proof) ©1993 Carillon Importers, Ltd., Teaneck, NJ

◆ The product as art, part one: put a frame around it.

to offer with a kind of refreshing naïveté. So Earnest Elmo Calkins, famed copy chief of Lord & Thomas, explained his new insights on the attraction of objects to the advertising community. In an article titled "Beauty in the Machine Age," he asserted the new epistemology:

> An exotic art cloistered in museums can never be a vital factor in modern life compared with that which springs from the daily interests of the people. . . . If we are to have beauty it must grow out of our modern industrial civilization. . . . A really beautiful factory building is worth more, has more influence on us daily, than a museum full of the choicest art of antiquity.
>
> • (1930:72, 77)

A decade later critics like H. L. Mencken were also aware of the shift:

> The American literati of tomorrow will probably come out of advertising offices instead of out of newspaper offices as in the past. The advertisement writers, in fact, have already gone far ahead of the reporters. They choose their words more carefully. They are better workmen, if only because they have more time for good work. I predict formally, they will produce a great deal of the sound literature of tomorrow. • (quoted in Shi 1979:173)

And artists too were discovering what Louis Chéronnet had explained in 1927:

The composition of the air has changed. To the oxygen and nitrogen we breath we have to add Advertising. Advertising is in some way an elastic gas, diffuse, perceptible to all our organs. . . . Technicians and "engineers" have certainly codified it and dominated it. But we have not been aware enough of its beauty, latent, profound, scattered, spontaneous. . . . The first domain of Advertising was the street. . . . Now it surrounds us, envelops us, it is intimately mingled with our every step, in our activities, in our relaxation, and its "atmospheric pressure" is so necessary to us that we no longer feel it.

• (quoted in Varnedoe and Gopnik 1991:299)

Until the "creative revolution" of the 1950s all sides held their ground, interested in what was happening across the street but not willing to risk the critical traffic. Madison Avenue could trivialize high art only by implication, and painters expropriated advertising almost surreptitiously. Surely, it was no coincidence that pop art erupted as William Bernbach, enfant terrible of Doyle Dane Bernbach, was contending that "persuasion is not a science, but an art." The term *art director* was coined, *commercial art* (a term of derision in Victorian times) was resuscitated, and design in general became not just fashionable to discuss but a major aspect of aesthetics.

The repertoire of highcult art used in Adcult is limited to perhaps only a hundred or so works we all recognize, not from studying the classics but from consuming advertising. The more middle class the venue, the more common the invocation of high culture as value creator. If the upper class owns the

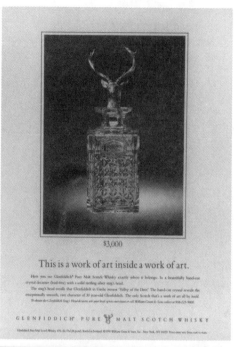

$3,000

This is a work of art inside a work of art.

GLENFIDDICH PURE MALT SCOTCH WHISKY

It climbed
up there by itself.

REMY MARTIN

*Remy Martin Fine Champagne cognac. Exclusively
from grapes of the Cognac region's two best areas.*

The art of writing

MONT BLANC

Neiman Marcus   BERGDORF GOODMAN

**MASTER THE ART
OF ENTERTAINING.**

Entertain with elegance.
Serve Boursin® to your guests.
Boursin® Spiced Gournay Cheese
is 100% natural cheese from one of
the finest fromageries in Normandy,
France. It's taste is exceptionally rich
and creamy, spiced with garlic and
fine herbs. Turn any occasion into a
special occasion with Boursin®,
the premiere brand of French imported
specialty cheese. When you want
to make a lasting impression

...There is only one Boursin®

boursin

◆ The product as art, part two: just call it art.

stuff, and the lower class couldn't care less about it, the middle class imbues it with value and treasures it. Magazines are especially rife with not just allusions to works but the works themselves. In fact, magazines are what most of us have for museums. By 1954 a copywriter from Young & Rubicam had already realized the value of art in magazines: "If we were to eliminate in any

◆ The November 18, 1991, issue of *People* is a museum of art. Fred MacMurray stands guard.

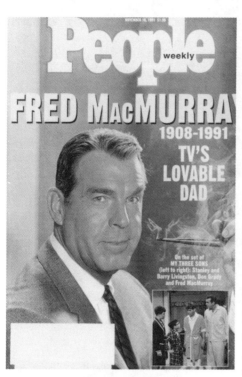

one issue of *Life* all advertisements that bear the influence of Miró, Mondrian, and the Bauhaus, we would cut out a sizable proportion of that issue's lineage" (Paige 1954:25). This has never been more true than today. With *Life* almost dead let us turn to the most middle-brow periodical of American culture—*People* magazine—for a glimpse of its gallery of ads. I have picked the November 18, 1991, issue at random, but any issue would do.

We know these works not because we know the art culture but because we have been inundated by Adcult. Gainsborough's *Blue Boy* is a stock image in advertising that connotes values inherent in eighteenth-century portraiture. We needn't know that Master Jonathan Buttall's fancy dress in the then-passé Van Dyck style and the very blueness were likely the results of Gainsborough's attempt to better his rival Sir Joshua Reynolds. All we need know is that the painting looks so opulent that setting anything near it raises the stakes. The Scoresby ad, however, takes a more circuitous route, from the comics of Milt Caniff to the benday art of Roy Lichtenstein and then back to the world of popular culture. If ever there was an apt example of the syncretistic nature of modern culture, it is here. Images migrate between Aesthetica and Vulgaria so quickly that if the all the words were removed from this ad we would be hard-pressed to locate the image as an ad.

Other images from the same issue of *People* move a little further from invoking masterpieces to borrow value. The Dole ad is visually layered over the medieval *Garden of Earthly Delights* and verbally echoes the Pears' Soap question, "Have you had your Pears' today?" It is an image worthy of a close reading. No emblem is more resonant than that of Arcadia, the promised land of milk and honey. Adtopia has simply replaced Arcadia. We half expect to see the Pillsbury Doughboy, Ronald McDonald, and the Coca-Cola polar bears running down the path. This ad also owes much to medieval painting in which the images of cornucopia are willfully and gleefully distorted to show the promise of the life beyond. Here is indeed a sun-kissed world (note the bursting sun in the *o* of Dole), a world of prelapsarian innocence in which all choices are possible ("All do's. No don'ts," the text tells us) and in which good health will be doled out to you all your livelong days. The young woman at stage center with the Alice-in-Wonderland posture is the new Eve at the crossroads of a life on the Dole. No snake, no Adam, just innocence eternal.

However, the Buick ad makes its evocation much clearer. The artist himself stands front and center, as if his work—and by extension all art—endorses the car itself. In fact, if you read the text, you even find the artist's name in the head copy, near the open paint cans. You haven't heard of Ed Lister of California? Well, you are not alone. Neither has NEXIS, the electronic news service. But who cares? He is an *artist.* He has paint brushes and dirty pants just like important artists. He may even have received a grant to make art. And who cares that the headline puns on the art-history period of impressionism, whereas Ed's own painting is ersatz abstract? The text asks us to decide whether the painting captures the essence of the Skylark (even Shelley had trouble here), which is a nice touch of postmodernism.

But again you don't have to understand art here but advertising. For Buick is playing on the trope of the car as the work of art, which was most clearly seen in a

• Gainsborough and Lichtenstein take note: ars longa, vita brevis, semper Adcult.

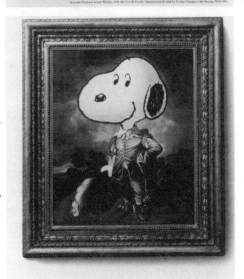

Honda campaign that ran a little before the Skylark ad. In it we saw the Honda Civic on the museum wall framed as a work of art. In a trompe l'oeil of special effects a gallery viewer enters the car and drives off.

About a year later Buick continued the metaphor of car as artwork by creating an ad that used a computer graphics metamorphosis technique (called morphing) from the feature film *Terminator 2.* Like a sheet lifted to unveil an important work of sculpture, a hook lifts the outer shell off a 1991

◆ Art lives in Adcult: the Arcadian vision Dole-style, impressionism Buick-style.

model (actually an airbrushed silk image of the vehicle) and beneath it is the 1992 LeSabre. In yet another illusion at the end of the spot a man pulls down a huge curtain with pastoral landscape and road seemingly painted on it, gets in the car, and drives into never-never land.

Moving still further from the invocation of specific attributes of high culture, but still depending on our association of art and value, we might consider yet other ads from the same issue of *People*. The artist's studio gallery is a common site to position your product, especially if you don't know what you are doing. So in the Sony ad, which has the sepia hues and ragged edges of an art photo, we see the hardwood floor and framed works that tell us we are in a modern art gallery. In the middle ground a gentleman in rumpled suit is tangled up in an old-style phone, victim of outmoded technology. He is displayed in the kind of simple-minded imagery of performance art. Reversing the gender roles might have occasioned a brouhaha. But in the foreground is the pert newcomer with her avant-garde cordless phone, gleeful that she, at least, is no longer hamstrung. "Don't be bound by convention," we are told in

a thoroughly modern misunderstanding of the history of art. But then again we are told in the copy to the left of the tele-pixie that this mass-produced phone has a "design that expresses your individuality."

An equally ahistorical but thoroughly modern approach to art is the Anne Klein watch, important not because it is a pleasing or well-made object but because it bears the artist's signature front and center on its face plate. After all, in brand central you don't buy a specific painting, you buy a Picasso; you don't buy a pair of jeans, you buy Calvin Kleins; so why

◆ What do you find in an art gallery? Works of Art, of course. How do you know what they are? They are framed and have the artist's name on them. When desperate use the *A* word.

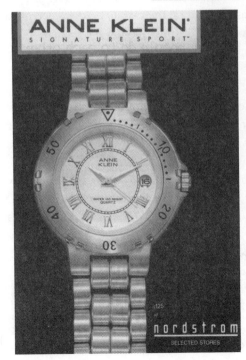

◆ "Good taste is always an asset." That's not the only asset.

"He's not married or anything. And he drinks Johnnie Walker Red"

Good taste is always an asset.

buy a watch, when you can have the metonymic Anne herself? The Noblia campaign in which "Art & Leisure" are "in time with each other" is another cliché. Not only does it evoke the Sunday *New York Times* (Arts and Leisure section) and the *New Yorker* (type face) but, as we have seen, just the mention of art is often enough to invoke value.

At a yet greater remove from art but still worth a comment is another ad from this 1991 issue of *People*, part of the infamous campaign run by Johnnie Walker Red. The invocation here is not to art culture but to what makes art culture, namely, the abstract quality of taste. After all, as the theme for this campaign makes clear, "Good taste is always an asset." But wait a minute. What we are doing in observing these two uproarious, albeit aging, vestal virgins in their white gowns is peering directly at their assets. The women may be commenting on the availability of a gentleman friend, but some gentlemen in the audience are doubtless contemplating their availability.[2]

Whereas individual magazines offer examples of the horizontal layering of Adcult over highcult, following the path of an individual painting into repeated commercial exploitations shows the same phenomenon vertically. Surely, no work of fine art has been so mindlessly coarsened as Leonardo da Vinci's *Mona Lisa*. Nothing comes close, not Munch's *Scream*, Van Gogh's landscapes, Matisse's cutouts, Mondrian's squares, Magritte's juxtapositions, Seurat's *Sunday Afternoon on the Island of La Grande Jatte*, Leutze's *George Washington Crossing the Delaware*, Wood's *American Gothic*, Whistler's

2. A more provocative ad in this campaign showed the up-close rear view of two other equally splendid women running on a beach in bathing suits. The caption was "He loves my mind. And he drinks Johnnie Walker." When women complained that the visuals subverted the text (or words to that effect), the agency ran a male hunk version with a less-revealing rear view. No matter. To make sure everyone was offended by Johnnie Walker's good taste, the Smith/Greenland agency prepared yet another version that showed two men talking on a racquetball court. The caption was "He works as hard as he plays. And he drinks Johnnie Walker." Now gays could be offended.

◆ Favorites in Adcult: Botticelli's *Birth of Venus* and Michelangelo's *David*.

Mother, or Henri Rousseau's sad-eyed jungle cats. In the Florentine spirit perhaps I should choose Michelangelo's *David* or Botticelli's *Birth of Venus*, but I chose the *Mona Lisa* because this peripatetic woman has traveled everywhere in Adcult. In fact, she has completely left the high-culture world to become a cliché. To be brutal, thanks to Adcult, Mona has become . . . a joke.[3]

To be sure, this is not the fault entirely of ad execs. The obsessive attention paid this painting in the nineteenth century surely helped ironize her out of highcult. We know so little of Leonardo, we know so little of the sitter: all we have are the elliptical comments by Vasari, the psychoanalysis by Freud, and the vampiric commentary by Wilde. If ever an image was ripe for exploitation, it was hers. What school child does not know her enigmatic smile? Marcel Duchamp was not one to pass it by. When he took a postcard reproduction of the *Mona Lisa*, added the goatee and moustache, and

3. We can "hear" the same phenomenon with certain strains of once classical music. For instance, Adcult has captured the finale to Rossini's *William Tell Overture*, the "Summer" section of Vivaldi's *Four Seasons*, the second movement of Beethoven's Symphony no. 9, Shostakovich's *Gadfly*, Straus's *Blue Danube*, Gounod's *Funeral March of a Marionette*, or Smetana's *Dance of the Comedians*. And who can ever listen again to Sousa's *Liberty Bell March* without seeing that giant foot come down from above, squashing the cartoon figures from *Monty Python*, or hear Liszt's Hungarian Rhapsody no. 2 without seeing that great piano virtuoso Bugs Bunny pounding it out with such rabbit aplomb?

◆ If she got residuals, we would know why Mona Lisa still smiles.

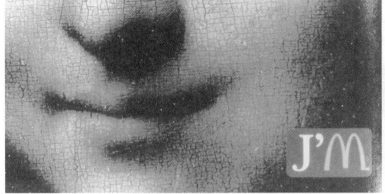

Naughty. But nice.

"Margaret, you've created a masterpiece!"

Just because a woman turns 50 doesn't mean she kisses her lip gloss goodbye.

To the contrary. Today, women over 50 are taking more pride in their appearance, because they're taking more pride in being over 50.

Modern Maturity encourages that pride, that self-esteem. We reach nearly half of all mature Americans. We pride ourselves in showing that life after 50 can not only be rewarding, it can be beautiful.

Modern Maturity

THE BEST WAY TO REACH MATURITY

inscribed the letters *LHOOQ* (French sounds that roughly translate "She has a hot ass"), he moved Mona Lisa from her privileged position in a nonce. This was the fur-lined urinal in reverse: he took the unique and made it common. By the time Andy Warhol ran her through his silk screen—along with infinite repetitions of film stars, tin cans, and dollar bills—she was already a "ready-maid."

I have no interest in cataloguing her modern appearance in popular culture. Paradoxically, her omnipresence in Adcult has rendered her so trite as to be overlooked. Her appearance is worldwide. She appears in ads for the English Caramilk chocolate bars, in the Italian Olivetti computer ads, and all through Japanese advertising. Just a bit of her life in Adcult USA has her hawking videocassettes, Italian food, a photocopier, olives, and cars.

By no means has Adcult been strolling through the mid-twentieth century with its hand in highcult's pocket. Modern art has been quite cozy with commerce, and postmodern art has been positively enamored of late. Or, to keep the tone intact but change the metaphor, what Katharine Hepburn said of Fred Astaire and Ginger Rogers could be said as well of high and low culture today. If Fred gave Ginger respectability while she gave him sex appeal, art has given advertising value in return for vitality. Like motifs in the Renaissance that wandered back and forth between the sacred and the profane, cultures of our modern world continually recombine. If you find the process invigorating, you call it *bricolage*; if not, you call it *tasteless*. But for most of us this never-ending exchange is so common as not to attract our attention.

Hey, Romeo, Meet Me at Wendy's

Although it is most evident in the visual arts, the migration of commercial names to the popular arts has been both sudden and far reaching. In a 1991 study only an academic would appreciate, *A "Brand" New Language: Commercial Influences in Literature and Culture*, Monroe Friedman actually does a head count of the brand names of known commodities that have become ligatures that hold fictional reality together. The professor turned almost two hundred of his students loose to number the streaks of the Adcult tulip. Because he is a psychologist, a research consultant to numerous federal commissions, and a statistician, Friedman did all kinds of sorting of his data to make sure they fairly represented the culture that was consuming them. So, for instance, when he is dealing with best-selling books since the late 1940s, he codes the 2,931,400 words scanned by copyright date, time, and place restrictions (eliminating historical novels and novels with foreign locales), as well as novels set in institutional environments outside the mainstream (mental hospitals, army bases, and the like). Figure 4.1 shows what he found about the frequency of brand names mentioned in popular American plays, novels, and songs, as well as British plays, in the rise of Adcult.

Certainly, two of the most egregious examples of brand-name-based entertainments in print have been the phenomenal successes of Ian Fleming and Stephen King. Everyone knows that James Bond drove an Aston Martin, that he was a bulk consumer of such brand names as Guerlain, Lanvin, Yardley, Rolex, and Cartier, that he agonized over his brand of gin, and that pages of prose surround his choice of champagne (Mouton Rothschild 1953, please). When 007 in *Live and Let Die* goes with his wish list to the FBI, he gets what he wants: "a Swank tie-clip in the shape of a whip, an alligator-skin billfold from Mark Cross, a plain Zippo lighter, a plastic Travel-Pac containing razor, hair-

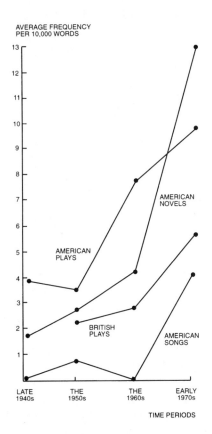
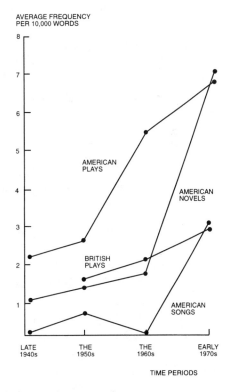

◆ Frequency of Brand Names in Popular American Plays, Novels, and Songs, and British Plays. SOURCE: From Monroe Friedman, *A "Brand" New Language: Commercial Influences in Literature and Culture,* pp. 78–79.

brush and toothbrush, a pair of horn-rimmed glasses with plain lenses, various other oddments and, finally, a lightweight Hartmann Skymate suitcase to contain all these things." Linguists may call this substitution of brand names for generics "taxonomic particularizing," but in Adcult this is not only a way to create the illusion of reality; it is reality. The names, not the objects, are what we know.

Stephen King, who refers to himself as "the literary equivalent of a Big Mac and fries," writes stories awash in brand names. Admittedly, there are few Rolls Royces and Rolexes here, but his tales tote a ton of names. Here are a few from just one novella, *Art Pupil*: Schwinn, Nike, *Time*, A-1 Steak Sauce, Motorola, Kool, Keds, Kodak, Scotch tape, Ring Dings, Coke, Hyatt, Diamond Blue-Tip matches, Krazy Glue, Porsche, Shell No-Pest Strip, Big Macs, *Penthouse*, Revlon, *Reader's Digest*, Wildroot Cream Oil, Budweiser, Lawn-Boy, IBM, Hush Puppies, Smokeenders, and Winchester. This novella is about a tenth the size of the usual King tome. It would take pages to list the brand names from the uncut version of *The Stand*.

Popular writers are not alone in tying their fiction to the world we know. As Tom Wolfe has mentioned, the phenomenon of "K-mart realism" is upon us because the only recognized world is the world of advertising. They are playing our song. If our rites of passage are through a thicket of brand names, why should we expect something different from our fictional counterparts? What is startling is that this has happened so quickly. Recall that F. Scott Fitzgerald scandalized part of his reading audience in the 1940s by using the brand names of cars instead of the more proper "high-powered motor car."

Although Friedman stops his research in the 1970s, he would find his thesis still in good repute. Take a look at Wendy Wasserstein's 1990s theatrical hit *The Sisters Rosensweig*. Not only do the sisters know each other through their branded objects, but the play itself turns on one sister's possession of a genuine Chanel suit. We are told the specifics of such items as Louis Vuitton handbags, Asprey candlesticks, Manolo Blahnik mules, Ungaro suits, Birkenstock sandals, Wedgewood and majolica pottery, Retin-A, Susie Cooper china, Portobello Road antiques, Ralph Lauren shirts, Fruit of the Loom underwear, *Newsweek*, Diet Coke, Tanino Crisci, Harrod's, the *Financial Times*, a Turnbull & Asser shirt, and even a Filene's bag thrown in for good measure. One sister—as you might imagine, the most American of the lot—vows that if she gets the cable television job she's after, "I'm marching myself right into Saks and treating myself to Bruno Maglis, Ferragamos, and Manulo Blanchikis." To get the joke not only do you have to realize that this last item is a mispronunciation of Manolo Blahnik, but you have to know what that is. (It's a snazzy shoe.) Such product placements are all unsolicited but not unappreciated. On opening night Chanel sent Wasserstein flowers, and after the opening Ferragamo sent shoes. And it's OK with most of us; we've come to accept product placement on television and at the movies. Why not on Broadway?

Why not, indeed. If you doubt our acceptance of Adcult, walk up and over a few blocks to the Museum of Modern Art. In the early 1990s the museum had a show entitled "High & Low: Modern Art and Popular Culture" that mapped out the muddy crossroads at which high culture and popular culture intersect. Predictably, critics excoriated the show. After all, if what you are supposed to separate insists on coming together, and especially if one of your own celebrates its junction, you have little reason to rejoice. With rare unanimity the critics of the *New York Times*, the *New York Observer*, the *National Review*, the *New Republic*, and the *Journal of Art* vilified the exhibition. In tightly organized galleries Kirk Varnedoe, director of the department of painting and sculpture at the Museum of Modern Art, and Adam Gopnik, art critic for the *New Yorker*, juxtaposed "low" vernacular source material (graffiti, caricature, comics, and especially advertising) with the art of high modernism. So why the big stink?

Although no one would admit it as such (and covered the truth with such fashionable bafflegab as Hilton Kramer's denunciation that this was "a show in which the intellectual fashions of the academic are cynically joined with the commercial imperatives of the contemporary art market," that it was too "archaeological," or that the distinction between high and low is arbitrary and we should only be interested in good as opposed to bad art), the embarrassing truth was that most of the popular culture in the show was more interesting than most of the highcult modernism. That was the point of the show, of course. The artists knew this, and that is precisely why they plundered from popcult—whoops, derived from the low forms—the vitality that made their work provocative. In a relevatory testament to the powers of art criticism, however, the exhibition catalog, an elephantine tome of 460 pages, hedged in print the truth shown in the galleries.

The show plundered no aspect of Vulgaria more than Adcult. Although there were a number of other categories—graffiti, caricature, and comics—the first division, advertising, embraced more pieces (both artworks and sources) than all the others combined. The massive catalog was central to the exhibition, for it explained in detail the artists' responses to newspapers, sales brochures, store windows, magazine ads, and billboards. It also had a section about something not made clear in the exhibition: the separate influences of words and images. The cumulative effect of exhibition and academic gloss was powerful. Little wonder that those who make their livelihood standing at the gate making sure no tainted or trivial effluent washes over high culture were shocked. What came through loud and clear was the undeniable and irrepressible vitality of commercial speech. It simply has not, and will not, shut up.

MODERN ART'S EDIFICE COMPLEX

Adcult first starts influencing highcult by taking over walls. At the end of the nineteenth century the most expressive advertising medium was the sides of

• The posted wall (Paris, 1908): visual pollution is Adcult inspiration.

buildings. If you were going to paint modern life, you were going to have to acknowledge its frantic vigor. The plastered-over wall, with images literally layered over each other, must have been startling. What in nature could compare to these frescoes?

The trip from poster to billboard to canvas was one of the central routes of modernism taken by the likes of Seurat, Toulouse-Lautrec, Bonnard, and Jules Chéret, all of whom painted such commercial objects as soaps, oils, and circuses, as well as concert announcements and bistro openings, with the enthusiasm and attention of fans. They were. Similarly, the appropriation of commercial material by Dada artists was no ploy or technique but a passion. This stuff was exciting.

Duchamp and Picasso made montage a method to interrupt the never ending stream of images and make the banal momentarily marvelous. European artists as diverse as Dali, Léger, Magritte, and Miró picked up literal advertisements and carried them over the threshold into artcult. They were not alone. Advertising was nothing if not democratic. In the United States Stuart Davis, Gerald Murphy, and Joseph Cornell were interested not only in advertising language but also the actual packaging of objects. Again they redirected attention to the commonplace through the transforming mirrors of art—not to mock but to marvel.

What was disturbing to many critics was the absence of irony. Highcult was not sending up Adcult; it was enjoying it. It is no coincidence that a disproportionate number of modernists served their formative apprenticeships by decorating the windows of Au Bon Marché and Samaritaine in Paris or Tiffany and Bonwit Teller in New York. The relation of window dressing to modern culture is a chapter in art history still not written. Likewise, numerous pop artists were card-carrying unionized commercial sign painters before becoming priestly members of the sacred sect of Aesthetica. Warhol, Magritte, Schwitters, Dali, Ruscha, and Rosenquist, to name only a few, earned part or all of their living from commercial art. It does no harm to remember that the idea of commissioning artists to create publicity did not start with Toulouse-Lautrec or Andy Warhol but with the Italian Renaissance.

The most important contribution of the "High & Low" show was not, as one detractor claimed, "terribly brilliant or profound. Full justice can be done to it in ten words: Modern art borrowed from mass culture, which it also influenced. Anything else said on that subject is merely elaboration" (Gardner 1991:37). Perhaps this belittled, but real insight was lost on critics although not on visitors. The power of the show was that it demonstrated that Adcult gave more than it took, and that pop art was hardly revolutionary or even new; it was in fact simply the consolidation of what had already been staked out. The so-called pop art of the 1960s was neither a surrender to, nor a manifesto about, the powers of Adcult. It was instead what art has always been: an acknowledgement of what is happening in the world around the artist. Pop was, to be a little vulgar, doing what most art has done since Florence. It was following the money.

The genius of pop art was, of course, that it never pretended otherwise. Let the Gloomy Gusses of abstract expressionism like Franz Kline, Barnett Newman, and David Smith mull things over down at Rothko's chapel; these commercial artists were heading for the street. No lugubrious rigors for them, no tortured disquisitions on the meaning of paint, no metaphysics of marginality for them. Pop art was simply that: *popular* art, art that made no pretense about distinctions, art that collapsed hierarchies, art that celebrated what we share, and, most annoying for those who cherish the romantic myth of the alienated artist, art dedicated to making money.

"To me," said Andy Warhol, "business is the highest form of art." If, to highcult pundits, advertising was the sulfuric gas of capitalism, to pop artists it was the divine afflatus. They reveled in it. Advertising was, after all, not just "the sponsored art of capitalism," not just "capitalism's way of saying 'I love you' to itself" or "the cave art of the twentieth century." It was the only true indigenous art of America. It was what we had. Pop appropriated not just the mentalité of Adcult but also the methods of production. Just as in the Renaissance, this stuff could be industrialized. *Imitation* was no longer a term of opprobrium. Appropriation became the method. Fine art could be dissolved into mass media, mass produced and mass consumed.

No critics were necessary; no priestly class of intercessionaries need apply. The subjects and the treatment of pop were as known to us as the stages of the cross were known to Florentines. Ballentine beer cans, Brillo boxes, Campbell soup cans, Liz and Jackie, Spaghetti-Os, VWs, Mott's apple juice, Kellogg's corn flakes, Del Monte peach halves, Lipton soup mixes, Lucky Strikes, Coca-Cola bottles, Dick Tracy and Mickey Mouse comic books, huge hamburgers and lipsticks—if it had life inside Adcult, it was captured in pop. Recall that before Andy Warhol became a foppish circus barker of the 1960s, he had spent the 1950s churning out magazine graphics, newspaper advertisements, menu illustrations, fabric motifs, record album covers, book jackets, Christmas card designs, photographs of department store window treatments, and enough illustrations of women's shoes to indulge a foot fetishist for a lifetime. The Florentine painter and friar Lippo

◆ Richard Hamilton, *Just What Is It That Makes Today's Homes So Different, So Appealing?*, 1956 (Kunsthalle Tubingen: Collection of Prof. Dr. Georg Zundel).

Lippi so loved his work that he spent hours reflecting in church surrounded by what he loved; after Warhol became famous, he spent more time shopping than painting.

Of course, pop was a dead end in the maze of highcult. Like Dada, it was bad *art*. It was meant to be. Pop was devoid of complex aspiration by design. By the end of the 1960s it had essentially answered Richard Hamilton's collage question of 1956: *Just What Is It That Makes Today's Homes So Different, so Appealing?* What is so appealing is packaged goods. Fast Moving Consumer Products, canned food, cosmetics, plastics, glitz, oversized packaging, emblems, audiovisual aids, blinking lights; in fact, what makes today's homes so different is that we don't have to deal with all the endless concerns of abstract expressionism.

Who cares about the sublime, the tragic, or the transcendent (who is looking at the celestial ceiling of Hamilton's comfy living room, anyway?) when there is so much good stuff down here? As Hamilton anticipated, when you have a sweet candy lollipop in your mouth, little else matters. Walter Benjamin, take a hike. In the credo of Claes Oldenburg:

> I am for Kool-art, 7-UP art, Sunshine art, 39 cents art, 15 cents art, Vatronol art. Dro-bomb art, Vam art, Menthol art, L&M art, Ex-lax art, Venida art, Heaven

Hill art, Pamryl art, San-o-med art, RX art, 9.99 art, Now art, New art, How art, Fire sale art, Last Chance art, Only art, Diamond art, Tomorrow art, Franks art, Ducks art, Meat-o-rama art. • (quoted in Rose 1975:166)

With a statement like that the conversation between high culture (art) and commercial culture (ads) was momentarily over. Depending on your point of view, pop art was either the surrender to, or the victory of, Adcult.

To a remarkable degree your estimation of pop will depend on how old you are. "Pop is about liking things," Andy Warhol commented, but he might have added, "especially certain things." The objects that pop liked best were the staples of Adcult. All it took to write a treatise on pop was a trip to the supermarket. Who among the pop artists did not make processed food a central icon in the painterly repertoire? Canned, bottled, pressed, sealed, and processed goods are as much a part of Warhol, Wesselmann, Rosenquist, Rauschenberg, Johns, Oldenburg, and Lichtenstein as holy Madonnas and crucified Christs were for the Florentines. Oldenburg's famous refusal to separate the commodities in a store from those put in an art gallery is more than a mischievous elevation of such subjects. It is an admission that they can't be separated. Art and commerce are one in Adcult, just as art and religion were in the Renaissance.

I don't mean to stretch this comparison too far, but if art does indeed reconfigure the world around it, then pop—short lived as it was—had a far more lasting influence than most other modern movements. In a prescient way Lichtenstein's 1962 painting that he called *Masterpiece* effectively forecast the future. In stereotypical comic images of a beautiful blonde and her handsome companion, the balloon dialogue tells the story: "Why, Brad darling, this painting is a MASTERPIECE! My, soon you'll have all of NEW YORK clamoring for your work." The important clamor for pop was not only that it created a new breed of gallery owner and collector (it did), and annoyed most highcult critics (it did), but that it changed the way we looked at the world around us. What it took from Adcult it more than returned by reshaping it. In the modern cant it privileged advertising, making it safe to discuss.

Highcult critics may babble that pop was a "subversive force" that "challenged" or undermined the "hegemony" of the art world, capitalist "commodification," and such through parody and spoof, but their rhetoric was as worn out as the ideology.

The cheery rebuttal was made with consummate insouciance by Larry Rivers, who asked of an interviewer: "Are we including Lichtenstein in this anti-materialism? Roy lives down the street here. He's got a big house, he's got a ranch in Scotland, cars. I don't want to hear any of that horse shit" (Kimball 1992:25). Indeed, as Lawrence Alloway (who coined the term *pop art*) argued, before all else it was the product of "an aesthetics of plenty." Part of pop's attraction was that it could elicit such comments as Sir Herbert Read's: "The

•Andy in
Adcult:
the artist
as endorser.

Andy Warhol gets Picture-Perfect Pictures with Sony Beta tape.

Andy Warhol, pop artist par excellence, looked slightly askance when we told him we'd like to transfer one of his original "Marilyn" prints onto Sony Beta tape and it would come out a Picture-Perfect Picture.

After all, every one of his prints shows incredible attention to color and subtle tonal relationships. And it's hard to imagine any video tape reproducing his vibrant colors perfectly.

But that's exactly what Sony Beta tapes do. They produce Picture-Perfect Pictures. As you can see from this *untouched* closed circuit transmission.

There's a good reason for this. We're the ones who invented the Beta machine and the cassettes that

go with it. We're the leader in the field. We set the standard. It's no wonder that Sony Beta tape is the largest-selling Beta tape in the world.

To create tape that captures brilliant color and delicate shading, we use a unique process. We polish each and every tape to a perfect mirror finish. We have a special formula for perfect binding of the magnetic particles to the tape, for longer tape and head life.

And like all Sony products, each and every tape is inspected. Not just at the end. But all along the way.

Andy Warhol is quite impressed with Sony's Picture-Perfect Picture. And who could be harder to impress than the perfect picture artist? **SONY**

Shown: Sony Trinitron. KV-1913HB and Sony Betamax recorder, SL-5400. © 1981 Sony Corp. of America. Sony, Trinitron, Betamax are trademarks of Sony Corp.

genuine arts of today are engaged in a heroic struggle against mediocrity and mass values, and if they lose, then art, in any meaningful sense, is dead. If art dies, then the spirit of man becomes impotent and the world relapses into barbarianism" (Mamiya 1992:157). Far more to the point than the glee of the artists in hearing these kudos was that American pop in no way subverted the mass values it may have trivialized. Bread and circuses are with us precisely because they are fun. The goal of most of pop was neither sardonic nor sacerdotal; it was celebratory. Pop art talked with its mouth full.[4]

Anglo-American pop had a unity about it rare since the Renaissance. Right from the start pop never was a movement in the conventional sense. No one person or group of people can be said to have started it. It had no single coherent manifesto. It did not even originate in one place. It didn't have to. Pop did have an ethos, a coherency inside Adcult, that can be seen in any number of places. It was merchandised by dealers like Leo Castelli and Sidney Janis, not as objects but as aspects of celebrity. You rarely saw ads for pop art shows with pictures of the objets d'art but rather with photos of the painter. Pop art was collected like pork bellies by people who understood art the way futures traders understand commodities. It was displayed with a minimum of framing devices. Go into the New York offices of the major ad agencies and there it is, all over the walls—in a sense, a wallpaper tribute to the cultural acceptability of the corporate endeavor. The New York office of Chiat/Day is a shrine to pop. Advertising as art and art as wallpaper.

Pop collectors had other goals in mind, naturally. Taxi magnate Robert Scull and advertising agency conglomerator Charles Saatchi always hankered

4. European pop was another matter. The Germans and the French were not so thrilled with the dissolution of fine arts into mass media. The works of Jacques de la Villeglé, Gerhard Richter, and Sigmar Polke, for instance, fairly reek with sarcasm. But then again, melancholy Western Europe never got the point of Euro Disney, either.

as much to corner the market as to own provocative things. Art was another derivative of the financial markets. Most collections went straight to the warehouse for safekeeping. These collector-speculators were ripe for vivisection, not by highcult critics like Greenberg, Read, Plagens, Rosenberg, Rose, and Kozloff (who looked down their noses at these parvenus) but by pop journalists like Tom Wolfe, who knew that the current pronunciation of the term *artmarket* emphasized the last syllables. The artists knew this too. That was part of the attraction. They enjoyed being brand names. It was perfectly in keeping that, after achieving more than his fifteen minutes of fame, Andy Warhol made a celebrity appearance on *The Love Boat* (one of his favorite shows), became a spokesman for Amiga home computers and Vidal Sassoon hair-care products (although he didn't use either), and—best of all—designed products for the Campbell Soup Company, the imagery of which he had once expropriated, much to the company's initial distress.

DOIN' THE KING TUT

About the time that pop artists were having fun industrializing art, American industry was starting to see some value in this art stuff. Art was no longer sacred. It was up for grabs and in Adcult the highest bidder wins. Whereas the value of art for pop was that it celebrated the commerce of the world around us, the value of art for industry was that it could at worst mitigate criticism and at best improve public relations. As other venues became too glutted with messages, large American industries found a new one, one that was ripe with value just waiting to be harvested. If advertising had shown how an individual art object could cover a product with meaning, think how hundreds of such objects could coat an entire corporation. If a product could own an art object, an industry could own an aesthetic category—or at least an art institution.

That institution was the modern art museum. Although most museums look as massive and stable as courthouses or banks, they are in truth held together by tissues of myth. They are also quite recent. Before 1870 the American merchant class was a relatively small part of our agriculture-based economy, and the few museums that served this class were mainly private galleries and teaching institutions in the Northeast. By 1930 most major American cities had at least one public museum, and scores were scattered in improbable small towns across the country. The reason was simple: economic growth created a new moneyed class in virtually every part of the country. Industrial capital provided the wherewithal to endow collections, and human nature did the rest. It's no fun being rich unless you can show it.

But nineteenth-century museums were hodgepodges: paintings by old masters and local talent, stuffed animals, live animals, wax figures, mechanical devices, light shows—whatever would gather a curious crowd. What these postbellum museums really resembled were the attics of European gentry. We can

◆ Charles Wilson Peale, *The Artist in His Museum*, 1822 (The Philadelphia Academy of the Fine Arts: Gift of Mrs. Sarah Harrison).

actually see this culture inadvertently portrayed in Charles Willson Peale's *The Artist in His Museum* (1822). We see Peale standing stage center, lifting a curtain so we can see what he has collected. At his right are display cases of stuffed birds, each in a reconstructed habitat, and on his left are the tools of his art: brushes and pallet. All that separates them is the tasseled curtain that Peale holds up as if to beckon us inside. This curtain is not to separate the pictorial from the natural sciences. Above the bird boxes are paintings, portraits of the heroes of the American Revolution. And in the foreground are several mastodon bones, a skeleton, and a stuffed turkey. The visitors in the background are in both a picture gallery and a natural history exhibit. The "value" in the objects is that they are the possessions of Peale and he is giving us a peek.

The curator of the modern museum would surely say to Peale, Make up your mind; your museum needs some "deaccession." For museums need themes the way literature needs genres, the way an orchestra or an acting company needs a repertoire. Their value is not that they include so much as that they exclude. What goes into them and what is kept out are acts of human choice. There is nothing in nature called art, but there is something central in modern Western culture called Art. Art depends on fine-line distinctions, and in the world before Adcult we can watch those distinctions being made with growing confidence and enthusiasm. At the same time music is being made classical, writing is being made literary, and theater is being made legitimate. Higher things depend on lower things. It is exactly this distinction that makes museums so attractive to corporate interests.

Historically, the modern museum has been the site of pitched battles for control, for social territory, for what modern criticism calls privileging. Who is going to decide what goes to the cellar: the curious onlooker, the educated patron, the new class of curators?

For that matter, who is going to determine what is heard: the musician, the conductor, the audience, or the benefactor? Who is going to determine what is printed: the avid reader, the editor, the critic, the agent, or the publisher? The answer, which evolved throughout the nineteenth century and was static until relatively recently, is that high-culture endeavors need a gate-keeper. From 1850 to 1950 the refrain was the same: art is salvation. The work of Art is sacred. The artist is a god. The critic is a priest.

Enter the corporation with its overweening need to distribute its surplus at the highest price possible. Inevitably, the value of art was there to be co-opted by the demands of capitalism. To perform this transition the museum itself had to be made businesslike. And it has, literally. If much of modern art resembles advertisements and vice versa, museums are looking more and more like department stores. Dead center in the museum is not Peale but the boutique shop. Here you buy a talisman, an advertisement (if you will) of your experience to show others and remind yourself that you have seen objects of inestimable value.

In America, museum shops are so important in merchandising the experience that the Metropolitan Museum of Art has some fifteen branches around the country. The Whitney has annexes in the Equitable building, in the Philip Morris building, and in the headquarters of Champion International in Connecticut—all of which the corporate hosts pay for. Even the Cathedral of St. John the Divine has a curio shop especially for crosses. If your museum is really maximizing return on investment, it also has an intimate eatery where viewers, aka consumers, can rest up between rounds. It should have a name like the Garden Café and be separated from an assortment of ferns and potted trees by a large slab of plate glass. Even the English have succumbed but in typically ironic fashion. A few years ago London's Victoria and Albert Museum plastered the tube stations with posters advertising "A great cafeteria with a nice museum attached."

Of course, to really market your relics you need catalog sales. Almost all big-city museums have them. They look as if they have come from FAO Schwartz. I hold a recent example from the Museum of Modern Art (please, never MOMA—too vulgar for proper connoisseurship) in my hands. Name an art object suitable for Christmas giving. It's here. Lamps, wallets, watches, clocks, wastebaskets, glassware, tableware, place mats, toilet brush holders, fly swatters, flashlights, and umbrellas float through the catalog's rich Florentine pages, joined by four pages of kids' products (spider robot, Babar coat rack) and six pages of holiday cards (Matisse, *Nuit de Noel*; Van Gogh, *The Starry Night*) and tree ornaments. Direct mail is not the only profit center. The Metropolitan Museum of Art has even established a bridal registry for the convenience of its affianced visitors.[5]

5. Like the department store, museums need more than bistros, boutiques, and catalogs. They need a chain of shops at various malls around America. New York museums like the Guggenheim and the Whitney have been trying to open up franchise operations in such places as SoHo, Austria, Spain, and even upstate Massachusetts and San Jose, California. The MBA, not the doctorate, is the entry-level degree in the curatorial business.

If the museum is being run as a business (for a $30,000 donation, almost anyone can rent a room to party at the Metropolitan), it is no surprise that decisions about what to show "on the floor" might come from the public relations department of some far-distant corporation. At about the same time that pop was exploding and Adcult was blossoming, corporations moved into museums. Museums became reservoirs of corporate PR for a number of extraneous reasons. First, the value of art objects, long dormant until the Eisenhower boom years, exploded. Art became worth something to a new breed of collector-millionaire, and this worth was reported on in the marketplace. *Barron's* started reporting weekly on the value of flatware and Old Masters. Christie's and Sotheby's became names as familiar as Bloomingdale's, even selling stock to the public. Next, the government, convinced we needed more of this stuff, provided insurance so works could be moved around inside this country from abroad. Collectors could increase the value of their fully insured holdings by shipping them around, gathering "good press," and so increasing their market value. Corporations could help out with their deep pockets. They could convince foreigners to let their objects out, protect them, increase their market value, and have them returned in a year or so. All they asked in return was that their corporate name travel alongside.

The blockbuster show, once humbly called the special exhibition, soon became one of the major food groups of museum survival. Especially after the Reagan years, when the deductibility of art objects lost much of its tax allure, here was one of the few ways to service the financial needs of collectors and museums as well as the advertising needs of such behemoths as Philip Morris, AT&T, American Express, Exxon, and the usual suspects. Unemployed holders of doctoral degrees in art history could even find cushy jobs in the cultural affairs subdivision of the public relations divisions of large cigarette, oil, communications, and alcohol companies and help out both sides. If ever there was a win-win game in Adcult, this was it.

Millions of people lined up to see the sponsored tours of works from the tomb of King Tutankhamen (more than a million people saw the show at the Metropolitan), from the Vatican, from English country houses, bits and pieces from the Princely Collection of Lichtenstein, as well as exhibitions of individual canonical artists like Picasso, Degas, Van Gogh, Monet, Renoir, Chagall, Caravaggio, Matisse, and Miró. In each case multinational corporations indelibly inscribed their name and presence on the event. The end of any modern blockbuster funnels the crowd into a special curio shop stocked with trinkets especially manufactured for the show. Most of this stuff is little more than billboards for the sponsor. Hundreds of thousands of posters, T-shirts, shopping bags, tote bags, even baseball caps (to be worn backward?) are sold, each with the appropriate "defining image" of the exhibit. Needless to say, the corporate logo travels along with that image.

So in the same sense that "Wonder Bread helps build strong bodies twelve ways" and "Colgate cleans your breath while it cleans your teeth," companies now claim chapters of art history. United Technologies claims Degas, AT&T stakes out David Hockney and Gauguin; Philip Morris has Frank Stella and the Vatican Collections; Manufacturers Hanover, Van Gogh; American Express, Grandma Moses; Ford, the Treasure Houses of Britain; IBM, Renoir; Mobil, Winslow Homer; and so forth.

Sometimes a little corporate serendipity comes in handy. Never forget that in the late fifteenth century the Medicis often insisted that their likenesses be included in paintings and frescoes. Botticelli's several Magi portrayals became eternal messages from his Florentine sponsors. "Wink, wink, I'm paying the bill," they seem to be saying. In Adcult art lends a hand in resolving corporate problems. So if Coors Beer is having a problem with its minority hiring practices, it sponsors a show of Latin American artists—"Expresiones Hispañas 88/89." Guess who was behind a show called "Making Their Mark: Women Artists Move into the Mainstream 1970–85"? Maidenform. Philip Morris and Occidental Petroleum were able to sponsor a show of Russian art of the Kazimir Malevich collection just as they were negotiating to sell twenty billion cigarettes to the USSR and divvy up oil leases. Because Mobil Oil planned a new refinery in New Zealand, it just happened to end up funding the American Federation of Art's traveling exhibition of Maori art. Mobil also gave $500,000 to keep the Metropolitan's Islamic Galleries open to impress the visiting Saudi Arabian Prince Sultan Ben Abdul Aziz with its concern for his culture. The Metropolitan Museum's Costume Institute sought out designer Ralph Lauren, whose fashion signature is a polo player on horseback, as a natural sponsor for its "Man and the Horse" exhibit. They got his $350,000 grant, and he plastered his polo player logo all over the show. Art is not all adbiz, however. The Philadelphia Museum of Art had a car company willing to sponsor a show if it would put a current model in the great hall. Was that too much to ask? It was.

IBM is the Giovanni de' Medici of Adcult, having given away millions in its palmier days when the mainframe was king. IBM used to have thirteen thousand square feet of exhibition space for art in its building at Madison Avenue and 56th Street (for a sizable tax advantage, to be sure), just as the wealthy Florentines had chapels in their homes. However, the more interesting role of junior Cosimo is played by Philip Morris. Although the company owns beer (Miller), soft drinks (7-Up) and packaged foods (Kraft, General Foods), its image problem lies in its cigarettes. All concur: it is difficult to feel good about a product that carries a warning that it kills. As colleague RJR Nabisco found with Joe Camel, even if you have a great campaign that really improves your market share, the do-gooders are all over you for doing precisely what you intended. But supporting art is a different story.

For years Philip Morris has occupied a special niche in corporate philanthropy. It has concentrated on the visual arts and, more than most companies, on the supposed cutting edge. One reason for supporting edgy museums rather than PBS, for example, is that cigarette companies and television do not mix well. But another rationale for sponsoring the visual arts is that good graphic design is critical to the success of Marlboro cigarettes, Miller beer, and the rest of the company's products. "It takes art to make a company great" is the company's advertising refrain. A little politics doesn't hurt, either.

Philip Morris sought perhaps the most unusual corporate favor when it was fighting a proposal before the New York City Council to limit smoking in public places. The city museums funded by the company received a sternly worded letter urging them to lobby against the legislation and even hinting that the company might leave the city. Art demands freedom of speech, and PM funds that freedom. The council gave some ground but finally passed a tough bill. Philip Morris will have to go elsewhere to protect our rights. After all, it trucked the Bill of Rights around the country in a special van that made it seem as if freedom was brought to you by Philip Morris (rather than the unvarnished truth that its livelihood depends on the First Amendment), and the company instituted its Thurgood Marshall Scholarship to show how deeply it cares for the plight of all Americans. Amount of the Marshall scholarship: $200,000. Amount to publicize it: $500,000. On second thought, perhaps a better Renaissance personage for Philip Morris would be Machiavelli. No matter. It is an irony of note in Adcult that the sinners are often the saints.

As might be expected, highcult critics and impoverished artists are not so thrilled about the inclusion of museum life in Adcult. For these corporations are doing something that the great private patrons never did. The Mellons, Morgans, Fricks, Gettys, Guggenheims, Rockefellers, Vanderbilts, Barneses, and Lehmans often had quirky demands and tastes, but they never gave a hoot for public acceptance. The collectors did not arrange focus groups. Instead they invoked aesthetic standards, admittedly often not their own but those of the gatekeeper-connoisseur they invariably employed to build the collections. The museums they endowed with their collections were charged to acquire and display the very best work available. That was all. Roger Fry, Bernard Berenson, and Harold Acton did not send out questionnaires. Corporations, however, are understandably concerned about nonaesthetic criteria—what in the current jargon might be considered the politically correct multicultural criteria of a target group—and are far more likely to support works that are "corporately compatible," in other words, not controversial.

From time to time word leaks out that some exhibition is to be delayed because of a lack of corporate underwriting. The Guggenheim, for instance, had assembled "Picasso and the Age of Iron" but had trouble locating a corporate sponsor. No one, it seemed, wanted to be associated with the Age of Iron, not even U.S. Steel. BMW passed up sponsoring an exhibition of "Masterworks from Munich," saying the company was "more interested in contemporary art because that is the image their car projects" (Vogel 1993:B4). Munich is not very sexy. A groundbreaking show of paintings by seventeenth-century Italian classicist Guido Reni couldn't find a sponsor for obvious rea-

Celebrating 25 years of lifting hearts, spirits, hopes. And, of course, each other.

DANCE THEATRE OF HARLEM

PHILIP MORRIS COMPANIES INC.

Supporting the spirit of innovation.

◆ A modern paradox: the major support of good causes in Adcult comes from nasty products: Philip Morris is concerned about dance.

sons. Who wants to look at all those moody saints? And the Art Institute of Chicago's critically acclaimed "Chicago Architecture: 1872–1922" had the same problem—too specialized, too little bang for the sponsorship buck.

Ironically, sometimes attracting too much attention can be equally detrimental if it is of the wrong sort. In 1989 the Corcoran Gallery of Art in Washington, D.C., raised a hornets' nest of concern by canceling a show that included homoerotic photographs by Robert Mapplethorpe, most notably one of a standing black man urinating into the open mouth of a recumbent white and another of a bullwhip inserted in the artist's anus. At the same time the sacrilegious images of Andres Serrano, especially one called *Piss Christ,* showing a submerged crucifix in a beaker of the artist's urine, were being shown in photographic exhibitions. Would any corporation ever want to be associated with either man's other work, although both have done what is acknowledged as important art? Would any modern corporation have wanted to be associated with Edouard Manet when he painted his naked Olympia staring straight out at the audience with no hint of embarrassment? Who would have wanted to sponsor his *Déjeuner sur l'herbe,* now one of the Louvre's treasures but considered indecent when first exhibited in 1863? Times change, as does patronage. But corporations are especially risk averse. Why take a chance when they can endlessly recycle such crowd pleasers as Picasso, Magritte, Van Gogh, and Matisse, or—God help us—more Edward Hopper, Georgia O'Keeffe, Thomas Hart Benton, and Andrew Wyeth? And what of whole movements utterly and purposefully lacking in corporate sex appeal like the abstract expressionists or even difficult artists like Vermeer?

One artist who has dedicated much of his oeuvre to lambasting the museum-industrial complex is Hans Haacke. *MetroMobiltan* (1985), a wall-sized reconstruction of the Metropolitan Museum's imposing façade, exemplifies Haacke's approach to the issue of corporate charades. He has placed an image from a Mobil-sponsored exhibit of Nigerian art on one of its three promotional banners. On either side are statements from Mobil justifying its sales of supplies to the then apartheid South African police and military. Behind and partially concealed by the banners hangs an enlarged photograph of a funeral procession for blacks shot by the South African police. Haacke has not found much corporate or museum support for his work. A work he did detailing slum lords of Manhattan, titled *Unfinished Business*, was made for a one-person show at the Guggenheim. The museum director canceled it at the last minute, explaining that opening the show would have involved the museum in "extra-artistic" issues. Before Adcult and corporate sponsorship, that was often the whole point.

If we have learned anything in the last generation about the business of art, it is that it is the business of art. It has always been that way. Art is always on the take. Only the coinage changes. Florins become dollars. The Medici become Mobil.

Well, the jig is up. In the last decade we have learned what the Renaissance masters always knew. Ya dance with who brung ya. For a while in the twentieth century it was thought that the government should pay the piper, that the National Endowments should take the piddling amounts at their disposal and inoculate us all with a good wallop of this stuff. Alas, it didn't take, and not because people like Senator Jesse Helms, prissy worrywart and general obstructionist to the public funding of private art, had the gumption to call most state-funded works worthless. The myth died because art—like the law or the news or canonical literature—is, in the last analysis, whatever certain groups choose to single out and call it by the special name. We didn't need the melancholy deconstructionists to tell us this. *Huckleberry Finn* is still at most public libraries.

In Adcult the special groups that are now doing the defining are competitive corporations, just as in the Renaissance the special gatekeepers were the competitive mendicant orders. The temper shifted after World War II as Western cultures sought new faith in materialism. One of the many precursors to Adcult's current absorption of art was the campaign of the Container Corporation of America that ran for more than thirty years. The "great idea" series that started in 1950 often featured a highcult illumination for a litcrit quotation or a big thought. So there might be a chrome "illustration" by sculptor Richard Hunt for a line from Nathaniel Hawthorne's *Blithedale Romance*, or a James Rosenquist oil-on-canvas rendition of Supreme Court Justice Louis Brandeis commenting on democracy. At the bottom of the page was a modest plug for a company, the products of which you couldn't buy by name even if you wanted to. Boxes are boxes. A can is a can. But Container Corporation wanted to separate itself as a corporation, and, because CEO Walter Paepcke and his wife were interested in the arts, it seemed a natural connection: value by association. Their choices were prescient, work by such artists as Jacob Lawrence, Willem de Kooning, Fernand Léger, René Magritte, Henry Moore, Man Ray, Larry Rivers, Leonard Baskin, Ben Shahn, and the omnipresent Andy Warhol. Reversing the usual pattern, these works commissioned by a corporation now reside in a museum, the National Museum of American Art, a testimony to the old-style art-industrial complex.

For an update have a look at Carillon Importers, a liquor importer. In introducing a little-known Swedish vodka named Absolut to this country, Michael Roux and TBWA,

● The ad as art, art as ad.

Carillon's advertising agency, decided to mix art and booze to sell the unknown by connecting it to the well known. Vodka has much in common with cardboard boxes in that most people cannot tell various brands apart. But vodka is different in that this is a product you can buy by name. Roux commissioned a still life of the Swedish vodka bottle from artist Andy Warhol for an advertising campaign that would feature only the painting and the two-word message Absolut Warhol. The campaign got the attention they wanted. Subsequently, other artists were signed up to paint their versions of the bottle. Among them: Ed Ruscha, Keith Haring, and Kenny Scharf. What started as a curious mixing of Warhol and an advertisement has grown into a multi-million-dollar annual program of commissioned or sponsored works, ranging from paintings to art pieces to fashion designs, usually with depictions of the well-traveled Absolut bottle. Who decides what is painted? You can guess. But more important: can the distinction be made any longer between what is done by the artists for their own account, so to speak, and what they do for the agency account?

The American Museum: From P.T. to E.T.

To put the absorption of art into Adcult in a slightly different light, what is the most recent museum to be built in New York City? It is the Museum of Television and Radio at 25 West 52nd Street, right next to its host institution, the Columbia Broadcasting System. The museum, a self-serving testament to the transformation of cultural hierarchies, was conceived of and primarily funded by William S. Paley. This institution is an almost complete effacement of "museum culture." What do you consume at the MTR? You punch up on a video monitor forty thousand television and radio shows complete with more than ten thousand commercials. Rather in the manner of Disney's Magic Kingdoms (or the Renaissance cathedral, for that matter) we sit in a pew and are shuffled through moments of packaged transcendence while a comforting voice assures us that this really is important stuff.

The experience of passing off masscult as highcult has not been lost on corporate America. A few blocks away in one of the most expensive retail locations in the Western world is the booming Warner Bros. Studio Store. This is essentially a museum store without the museum. Visible from the street is a glass elevator that ascends with a push from a man-sized Superman. Batman's jet with a fifteen-foot wingspan descends from the ceiling every half hour to do laser-beam battle with villains on a huge video wall, and a Marvin the Martian spaceship takes kids on simulated visits to the planets. Wherever you turn in this sculpture garden of Adcult are giant figures of cartoon animals and DC Comics superheroes. Bugs Bunny and the Looney Tunes and Merrie Melodie characters mingle with Batman, Wonder Woman, Elmer Fudd, and *Mad Magazine*'s Alfred E. Neuman. This is not a retail store, it is a retail experience. Everything is labeled, provenance accounted for.

The first floor, oak paneled to recall Jack Warner's old studio offices, features Hollywood-inspired merchandise and accessories, including books, posters, and novelty items related to such legendary Warner stars as Bette Davis, James Cagney, James Dean, Joan Crawford, and Humphrey Bogart. The room is just like the reconstruction of Frank Lloyd Wright's prairie house over at the Metropolitan, except that you can walk through Warner's office. The second floor has the main apparel department and touch-screen video games for shoppers. The third floor has collectibles with a gallery featuring authentic animated cartoon celluloids, paintings of Wile E. Coyote as Whistler's Mother and Daffy Duck as the Mona Lisa, bronze statues, and other sculptures and jewelry. The appeal of such an establishment is the appeal of museums: they exhibit objects worthy of collection. They already have value. Better yet, now *you* can buy them.

To the north is the Sony Building at 56th and Madison, complete with its museum store. A few blocks to the south, Coca-Cola is also trying to cash in on its status as an American icon. Its museum store is free standing. The main Coke museum is in Atlanta. On sale are Coke glasses, T-shirts, piggy banks, and, of course, copies of old advertisements. As I write this, Disney is negotiating to rent retail space on Fifth Avenue for its flagship store-museum by buying out the leases of Le Côte Basque, Goldpfeil, and Bally of Switzerland: the mouse triumphant.

To a considerable extent the collapse in hierarchies that has produced such enigma as advertising struggling for the condition of art and vice versa, and museums masquerading as department stores and vice versa, is at the very center of Adcult. The media themselves—which used to be organized vertically with print at the top, then film, television, radio, and comics in descending order—have been so shaken up that a Pulitzer Prize can go to a comic about mice, albeit intensely human mice, whereas most of what is atop the *New York Times* best-seller list might be better used as bedding for mice.

Consider books and movies in relation to TV, for instance. Here is Leonard Goldenson, one of the founding fathers of network television (ABC) and broadcaster of *Charlie's Angels* and *Love Boat*:

> Of course there are lousy programs—perhaps 40 percent of what's on the schedule at any given time is junk. . . . Moreover, no one claims that more than 60 percent of all the books published in America are wonderful, enlightening, inspiring works of art. Many, including many bestsellers, are worse trash than anything on television. Yet that's what people want to read, so publishers give it to them. Television is no better and no worse than book publishing.   • (1991:123)

Goldenson may be too hard on himself. Jeff Jarvis, then an editor at *People*, actually compares the best-sellers with the most-watched television shows:

> By my count, there were seven great shows [in the 1987 top ten Nielsens], two good ones, and one that's merely mediocre. Compare those shows to the books on a recent *New York Times* list of best-sellers, filled with trashers and romancers by the likes of Danielle Steel, Sidney Sheldon and Stephen King. The obvious conclusion: TV viewers have better taste than readers.
>
> • (1987:9)

And here is John J. O'Connor, TV critic for the *New York Times*, comparing movie blockbusters to television:

> For decades, some of the more patronizing and printable catch phrases have been reserved for television. The pecking order of popular culture over the years settled into a widely accepted hierarchy. At the bottom, there was television entertainment—formula-ridden, silly, pointless, and forgettable. Far above, there was the art of film, occasionally called cinema—probing, elevated, provocative, memorable. Those distinctions never did hold up very well under close scrutiny. Now as television entertainment enters the 90s growing both more adventurous, and pointed, they are being obliterated. . . . One thing would seem certain. A significant sea change has taken place in popular culture. It is now the typical Hollywood film that is becoming pointless and forgettable. And it is television that is showing distinct signs of being provocative and, on occasion, memorable. The old pecking order is very much on the verge of collapse.   • (1990:B1, 27)

All the mass media are behaving like one vast delivery system in Adcult, each behaving like the others, all striving to program images for whatever finds the largest demographic pocket. The Great Chain of (media) Being is no more. Advertising is the prime reason.

Little wonder, then, that artists don't know where they belong. In the old days before Adcult became the dominant culture there was a public and a private world of art. The public world unfolded before an educated audience in such places as the Museum of Modern Art and the Whitney, art coverage in magazines such as *Time* and *Life*, the lineup at international shows like the Venice Biennale, and exhibits at blue-chip commercial galleries such as Sidney Janis and Leo Castelli. The private world was the artists' own studio culture, reviews in art magazines, and inside art departments of certain schools, usually in New York, like Brooklyn College and Queens College.

There was often a tension between these worlds. But there was no doubt which group held sway. There is a perhaps apocryphal story of how delighted a recently famous Jackson Pollock was when Earl Kerkam, a painter of figures and still lifes who had an archetypical art world reputation, told him that some recent work was "not bad." Better to be casually praised by a caesar than be king of the rabble.

No more. In a world in which rap singers are called recording artists, a world in which an ordinary hunting net placed under a pool of lights at the Center for African Art elicited phone calls from interested dealers, a world in which the California Institute for the Arts (funded by Disney money) produces graduates keenly knowledgeable about how to mass-produce what sells, a world in which an enterprising artist named Neville Brody charges various businesses $139 to get their names mentioned in posters and then franchises the operation in various cities around world as part of Art Project 1123 (90 percent of companies pay), that the most important current artists have made Adcult their subject matter is not surprising. The proximate relationship of postmodern art is not with art history but with advertising culture. Here, for instance, is an advertisement for a new kind of museum (on diskette) for a new kind of art (images created for magazine display), from a new patron (a company), for a new purpose (to increase the consumption of vodka).

In the affirmative action spirit of the times let me mention a few gender-equal examples to show the current influence of Adcult. How can you look at the work of Barbara Kruger or Jenny Holzer and not see the influence of advertising design? Futura bold italic white lettering on red banners plastered over ambiguous black and white photos has moved from the ads of the 1930s to tabloid headlines to Kruger's knock-offs, then back to the covers of midcult magazines like *Ms.*, *Newsweek*, the *New Republic*, and *Esquire*. Holzer's electric display boards have streams of pith flowing across them. Thoughts represented may be intensely personal, but because the medium is so electronically processed little of the artist remains. In this send-up of Adcult's often frantic declarations the LED ticker tape blazes such observations as "Raise boys and girls the same," "Lack of charisma can be fatal," "Boredom makes you do crazy things," "A man can't know what it's like to be a mother," "Confusing yourself is a way to stay honest," and "What urge will save us now that sex won't?"

How can you look at the self-promoting devotion to gloss and glitz by the likes of Jeff Koons and Julian Schnabel and not see that they have zero interest in the art world inherited from Baudelaire or Daumier but a consummate interest in Madison Avenue? These artists have no complaint with the philistines. They are the philistines. And proud of it. The objects they choose to memorialize, and the in-your-face scale they invoke, tell all. For Koons this includes silk-screened

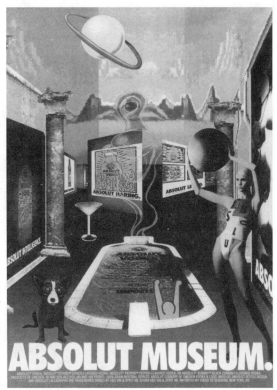

◆ The campaign as museum, museum as campaign.

liquor advertisements on big canvases, vacuum cleaners encased in Plexiglas boxes, a seven-foot-tall toy bear in a striped T-shirt inspecting the whistle of a London cop, a stainless steel cast of an inflatable plastic bunny, and a bigger-than-life ceramic sculpture of Michael Jackson and his pet chimpanzee, both of whom are in whiteface. Schnabel, on the other hand, is noticeable more for size than subject matter. His paintings are mammoth, sometimes more than sixteen feet square. How could you own them? Where could you put them? That's the point. He attaches all manner of things to them—broken crockery, animal hides, deer antlers—but they impress not for content but for lack of it. They are signage. They are billboards. They are sensational gestures. Eye stopping is all. That he was a favorite of corporate sponsors for whom eye stopping is stock-in-trade goes without saying. Ditto that one of his major collectors was Charles Saatchi.

The works of Kruger, Holzer, Koons, and Schnabel are not so much over the top as they are far down the other side. The cruelest words in Adcult obtain: been done. More interesting things are happening elsewhere. For if art has been appropriating advertising, advertising has returned the favor ten-fold. To a great degree this has come about because of photography. Like the department store window with which it shares many similarities, the photograph fixes objects for public consumption. It shows you not so much what to see but how to see it.

◆ Richard Avedon, the artist, not the commercial photographer, has a show sponsored by Kodak and *Harper's Bazaar*.

THE ART OF AVEDON

Richard Avedon's photographs first appeared in Harper's Bazaar. Fifty years later, they appear at the Whitney. Harper's Bazaar has helped make possible "Richard Avedon: Evidence 1944-1994". A major retrospective at the Whitney Museum of American Art, on view through June 26, 1994.

BAZAAR
fashion's new testament

I dare say that most viewers could not tell the difference between the photography of the late Robert Mapplethorpe and those homoerotic shots by Bruce Weber that Calvin Klein uses to advertise his Obsession body-care products. In one recent example the ad is spread over two pages, one given over entirely to a black-and-white close-up of a male torso. There's no head or face to make the portrait individual. It shows only an anonymous naked body, almost to the groin. The details may be absent, but that sensual delight Mapplethorpe took in the male physique is much in evidence. Although Mapplethorpe seems to be on one side of the divide (art) and Calvin Klein on the other (commerce), it is often impossible to tell whether Annie Leibovitz and Irving Penn are on commission when they open and close the shutter or whether they are doing it for Art. But that's no longer the point. The images are interchangeable. The point is also who cares? Only the sponsor does, which explains why such commercial photos have the shutterbug's name prominently displayed at the side, just like the signature of a painter.

The case of Richard Avedon may be instructive. Here is a first-rate fashion photographer who started his career doing layouts for *Harper's Bazaar*, graduated to the advertising campaigns of Revlon and Calvin Klein, and then jumped the tracks to produce art images. His famous art portraits, however, are not of everyday folks but of celebrities—Marilyn Monroe, Audrey Hepburn, Charlie Chaplin, and George Wallace. And these celebrities are not shot in the Bachrach or Karsh style but in the high-gloss style of Adcult. They are just short of shrill. Attributes are magnified. Skin pores the size of craters. How do we know this is art? Because Avedon has also photographed coal miners, asylum inmates, cross-dressers, and drifters. Only a real artist would do that. More important, the *New Yorker*, the vade mecum of middlebrow Adcult, gives Avedon almost weekly space, announcing him in the table of contents simply as *Avedon* (as if he were Madonna or Cher, for goodness' sake). When the Whitney Museum of American Art arranges a retrospective, the show title is "Richard Avedon: Evidence 1944–1994." Exactly what the word *evidence* means is evident from the catalog, aka press kit. We are assured repeatedly that Avedon is "a major figure in post-war American art." Best part of the show? Page 157 of the exhibition catalog. Avedon directing a catalog shoot for Bloomingdale's from his sickbed cot in a studio, like some Roman soldier unwilling to leave the battlefield. Corporate sponsors of the Whitney show? Eastman Kodak and *Harper's Bazaar*.[6]

✦ Two works of arts collide and pollinate: the Pygmalion myth in Adcult.

If advertising is the sponsored art of capitalism, the photograph is the central medium of display. Not by happenstance did Benetton submit some fifty-six close-ups of naked adults and children taken by creative director Oliviero Toscani to the avant-garde section of the Venice Biennale. The whole point was that there was no difference, as the futurists had predicted, between art and advertising. Far from being a sign of decadence it is actually testimony to the profitable convergence of postmodernist curiosity and aggressive marketing. Take the ad launching Fendi perfume featuring a photograph of a beautiful model, eyes closed, about to kiss the lips of an ancient statue of a man. The image, photographed in Rome by fine-art photographer Shelie Metzner, plays on the Pygmalion myth. Here we have the distaff version, complete with the implication that Fendi will work Aphrodite-like to aid the youth in bringing the statue to life with a kiss. The art in advertising and the art as advertising momentarily merge.

6. Si Newhouse's Advance Publications owns the *New Yorker*, which gave Avedon more-than-usual space in the week of the show's opening. The copublisher of the exhibition catalog, with an essay by *New Yorker* art critic Adam Gopnik, is Random House, which is owned by Newhouse. Among the six speakers at a Whitney symposium connected to the show were Random House's CEO Harold Evans and writers Brendan Gill and Ingrid Sischy who write for . . . the *New Yorker*. The curator of the show was Jane Livingston who does not work for the Whitney but for Avedon, who used a grant from Kodak to pay her for the show and the catalog. Synergies, anyone?

◆ The contrived art photograph becomes the ad for a masscult magazine of urban decorating.

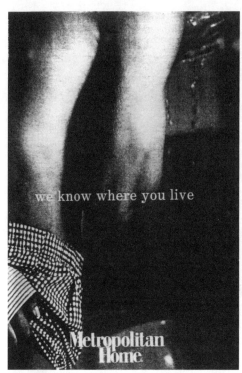

A slightly less clear version of this appears in the 1993 campaign for *Metropolitan Home*. If you did not know that *Metropolitan Home* is dedicated to showing the snazzy side of urban life, you would probably think the images advertised products like perfume, fabrics, sheets, or—with the line "We know where you live"—a home security company or, worse yet, the most recent stalk-and-slash horror film. The ambiguity is purposeful, but if you saw the same image and line absent the sponsor's name in an art gallery, chances are you would think, how provocative, how daring . . . how artistic. That the photographer, Peter Arnell of Arnell-Bickford, is indeed an art photographer, and that his slice-of-life images are his highcult interest, betray what is going on here. The art comes first. The advertising tags are added later.

That advertising has co-opted the traditional function of art and is now defining the objects of desire could have been expected. That it occasionally has been able to invest in these commercial objects the sense of the ineffable, the mysterium terrendium that is associated with the transcendent, might also have been predicted. For if materialism is the modern religion, why should advertising not be its bible? And why should our best talents not be used in its employ?

When David Lynch does ads for Calvin Klein's Obsession, using passages from D. H. Lawrence, Ernest Hemingway, and F. Scott Fitzgerald, the aura of art culture is subsumed by Adcult. When an artist like Ridley Scott lends his genius to Apple Computer, when John Frankenheimer does ads for AT&T, when Jean-Luc Godard is employed by a French jeans company, when Woody Allen makes spots for Campari, when Spike Lee produces campaigns for Levi's, Nike, the Gap, and Barneys, and when Federico Fellini sells his services to Coop Italia (a grocery chain), the visionary imagination that had served the church and the state is now serving industry. When the entire fifth floor of the Centre Georges Pompidou in Paris is dedicated to the "Art of Advertising, 1890–1990," and when the Museum of Modern Art in New York sponsors a show called "The Art and Technique of the American Television Commercial," you know that Adcult is no longer the culture of the Visigoths but the culture of Rome.

5 ✦ TAKES A LICKING, BUT KEEPS ON TICKING

THE FUTURE OF ADCULT

When the historian of the Twentieth Century shall have finished his narrative, and comes searching for the sub-title which shall best express the spirit of the period, we think it not at all unlikely that he may select "The Age of Advertising" for the purpose.

• *PRINTERS' INK*, MAY 25, 1915

These humbler adjuncts to literature [advertisements] may prove more valuable to the future historian than the editorial contents [of large magazines]. In them we may trace our sociological history, the rise and fall of fads and crazes, changing interests and tastes, in foods, clothes, amusements and vices, a panorama of life as it was lived, more informing than old diaries or crumbling tombstones.

• EARNEST ELMO CALKINS, *AND HEARING NOT*, 1946

☞ *HAS* there ever been an institution so reviled as modern advertising, so hectored, so blamed for the ills of society? Who but fools, toadies, and industry flacks have ever come to its defense? Arnold Toynbee summed up the view of many when he dourly commented, "I cannot think of any circumstances in which advertising would *not* be an evil" (Ogilvy 1963:149). Yet has there ever been an institution so responsible for conveying not the best that has been thought and said but the most alluring, the most sensitive, and the most filled with human yearning? As I have argued, the only institution comparable in scope and magnitude was the Holy Roman Catholic Church of the early Renaissance. Long before Philip Morris, Procter & Gamble, and General Motors, long before N. W. Ayer, J. Walter Thompson, and Young & Rubicam, the most effective advertiser and carrier of culture was the church. Although it has been observed that this institution was neither holy, Roman, nor an empire, no one has ever denied that as a social force directing the attention and faith of a mass audience to a specific pattern of consciousness *and* consumption the church was without equal—at least until Adcult.

Is Adcult's time now up? Now that the culture of consumption has replaced the culture of contrition is it time for a new world order? Will some new system "afflict the comfortable and comfort the afflicted"? Has advertising, in its own terms, lost *it*? Who knows? For an apt image of how we once perceived the force of modern advertising, we need look no further than the enormous sign of the all-seeing optometrist in *The Great Gatsby*, Dr. T. J. Eckleburg. From high above the Valley of Ashes this billboard is the observing presence of decay that knows all, sees all, and cares not a whit. He is interested only in generating business, more business. To George Wilson, yeoman of the American dream, these are the eyes of God. The rest of us are not so sure.

Advertising no longer hovers above the fallen world of goods like a tsunami at the edge of Japanese paintings. It has flowed into our world. It has been absorbed. Advertising is not part of the dominant culture. It is the dominant culture. We have come to trust what it says not necessarily about goods but about itself. In other words, we may not know what it does, but we all know what it is. Ironically, the price of recognition and even acceptance is the loss of what it was supposed to do, namely, arrest our attention by confronting us. Adcult, again like Christianity, is always at its purest, its most vital, when it is countercultural and confrontational. "Without Contraries is no progression," wrote Blake. But who now opposes Adcult? When university professors write about a subject, one thing is certain: the wave has passed.

I'll skip an unthinkable but potential cause for the eventual demise of Adcult: mass consumption becomes too expensive. Advertising can flourish only in times of surplus. Such threats as the greenhouse effect, poisoned rivers, overflowing landfills, worldwide famine, and especially overpopulation may deplete surplus. Marxists have made a comfy living claiming that we are living in what they clairvoyantly call "late capitalism." Who knows? They may be right. There is no doubt that the economic waste in Adcult is staggering. It has been estimated that it costs nearly $250 to get a consumer to switch brands of toothpaste. Even so, the enormous waste in Adcult may be the concentration that it requires of its audience. But there are other reasons to think that the prime of Adcult is over.

Popular Culture

The history of advertising yo-yos between hard and soft sell. During hard times we get the hard sell, during affluent times the soft. Until we got video, cable, and the remote control, we could observe the yo-yoing in approximately fifteen-year cycles. Hard or soft, however, the one thing advertising has not been is ironic. But it seems to me that irony is becoming more and more a staple of Adcult and that irony is the deflation of Adcult. This irony often becomes parody, as if the only way to get through the clutter is to give

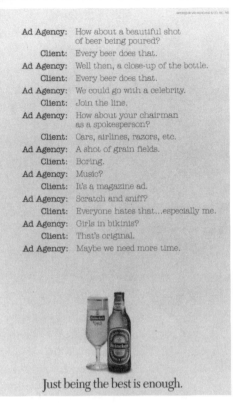

✦ The jig is up, part one: the self-effacing advertising agency acknowledges its existence, for better or worse.

up the charade and come out in front of the curtain. The Heineken, Merit, Taurus, and Simple Shoes ads show what I mean.

This "I'm your pal" persona collapses the usual voice of advertising, which is the strict "I'm your doctor; I know what's best for you." The ads on MTV and in *Rolling Stone* preview the future of selling to a generation that has been sold out. Although "Perception is reality" is certainly true, ads need not acknowledge that, let alone flaunt it. In giving up the guise of deified expertise to assume the new role of wise-cracking buddy, advertising may not be throwing in the towel, but it is coming close. Priests wear black robes for a reason.

To be sure, this dropping of the façade is the result of horizontal and vertical saturation. All this generation sees, and has ever seen, is endless advertising. If you want to be noticed, you now have to sell so softly that the product is almost overlooked. The product is no longer the hero; it often is not even a participant. The mystery is gone. As is typical of postmodernism, the authorial voice often gains attention by confessing its presence and admitting base motives from the get-go. Many of the ads on MTV—postmodern television, it calls itself—follow this path to the audience.

Here is a series of three Bugle Boy ads from DDB Needham Worldwide that aired on MTV recently. For thirty seconds we see pneumatic, bikini-clad women frolicking across the upper two-thirds of the screen. The spots are made with rock video techniques, quick cutting, weird angles, and abrupt close-ups. Scrolling across the lower third is the text, which runs in white against black. Here is what it says:

> Attention all guys. This is a commercial for Bugle Boy's new Color Denims. At least that's what we told Bugle Boy. They wanted to show a bunch of male models. We said showing nothing but beautiful women would work better. So if this is the sort of thing you want to see more of, buy some Color Denims. Otherwise Bugle Boy will force us to put men in the commercials. Like this [cut to male models] . . . None of us want that. Do we?
>
> Attention all guys. Although Bugle Boy is pleased by our response to the first commercial, they're still not convinced you know enough about their new Color Denims. We told them showing nothing but beautiful women should subliminally convince you the product is available in many colors and styles. Of course they'll probably check. So, if anyone asks, tell them you understood. Otherwise, we'll be forced to put men back in the commercials [cut to men] . . . Not a pretty picture, is it?
>
> Attention all guys. First the bad news. Bugle Boy is demanding we show their new Color Denims in this commercial. Now the good news. Nobody said we had to put them on men. [cut to women wearing Color Denims]

Although the trading of soft porn for soft sell is how jeans are sold, the premise of the ad agency in active collusion with the male viewers is startling. The quid pro quo is not implied, it is stated. If you'll buy the product, we'll show you what you want, and we'll keep running the ads so long as you keep purchasing. The product is not the hero, the ad agency is. No need to buy the jeans because you like them. Buy them because you like these pictures.

In a way, DDB Needham Worldwide one-upped Calvin Klein, which almost owns this genre of advertising. Calvin Klein ads show us images of young women in jeans fondling themselves, or young love makers on the beach or in a swing doing what cannot be misinterpreted. If there were no printed text, we would decode these ads as mild pornography. Nothing is more typical of this approach than Klein's 116-page "polybagged outsert" in *Vanity Fair* some years ago. Here, in photos by Bruce Weber, was a story of a rock band like Guns 'n' Roses and its fans before, during, and after a concert. This is the Bugle Boy ad in stop action. Among the more provocative images: a muscular Klein type clutching jeans to groin in shower; a shirtless man looking into mirror and applying eye makeup; a young woman pulling a young buck by his unbuckled belt; a nude woman, her hand cupped on her breast; and a final image of a young man at a urinal looking over his shoulder and smiling wistfully. Stuart Elliot of the *New York Times* did the body count (1991:D17). His sex tally: nude male posteriors—2; nude female posteriors—4; bare-chested men—27; topless women— 2. The product, however, is not mentioned.

Agencies are creating ads like this because their targeted audience responds. This audience has seen the rabbit pulled out of this magician's sleeve so many times that pretending that it's really in the hat won't work. The young audience essentially says, "OK, pull it out of your sleeve, but do it well, make a joke, and don't take it seriously." The Energizer rabbit even plays off this by marching through commercials of other products as if to say, "The jig's up, we all know it's just advertising." So too the Subaru ads that make fun of zero to sixty acceleration, the Swedish Bikini Team beer ads that send up bimbo beer commercials, and the Pepsi ads that mock taste tests by showing chimpanzees as subjects. In fact, if you watch MTV, you will see that more than half the ads are essentially subversions of mainstream ads. When Wayne and Garth hold Frito-Lay products up to the camera during *Wayne's World* and blather about how disgusting product placement is, the audience gets the joke immediately. My generation instantly recognizes and criticizes product placement; to Generation X it is commonplace and risible.

If much modern advertising has taken to self-parody, it is because the audience likes it. What was the favorite genre of *Saturday Night Live*? What locked the viewer in place during the first half-hour? It was the blurring of the lines between entertainment and advertising. Where first we expected the advertising break to appear, we found Eddie Murphy as Buckwheat, hawking a record; John Belushi, as an out-of-shape athlete whose training-table mainstay is Little Chocolate Doughnuts; Bill Murray, peddling mineral water "dredged from Lake Erie" or demonstrating the Bass-o-Matic; or Roseanne playing an apathetic operator who shrugs off a credit-card customer's problems. Part of the fun was that although we instantly recognized the visual style of ads, we didn't always know if a parody would follow.

The gist of parody is that we recognize the butt so well that it never has to be expressed. That means that it has been internalized, which means that it is no longer arresting attention. Many a viewer of *SNL* can remember not only the send-up, but the butt of the following:

- Shimmer, the floor wax that's also a dessert topping
- The Royal Deluxe II, the car that offers so smooth a ride that a mohel can perform a circumcision in the back seat during a drive over a rough road.
- Super Colon Blow, the cereal with as much fiber in one bowl as 2.5 million bowls of oat bran
- The Kannon AE-1, a camera so simple even Stevie Wonder can use it

True, advertising parody has been around a long time. In the 1920s *Ballyhoo*, a magazine devoted to satirizing advertising, was a favorite on college campuses. But parody did not become a serious subgenre of Adcult until the late 1950s. My generation grew up with the playful parodies of *Mad Magazine* that wonderfully subverted the Bufferin, Crest, Breck, and Tarreyton campaigns. No one who ever saw the Bofforin (misspelled on purpose) cutaway of the digestive system, the Crust kid as juvenile delinquent with no teeth holding the "no cavities" message from his dentist, the Blecch portrait of Ringo Starr with the golden locks and busted-up nose, or the black-eyed Carry-on smoker who has been pushed around by the government one too many times could ever see the original ads the way they were intended.

About the same time that *Mad* was having at Madison Avenue in print, Ernie Kovaks was doing the same on television. But it was Stan Freberg on radio who turned the momentum of advertising against itself and made it at least momentarily postmodern. Freberg's ads were not just parodies, they were ads. The minute you heard his voice, you knew the playful ironist was close at hand. He always gave the impression that he was broadcasting his messages from somewhere off-shore, far from agency control. Freberg made his radio advertising debut in 1956 for Contadina, a small San Jose-based tomato-paste maker, with the long-lived jingle, "Who puts eight great tomatoes in that little bitty can?" Later, in a series of commercials called "Clark Smathers: A Kaiser Aluminum Foil Salesman Faces Life," Freberg painted a grim picture of a man who couldn't afford to clothe or feed his family, pay for an operation for his wife, or buy his daughter shoes "because the mean old grocer wouldn't stock Mr. Kaiser's foil." Freberg's tongue was always firmly in cheek, as with his intentionally provocative bit about the nine out of ten doctors who prefer Chun King chow mein (all but one doctor was Chinese), his mini-musical for Butter-Nut coffee called "Omaha!" and the only honest airline ad ever made. His voice-over for Pacific Air Lines: "Hey there, you with the sweat in your palms. Do you wish the pilot would knock off all that jazz about 'That's Crater Lake on the left, ladies and gentlemen,' and tell you instead what the devil that funny noise was you just heard?"

What made all Freberg's commercials so funny was that they poked fun at what he was doing. He was trying to sell something. But wait! He was one of us! What he was doing in the 1950s and 1960s has become commonplace. Such parody, especially when widespread, carries not only the seeds of discontent but the symptoms of exhaustion. Seeing the priest in suspenders and shorts—literally defrocked—has drawbacks. To get our attention the industry is more interested in mocking itself than in making the sale.

This may not be good for advertising. The power of organizing systems is often tied up in their confrontational natures. Christianity was never a greater force than when in conflict with another culture. It has never been as vigorous as when it tangled with the Romans. American culture may well have needed the Soviet Union to give it the cohesion necessary to organize its various selves. The cold war may prove to have been the American moment. We may need the myths of the heathen and the evil empire more than we realize. Highcult is hopelessly dependent on the vulgar. So advertising also may never be as concentrated and dynamic as it was in the first half of the twentieth century, when it pushed hard against other established value-creating cultures. The ad exec, like the heathen and the Soviet, has become a regular person.

We can see this by briefly looking at the ad man in popular culture during the 1950s. Naturally, we would expect hostility from highcult because advertising was besmirching print. Prose fiction was chockablock with criticism. From Sinclair Lewis ("Advertising is the cheapest way of selling goods, particularly if the goods are worthless") to F. Scott Fitzgerald ("Advertising's contribution to humanity is exactly minus zero") to Herman Wouk ("Advertising blasts everything that is good and beautiful in this land with a horrid spreading mildew") there was little love lost.

Hollywood soon climbed aboard this bandwagon. In movie after movie ad execs are portrayed as shifty rascals sneaking around our consciousness—picking, poking, prodding us to action against "our better natures," although they have none of their own. They have no moral compass. In Reginald Rose's *Twelve Angry Men* (1957) jurors attempt to reach a verdict in a murder trial. Although eleven jurors have various principles, including careless expediency, the ad exec makes and unmakes his decisions on the basis of—in his words—"Let's run it up the flagpole and see who salutes." He can't make up his mind because he hasn't got one. Often this lack of moral center is played out as sexual farce, with the advertising man using the tricks of his trade to seduce the innocent damsel. The result is often happy, but the methods are deception and subversion. Have a look at *Take a Letter, Darling, Marriage on the Rocks, The Way We Live Now, The Arrangement, Kiss Me Mate, A Letter to Three Wives, Madison Avenue*, or *The Wheeler Dealers*, and you will see that this rascal is up to no good. More often than not, once successful, the ad man concludes the escapade by promising to leave the Avenue forever. What's fair in love and sales, he learns, is not fair in life.

In a sense, the cauterizing text for this view of advertising was Frederic Wakeman's 1946 novel *The Hucksters*. The plot is hardly complex: Victor Norman is back from the war (his name makes the point), he returns to his old advertising agency to tide himself over until he can find an honest job, falls for a married woman, writes great ads but feels he is selling out, then gives it all up and wanders off into the sunset, forsaking even his heartsick love. He didn't fight the Nazis to end up lying to his own country. And he's not about to steal some other guy's wife just because she's crazy about him. The book was a great success, in part because it supposedly was based on Wakeman's experience as copywriter for Foote, Cone & Belding. *The Hucksters* was a number one best-seller, a Book of the Month Club selection, condensed by *Reader's Digest,* and then sold to MGM for the then exorbitant $250,000.

The movie, starring Clark Gable and Deborah Kerr, hosed the book down some to allow for a happy ending (the lovers go off together into the sunset). But it did not touch the character who personified the ad man in popular culture. In both the book and the movie Evan Llewelyn Evans is central. Clearly based on FC&B's most illustrious client, George Washington Hill, ayatollah of the American Tobacco Company, Evans was played with devastating wickedness by Sidney Greenstreet. Anyone who read the book or saw the movie will not soon forget Evans's Introduction to Advertising 101.

In the central scene of both book and movie Victor accompanies the dyspeptic head of the agency, a Mister Kimberly (based on Emerson Foote), to be introduced to Evans. For legal reasons Wakeman substituted Beautee Soap for Lucky Strike cigarettes. In the cavernous office at the head of a large oval table and surrounded by flunkies is the small and dapper Evans. He wears a black alpaca coat, a white linen vest, and a bandanna around his neck. On his head is an old straw hat, the kind worn in southern fields. Victor starts to shake hands, but Evans will have none of it (germs), and so Victor takes his seat.

> In the expressive silence, Mr. Evans raised his straw-covered head once more, hawked and spit on the mahogany board table.
>
> No one spoke. Very deliberately, he took the handkerchief out of his sleeve, wiped the spit off the table, and threw the handkerchief into a wastebasket.
>
> "Mr. Victor," he said.
>
> Allison [a secretary] leaned down and whispered.
>
> "Mr. Norman," he said, shouting in a deep bass. "You have just seen me do a disgusting thing. Ugly word, spit. But you know, you'll always remember what I just did."
>
> Taut silence.
>
> Then Mr. Evans leaned forward and whispered hoarsely, "Mr. Norman, if nobody remembers your brand, then you ain't gonna sell any soap."
>
> Pregnant pause.
>
> "Mr. Norman, that's just what we're in business for—to sell soap. Beautee soap. I don't want you to ever forget that. You got to eat, drink, sleep and yes, by God, dream soap. Because even if you build the most glamorous, high Hooper rating show on the air—it ain't gonna do us a damn bit of good unless

you figure out some way to sell soap on it. You gotta make the people remember you. Check?"

"Check!" said Mr. Kimberly.

"Check," said Allison. Only son Paul and new-man Vic failed to echo it.

"And the way I look at it. You got your people and I got my people. And we both gotta keep goosing 'em to make 'em sell more soap. Beautee soap."

He made a goosing motion.

"Right?"

"Right!" they all said again, following the chain of command. It was a ritual.

"Now one other thing, Mr. Forman."

Allison leaned down and whispered again.

"Now one other thing, Mr. Norman. I believe in selling by demonstration. Any other way. . . . "

He looked around, found a water carafe at his right, grasped it.

"Any other way," he repeated, turning the carafe upside down on the board table, "is all wet. See what I mean?"

The water ran on Brown and Regina Kennedy [Evans's flunkies]. Neither made a protective motion. Allison leaned forward and mopped up with his two handkerchiefs. Evans watched dispassionately until Allison had finished. Then he leaned forward again, this time hoarsely whispering.

"Also, Mr. Norman, this company gives your agency ten million dollars a year to spend in advertising. And do you know why? I'll tell you a secret about the soap business, Mr. Norman. There's no damn difference between soaps. Except for perfume and color, soap is soap. Oh, maybe we got a few manufacturing tricks, but the public don't give a damn about that. But the difference, you see, is in the selling and advertising. We sell soap twice as fast as our nearest competitor because we outsell and out-advertise 'em. And that gets me to the most important part of this meeting."

He blew his nose loudly and continued.

"We get our results by work. By chin-chin and by compass direction. When we want something, we work it out. When we don't know where we're going, we chin-chin until we do. That's the time for ideas, suggestions, new plans. But once the compass points north and we know where we're going, we stay on the beam. And we don't want anybody associated with us who's off the beam. I ain't interested in ideas that are off the beam and I ain't interested in people that are off the beam. Check!"

"Check," went around the board table like a whipcrack.

The old man got up. "That's about all I had to say. Except"—he took off his alpaca coat, walked around and put it over Vic's shoulders—"except I want you to realize you're wearing the Beautee soap coat now. I hope it fits you well."

"Thank you, sir," said Vic.

"Remember, two things make good advertising. One, a good simple idea. Two, repetition. And by repetition, by God, I mean until the public is so irritated with it, they'll buy your brand because they bloody well can't forget it. All you professional advertising men are scared to death of raping the public; I say the public likes it, if you got the know-how to make 'em relax and enjoy it."

• (Wakeman 1946:21–24)

I quote at length because this is the most glorious depiction of the wickedness of advertising ever to appear in popular culture. Other villains would have to move over to make room for this one, or he would make even them buy soap. Of course, matters have changed some since the 1950s. If you look at recent movies like *How to Succeed in Advertising, Crazy People, Defending Your Life, Putney Swope, How to Succeed in Business Without Really Trying, Nothing in Common,* or *The Coca-Cola Kid,* you will see the tone is now invariably ironic. This is an ad man, wink-wink. We know what he's up to. The ad exec has become a slightly crazed buffoon, not a nefarious seducer of the innocent. He is, quite simply, not for real and therefore need not be taken seriously. At the end he does not hang his head and go off to a Vermont farm. Why should he? He has not been evil, just nuts.

Surely the fact that Michael Doonesbury, protagonist of the Gary Trudeau comic strip, is a copywriter who must balance his principles and his portfolio, or that the everyday heroes of television's *thirtysomething* were forever going up against the Evansesque martinet Miles Drentell, show that our sympathies have softened. Darren Stephens in *Bewitched* was an ad man but was hardly to be feared. Indeed, he was a very dim bulb. When the Nick at Night network offered a three-hour celebration of *Bewitched* in 1994, it entitled the block programming "How to Get Ahead in Advertising." In each episode Darren was shown as a sweet noodlehead, successful only when Samantha added the magic. Little need be said of NBC's dreary and short-lived *Nothing in Common,* other than that the endeavor was a poor rip-off of the theatrical movie of the same name, that it took place in a fictional Chicago ad agency, and that advertising was portrayed as being about as dangerous as a Shriners' parade. More recently, however, Angela Bower, heroine—mother— sexy date *and* finally owner of her own agency on *Who's the Boss?* is nothing if not a complete reversal of George Washington Hill. She is eternally juggling son, mother, Tony the male housekeeper, and clients with boundless concern and goodness. Although *Who's the Boss?* may show that only a woman can be an unambiguously "good" executive in advertising, at least it shows that goodness is possible. If popular culture is a trustworthy mirror of contemporary anxieties, we must conclude that ad execs-sellers are no longer a major villain. In fact, they are just doing a job like the rest of us working stiffs. Little wonder that we have lost the pejorative eponym *Babbitt.*

*A*UDIENCE

As advertising has lost some of its wickedness in popular culture, it has lost some of its thrill for consumers. This may be hard to believe because there is so much of it, but commercial speech is much less powerful than it was. As the din has increased, fewer messages are getting through. When a great copywriter like Howard Gossage jokes, "The object of your advertising should not be to communicate with your consumers and prospects at all, but to terrorize your competition's copywriters" you know that even the priests are losing faith (Hampel 1988:25). If so, what about the audience?

Recent studies have shown that consumers use less advertising in decision making. Advertising is not supplying the reason for purchasing as it did a generation ago. A cross section of Americans studied between 1982 and 1992 showed that 15 percent fewer people relied on advertising in buying appliances, 10 percent fewer in buying furniture, 7 percent fewer in making banking decisions, 9 percent fewer in buying automotive supplies, and 17 percent fewer in purchasing clothing (Bernstein 1992:25). Is this because so many messages are being shoved into the pipeline that few get through, or is the problem more systemic?

Part of the problem is in the audience on both sides of the demographic arc. On the one hand, baby boomers are running out of boom. Aging yuppies are turning into grumpies. They still consume—wide-seated jeans, miniature Oreos, graduated bifocals, comfy walking shoes, girdles (now called hip slips, thigh slimmers, or body shapers)—but they are more concerned about being fully vested in their retirement systems than being fully participating citizens in perpetual debt. Women, for whom so much of Adcult was created, are simply shopping less. Not only do more than half the women in America work outside the home, they are growing older. Within the next few years some forty million women will be in their forties. This triple whammy means they will be hard to reach, they will find it hard to shop, and, worse yet, they will have already made most of their brand choices.

Thankfully, Madison Avenue has a new concern for hand wringing. On the other side of the demographic curve is the mysterious and potentially adnoxious Generation X. Are these people a serious threat to Adcult? Certainly, the first warning is implicit in the act of labeling. After all, we've just had the Me Decade, the Mauve Decade, the Silent Generation, the Swinging Sixties, the Decade of Greed, the Nuclear Age, the Electronic Age, and the Age of Aquarius. Why should we think Generation X is anything more than the generation du jour?

More indicative of what is going on is how the advertising industry has latched onto Douglas Coupland's 1991 novel, *Generation X*, to explain not the audience so much as the industry. If women can be seen passing through the Adcult python like the proverbial rabbit, the X'ers, Posties, Baby Bummers, Slackers, or whatever jumped out while the python wasn't looking. Supposedly, some forty-seven million 17- to 28-year-old Americans became snake proof overnight. Not only that but the condition is epidemic. The X'er kicking rocks in Peoria en route to his McJob supposedly has more in common with his fellows in the Ginza, in Piccadilly Square, in Pushkin Square, at Notre Dame, and

If you don't think your tastes change, let's think back to that haircut senior year.

Dewar's

{ Oh yeah. I stand around the gazebo in my underwear all the time. }

Jack Purcell
CONVERSE

• The jig is up, part two: Generation X advertising.

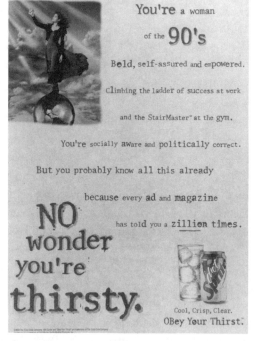

You're a woman of the **90's**

Bold, self-assured and empowered.

Climbing the ladder of success at work and the StairMaster® at the gym.

You're socially aware and politically correct.

But you probably know all this already

because every ad and magazine

has told you a zillion times.

NO wonder you're thirsty.

Cool, Crisp, Clear.
OBey Your Thirst.

at the Brandenburg Gate than he does even with his older siblings. The usual culprit, MTV, is to blame.

Worldwide TV has rendered this generation not just sublingual but subcultural. How else to explain the inability of multinational advertising agencies to create much in the way of international campaigns for their multinational clients? These postboomer boomerangs have been so polluted by desire unmet, so overwhelmed by promise unkept that they override any claims, even those based in their own slightly dreary reality. These kids, we are supposed to believe, deconstruct ads faster than Yale critics on amphetamines.

Does this sound like a scapegoat for an industry that has lost touch? Every major agency has a special presentation on selling twentysomethings,

BANANA REPUBLIC

claiming that only they can "get under their radar." Some even have resident X'ers, in-house stoolies on the take, betraying their brothers and sisters for arcade money. However, the ads themselves make us wonder. Will showing X'ers, in droopy drawers, baseball hats turned backward, mumbling in rap-rhythmic speech really work? The Burger King "BK TeeVee" spots with Dan Cortese, the Subaru Impreza's campaign in which an X'er compares the car to hard-core music, the Converse sneaker ad in which a spokesman yells, "We don't want to be in a beer commercial," the Gap counterculture icon series that uses Anthony Kiedes (of the Red Hot Chili Peppers), the Sprite ad in which a young black man remarks that he is sick of some celebrity selling him something, the Chrysler Neon "Hi" campaign with concocted graffiti, the brainless chatter from the Budweiser pool player comparing the relative values of sitcom starlets from *Gilligan's Island* and *I Dream of Jeannie* ("Is Ginger better than Mary Ann?" "Is Mary Ann better than Jeannie?"), or the Dewar's Scotch ad ("You finally have a real job, a real place and a real boyfriend. How about a real drink?") seem pretty much business as usual. Coke is even testing a new drink called O.K. with the slogan, "Things are going to be OK." I suspect this will have as much traction as a minister saying, "Well, maybe all this after-life stuff is just made up to make us feel better." Unitarianism is not a very forceful brand of salvation, and the target audience is quite small.

The claim that Beavis and Butthead, Bill and Ted, Wayne and Garth are immune to advertising is claptrap. Although they may not buy Ferragamos or earrings, X'ers are consuming Doc Martens and nose rings. If their expectations are diminished, it is because we are comparing them to the wrong generation. X'ers may not have the disposable income of the baby boomers, but what generation ever did? The boomers were the exception. And the claim that the X'ers are the first generation unable to improve their standard of living relative to the previous generation is hogwash as well. The same was said during the depression. The generation Gertrude Stein so confidently located as lost awoke to find itself awash in tail fins and refrigerators.

When a supposedly lost generation enjoys reading *Wired*, *Adbusters*, and *Details*, listening to a singing group called the Spin Doctors, going to movies like *Slacker*, *Naked in New York*, *Bodies*, *Rest and Motion*, and *Reality Bites*, and hanging ads on their bedroom walls, the problem is not revulsion. Although they may diss advertising claims, they are very much caught up in the ethos of Adcult. If anything, Generation X loves advertising, not wisely but too well. When Liz Claiborne and Ralph Lauren manufacture a line of grunge clothing, you know the machine is still in gear. This generation is not passing through "prime brand option time" (as one agency describes it) unscathed. True, Anita Roddick has built up one of Britain's best-known brands, Body Shop, without a single advertisement. And true, a study commissioned by the Robert Wood Johnson Foundation called "Reaching the Hip-Hop Generation" (based on small group meetings with three hundred black teenagers in various cities over two years) found that some inoculation against advertising had occurred. For instance, the respondents knew that Magic Johnson, Jesse Jackson, and then-President Bush were only "playing the game" of celebrity endorser (Harrington 1992:F7). But I suspect that advertisers knew that already. If commercial speech has lost some of its power, it is not just because the audience has become deaf but because the agencies have been saying the same boring things for too long.

Sponsors

With greater misgivings than ever, manufacturers are questioning whether advertising works. Lord Leverhume and John Wanamaker—both of whom supposedly said that half their advertising budgets were wasted, they just didn't know which half—are being joined by a multitude who wonder whether the figure might be much higher. Studies commissioned by the Association of National Advertisers concluded that, although advertising is a reliable way to increase short-term sales, it does not do much to boost market share and profits. Because ad budgets are usually allocated as a fixed percentage of actual or anticipated sales, sales appear to cause advertising, not vice versa.

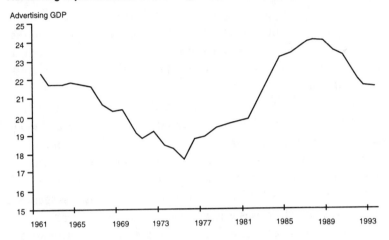

Advertising Expenditures as a Percentage of Gross Domestic Product

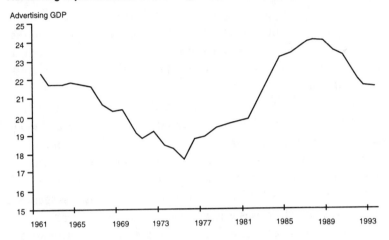

Year-over-Year % Change for Gross Domestic Product, Advertising and Personal Consumer Expenditures

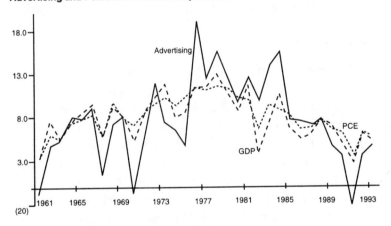

✦ Advertising Expenditures, 1961–1993.
SOURCE: Goldman Sachs U.S. Research with data from McCann-Erickson and U.S. Department of Commerce.

Advertising may in fact be the least effective part of the marketing mix, with distribution, pricing, and promotion having much more power to influence which goods the public buys. A study done by New England Consulting Group found that "given a fixed budget, you're better off exiting advertising entirely" unless you *know* you have a top-notch campaign (Crain 1994:21). Another study, this one commissioned by advertisers and undertaken by Information Resources, concluded, "There is no simple correspondence between advertising and higher sales" and that top-scoring ads on recall tests don't necessarily translate to higher sales. In fact, "the relationship between high copy scores and increased sales is tenuous at best" (Lipman, "Research Tactic," 1991:B1). Just because you recall the Doritos ad does not mean you'll buy the product. It's not surprising that the last few years have marked a huge shift away from traditional sites toward couponing, direct mail, discounting, in-store displays, and other promotions. For many products advertising has become only one of many marketing choices and a relatively expensive one at that.

The numbers support this sense of diminishing confidence. In 1991 spending on advertising slowed for first time in thirty years, and even though a recession makes advertising budgets vulnerable, the percentage of budgets allocated to advertising may never return to the levels of the 1980s. In 1980 advertising made up two-thirds of marketing expenditures, in 1990 no more than one-third. Another way to look at it: in 1960 American business spent $12 billion on advertising, which was 2.32 percent of GNP. In 1990 GNP was ten times bigger and ad expenses were eleven times as great (Mayer 1991:219). Yet another way to express this at-best steady-state environment is by showing advertising expenditures as a percentage of gross domestic product (GDP) or comparing them with consumer spending, as in figure 5.1.

Advertising Agencies

Advertising is a relationship business. Like a dance, it is based on predictability. The pas de deux between client and agency has become more and more like Texas line dancing in which the client locks arms with a number of agencies, faces front, does a few repetitive steps, and then sits down to watch a video replay. In fact, if you were to note the abrupt changes that have occurred since the mid-1980s between such historically advertising-dependent businesses as Burger King, IBM, Diet Coke, American Express, Subaru, Reebok, BMW, and Colgate-Palmolive, you might wonder whether the appropriate metaphor might be slam dancing. This fractiousness in the agency-client relationship is repeatedly shown in the Salz Survey of Advertiser-Agency Relations, which questions both parties on how they are getting along with each other (Elliot, "Agencies and Clients," 1994:D18). In a word: *edgy*.

Agencies continually complain that they are no longer considered partners, that they are being treated like suppliers. This hesitancy to get heavily involved is partly the result of the client's observation of the waste and bloat in the leveraged buyouts and conglomerations of the agencies in the 1980s. Imagine the consternation on the clients' side when Saatchi & Saatchi bought out the venerable Ted Bates Agency for $507 million in 1986 and $112.5 million went into the pocket of agency chairman Robert Jocoby. Clients of both agencies must have wondered how much of their money was tied up in this transaction. So did everyone else.

Any compensation system that is tied to a percentage of media buying instead of to increased sales has to be perpetually suspect. Fred Allen's well-known jeer—"An advertising agency is eighty-five percent confusion and fifteen percent commission"—is still appropriate. How often will an agency tell you that you have enough advertising? Or too much? Although task-based and cost-plus remuneration systems have been tried, the industry has no standard for payment. Every few years a hungry agency will proclaim "guaranteed results" or "incentive compensation," but Maxwell Dane (the first *D* in what is now DDB Needham) knew better. Back in the late 1960s he proclaimed:

> New methods of compensation are always being tried . . . and I say great! Let's never be complacent about what we're doing. For example, several agencies had widely publicized deals with advertisers to share in increased sales. When they vanished hardly a word was said about them. They didn't work and never will. If sales go up appreciably, the advertiser rumbles that he is paying too much and there are plenty of agencies who will take over the account on a more conventional basis. If sales go down, pity the poor agency.
>
> • (quoted in Hanlon 1993:18)

As clients do-si-do through agencies today, they often send a packet of questions to prospective partners. One question invariably has to do with willingness to negotiate compensation. Aware that the client is always going to be concerned about what the agency is doing for its money, rather than what the advertising is doing for sales, agencies have to behave as if they are always doing something.

This do something—anything!—mentality results in the Hawthorne effect. The phenomenon was observed some sixty years ago in a Western Electric plant near Chicago called the Hawthorne Plant. Production studies found that workers who assembled telephones responded to thirteen variables, such as light, temperature, rest, nutrition, and the like. Change any variable, announce it was made in the workers' interest, and short-term job satisfaction rose. The Hawthorne effect may explain not only why campaigns are often replaced before they have done their work but also why agencies are shifted before they have understood the product. All parties have a vested interest in doing something—anything!

One argument for consolidation in the 1980s was the prospect of global advertising. Theodore Levitt of the Harvard Business School has made a career of assuring Madison Avenue that the global village is just around the corner. Ironically, while the fall of national barriers increased the squabbling of central European states, the breakdown of discrete cultures produced often fierce individualism. Cable, satellite transmission, fiber optics, and all the delivery systems that were to make one worldwide brand, one delivery system, and one advertising campaign a bonanza for international agencies have not panned out. Ironically, global advertising may have even become more difficult. The holding companies did better naming themselves—Omnicom, Eurocom, Interpublic, and sticking *Worldwide* after their names—than

● Western-style
advertising in the
Soviet Union:
a smile is
still a smile.

МИР ГОВОРИТ «КОЛГЕЙТ»–
ПОДРАЗУМЕВАЕТ ЗУБНАЯ ПАСТА.
МИР ГОВОРИТ ЗУБНАЯ ПАСТА–
ПОДРАЗУМЕВАЕТ «КОЛГЕЙТ».

advertising for their clients. Who in Adcult would have known that the closer people get, the worse they look to each other?

The old bromide to think globally, act locally has never been more true than in global advertising. Although half the world thinks you can advertise soap by showing a woman luxuriating in her bath, extolling the percentage of skin cream in Dove soap to her husband, the other half of the world is repulsed. Why is she taking a bath? What is skin cream doing in soap? What is skin cream? And what is her husband doing invading her privacy? It is hard to predict which products can make it across cultural borders with out being stopped, frisked, and deported. When McDonald's and Coca-Cola placed the Saudi flag and a passage from the Koran on their throwaway packaging during the World Cup promotion, the gaffe cost them millions in goodwill, to say nothing of the cost of destroying the Happy Meal packaging. The French have insisted that no foreign words (read English) appear in ads. Cultural hackles can be raised not just by words (as with Chevrolet's introduction of the Nova automobile in Latin America where *nova* means it doesn't run or IBM's billboards in Czechoslovakia, where using the language of the Slovaks angers the Czechs) but also by shapes, gestures, and even color tones.

There are exceptions, however. Products that symbolize America cross borders with ease. Coke, Hershey bars, Levi's jeans, Marlboro cigarettes, Nike shoes, and Wrigley gum are bought worldwide simply for being American. The packaging is the ad. Some products make it across because they symbolize elegance, like Seagrams's Chivas Regal or technological superiority like Xerox's. Whereas airline advertising is relatively simple, cosmetics are tough, and food tastes are almost impossible to communicate. Yet who could have predicted that Tony the Tiger could roar for Kellogg's Frosted Flakes and not be stopped in his tracks? These sugar-coated flakes are one of the few world-wide foods.

Media

An irony often noted is that the mass audience put together by advertising is now splintering, thanks to the new media supported by advertising. Ad execs wistfully recall the 1950s and 1960s, when 93 percent of homes using television were watching the networks and an advertiser could reach two-thirds of all homes by buying space in *Life, Look,* and the *Saturday Evening Post.* Print media are still able to deliver a predicted audience, but television is in chaos. Cable, and especially the clicker, have made ad-avoidance a pastime. Advertisers of FMCGs may have to return to advertiser-sponsored and/or -produced programs in order to integrate ads and programming. They may also have to depend more on such traditional media events as the Super Bowl and the Oscars, which can deliver predictably large audiences. Adcult is running out of space to colonize. Many people were shocked when Penn State entered into an exclusive $14 million, ten-year deal with Pepsi to make the soft drink the official school beverage. How could a school sell out? In the advertising business, however, the distress was that Pepsi would prefer to rent a college than rent an audience in the traditional media.

And who knows what will be coming down the much vaunted information superhighway? Interactive capacity may well spell the end of the carpet style of advertising, in which advertisers hope to pick up a few customers by covering many. With the proliferation of information "tubes" such precise targeting may be possible that Ford could put an Escort commercial in one neighborhood and a Lincoln town car in another. Conversely, customers may be able to insert a virus in their media receivers to screen out ads or to have other ones inserted. Viewers may even have to request advertising. The audience may target the ad rather than have the agency target the audience. This will produce more information-rich advertising, but it may be selling-poor. Already, services like FreeFone and HomeFax exchange phone and fax expenses with certain customers for accepting ads "along the wire." Collaboration will be the future of commercial speech, and it will have a profound effect.

Hardly a day goes by that we don't see signs of this restlessness in Adcult. Take road signs, for instance. Since Lady Bird Johnson lobbied for the Highway Beautification Act of 1965, the federal government has regulated signage along the interstate system. Eventually, states like Vermont, Oregon, and Hawaii decreed that certain off-premises signage could be completely regulated. Goodbye to billboards. Now still-smaller units of government like cities and towns are attempting to control by-the-road urban advertising. This erosion of Adcult's once unquestioned presence is happening all over. Exercisers at health clubs have boycotted treadmills placed so that the exerciser can see only the monitor of an advertising network; people hang up if advertising is played while they are on hold, and so many patients have rebelled when forced to read and view special programming at the doctor's office that Whit-

tle has called it quits. And in the inner city, advertising commandos have organized to remove not just tobacco and liquor ads but also actual products like PowerMaster beer, as well as Dakota and Uptown cigarette brands, that target ethnic, minority, and underage groups.

It used to be that if an ad was offensive, you would complain. Then you might deface it. "This ad is demeaning to women" was written across countless signs. If you were really dedicated, you might try to remove the ad. Now the rise of "culture jamming," or "subvertising," is gaining popularity. You use the ad's force against itself in a kind of cultural jujitsu. This is clearly the hope of a Canadian group called Adbusters, which attempts to neuter the influence of liquor and cigarette advertising by commandeering the ad itself. These subversions are already appearing on dormitory walls.

Adbusters is in regular contact with the legal departments of the parodied agencies. Because ads are intended to be consumed in the public domain, they are not accorded the special copyright protections of works of art. Understandably, no one wants to go to court to find out precisely where the line is between private and public, because doing so would lead to the question of exactly how much protection is accorded speech that sells dangerous products. TBWA, the agency that did the Absolut ads, was especially irritated by Adbusters. But true to the nature of sabotage, Adbusters would change the ad slightly, as with adding an *e* to *Absolut*, or run the parody only once.

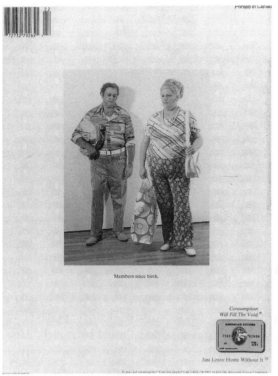

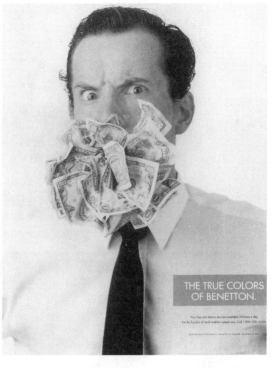

◆ Culture jamming, as performed by Adbusters of Canada. When Absolut threatened suit in February 1992, Adbusters challenged Absolut to a debate about alcohol advertising. By April Absolut had dropped the suit, and the spoofs are now omnipresent on campuses.

Advertisers' increasing proximity to the courts is a sure sign of distress, however. As is true of much else in our society, the courts have not really addressed the big questions in Adcult. Nor should they. The Supreme Court is warily hoping that resolving the small questions—should the display boxes containing advertising circulars be afforded the same protection as boxes containing newspapers? can you put a political sign in your front yard? what happens when a radio station in one state broadcasts lottery commer-

Marlboro Country.

ABSOLUTE ON ICE.

NEARLY 50% OF AUTOMOBILE FATALITIES ARE LINKED TO ALCOHOL • 10% OF NORTH AMERICANS ARE ALCOHOLICS
A TEENAGER SEES 100,000 ALCOHOL ADS BEFORE REACHING LEGAL DRINKING AGE

cials into a state that prohibits it?—will stave off the big questions.

The big question, which will be raised for some time to come, is whether speech about dangerous products should be muted. Alcohol and tobacco are the usual suspects, but the lottery and state-supported gambling should be included. Should Smooth Joe, the Camel dromedary with the scrotal head, be able to speak at times when he will be clearly heard by the kiddies? Should a potent malt liquor called PowerMaster be marketed just to urban African Americans? Should state lotteries, which are clearly a regressive tax in which the state retains about 35 percent of ticket sales while spending almost 15 percent on promotion, be allowed to use outrageous magical thinking in their advertising? In each case the ad budgets are huge, and most of that advertising is directed at those least able to afford addiction. Behind liquor, lotteries, and cigarettes lurks a vast world of goods that may be dangerous. And what of political advertising?

Branding

Branding—the very heart of advertising—has become problematic. Branding was supposed to create long-term value. It was supposed to inhibit, or even stop, what was thought to be the natural rise, shine, evaporation, and fall of consumer products. *Brand stewardship* was the explanation given for the mergers and takeovers of the 1980s. What this term often meant was buy and consolidate the competition. In Darwinian terms fewer brands mean less competition, lower promotional costs, and more profit.

If branding really worked, what was Philip Morris doing cutting the prices of its premium cigarettes to recapture market share on April 2, 1993? Brand management was supposed to defend against exactly this. "Marlboro Friday" will not be soon forgotten on the stock exchange or along Madison Avenue, because it demonstrated that when consumers were given a choice between lower price and brand loyalty, loyalty lost. Worse yet, in the game of chicken between buyer and seller, the seller blinked. Michael Miles, CEO of Philip Mor-

Premium Quality.

New Low Price.

We recognize that today, more than ever before, consumers are looking for greater value in everything they buy. So, Philip Morris USA has made it easier for smokers to enjoy even better value in our premium quality brands – Marlboro, Merit, Virginia Slims, Benson & Hedges and Parliament – by lowering the price to our customers.*

Look for the new lower price where you shop.

* Based on Manufacturer's Price Reduction.

✦ If advertising worked as advertised, this would never occur: the beginning of Marlboro Friday, when Philip Morris shares lost 23 percent of their market value.

ris, lost his job and Adcult lost a seminal myth. The sheriffs of Marlboro Country could not contain the threat of the encroaching low-cost generics by their usual method of raising prices and increasing advertising. If branding really worked as advertised, why would Madison Avenue feel compelled to run an ad such as the one by the Coalition for Brand Equity in the *New York Times* and the *Wall Street Journal*?

Next, brand extension, or introducing goods by adding the cachet of an established brand, was thought to be one advantage of branding. So Oreo cookies are translated into Oreo ice cream; Coke becomes Cherry Coke, then Diet Cherry Coke; Camels appear as Camel Filters, then as Camel Filter 100s, Camel Light Filter 100s, Camel Special Lights, and Camel Wides; Tide in powder form becomes Liquid Tide, and Miller Beer brews Miller Lite, Miller Ice, and so forth. Clearly, the producer can shortcut the introduction costs of new goods by using such piggybacking. But this has been a two-way street, with anemic extension products sapping the home product. Think of the rousing failure of Kodak Floppy Disks, Milky Way Ice Cream, Arm & Hammer antiperspirant, Life Saver gum, and even Euro Disney, all conceived and planned by the masters of Adcult. The surest thing that can be said of brand extension is that it is a crap shoot.

Branding itself, so important to retailers because they could be assured of consumer interest, ironically allowed discount retailers to cannibalize the value of cooperative advertising. Wal-Mart, for instance, does relatively little

The fastest way to wreck a Ferrari.

product advertising, carries only name brands at lower prices than other retailers, and makes its money by bickering with the producer for lower bulk rates. Your local electronics store, which helps to advertise Sony televisions sets, is also creating value for the product at Wal-Mart. Little wonder that Sears threw in the towel and created Sears' Brand Central.

Worse still, the appearance of generic, unbranded, or no-name products, so popular in the 1970s when inflation was soaring, reflected the notion that even price won't do the job alone. What would happen if store brands took over shelf space? A&P tried this and almost went under. But what if store brands were recognized as of value equal to both the generics and the nationally branded products, as is the case in Western Europe or in certain specialty stores? This has happened in bookstores; large national chains like Waldenbooks and Barnes & Noble have taken to reprinting the classics under their own colophons and displaying them as you walk in the store. Who cares who published *Moby Dick*? This unbranding hasn't happened with package goods, because the storekeeper has had little control over what is on the shelf. This may change. Until recently, producers, not retailers, held the knowledge about the Fast Moving Consumer Products. Procter & Gamble, Kellogg, Philip Morris, Colgate-Palmolive, Gillette, Campbell, Nestlé, Unilever, and RJR Nabisco adjusted the store mix, coddling certain products until they found an audience, moving about the real estate as if they owned it. In a way they did.

But the balance of power is shifting back to the retailer with the introduction of more efficient inventory methods. The Universal Product Code and the optical scanner mean that the storekeeper can tell the manufacturer what is moving through the store. Once the consumer knows that most shampoos are made by two or three manufacturers, and that they are essentially interchangeable, the store brand may finally make a comeback.

Certain national brands—brands like Camay, Chun King, Bayer, Michelob, Lunch Bucket, Miller High Life, Prell, and Sanka—are in distress, not because the producer is cutting them loose, or because the consumer is not buying them, but because the retailer is balking. Such products are not moving fast enough. When you realize that every night, as the chain grocery stores download the data of the day, the retailer is getting the freshest FMCG information, you realize as well that the decision making is shifting back to the owner of the rack space. Manufacturers often have to pay "slotting allowances," underwrite expensive in-store displays, or even give gross-margin guarantees. Big FMCG companies now spend about twice as much on such promotions as they do on advertising. One wag has even suggested that most FMCG companies' advertising budgets would be better spent bribing the forty or so retailing executives who decide what gets onto most shelves.

This shift in power is ironic because the whole purpose of advertising in the early days was to put the information in customers' minds so that they would enter the store demanding Uneeda biscuits in a package rather than biscuits in the barrel. Consumers would force the storekeeper to stock the item by asking for it "by name." Now storekeepers at Wal-Mart, Safeway, Builders' Emporium, Circuit City, and the other national specialty stores are reasserting their power. Who knows? If it is in their interest, we may be buying out of the barrel again.

By no means am I predicting Adcult's imminent demise. So long as goods are interchangeable and in surplus quantities, so long as producers are willing to pay for short-term advantages (especially for new products), so long as manufacturers have a need to reach over the heads of the retailer and talk to the consumer, and so long as occasional ads do indeed cut through media clutter and connect with an audience, advertising will remain a central marketing tool. But as we have seen, Adcult does not exist solely because of distribution concerns. It has become the dominant meaning-making system of modern life because of our deep confusion about consumption, not only about what to consume but how to consume. The idea that advertising creates artificial desires rests on a wistful ignorance of history and human nature, on the hazy feeling that there existed some halcyon era of noble savages with purely natural needs. Once fed and sheltered, our needs have always been cultural, not natural. Until some other system codifies and satisfies those needs and yearnings, advertising—and the culture it carries with it—will continue not just to thrive but to triumph.

SELECTIVE BIBLIOGRAPHY

☞ This bibliography is by no means complete. However, it does reflect the bias of *Adcult*. In the spirit of the endeavor I have shamelessly lifted material from many popular culture sources—most important, the advertising columns of the *New York Times*, *Wall Street Journal*, *USA Today*, and *Advertising Age*. The pithy one-line comments from pundits about advertising that are sprinkled throughout the text were gleaned not from reading primary material but from looking under *advertising* in popular collections of quotations. Because these comments are considered to have passed into general knowledge, the collector rarely gives a complete citation.

Abrams, Ann. "From Simplicity to Sensation: Art in American Advertising, 1904–1929." *Journal of Popular Culture* 10 (3) (1976): 620–28.

Andrews, Peter. "Peddling Prime Time." *Saturday Review*, June 7, 1980, pp. 64–65.

Archer, Gleason L. *History of Radio to 1926.* New York: American Historical Society, 1928.

Atwan, Robert. *Edsels, Luckies, & Frigidaires: Advertising the American Way.* New York: Dell, 1979.

Bagdikian, Ben. *The Media Monopoly.* Boston: Beacon, 1983.

Baker, C. Edwin. "Advertising and a Democratic Process." *Pennsylvania Law Review* 140 (6) (1992): 2097–143.

Baldrige, Letitia. "A Wedding with Heart." Advertising Supplement to the *New York Times Magazine*, June 14, 1992, p. 1Aff.

Barnouw, Erik. *The Sponsor: Notes on a Modern Potentate.* New York: Oxford University Press, 1978.

Barthel, Diane. *Putting on Appearances: Gender and Advertising.* Philadelphia: Temple University Press, 1988.

Barthes, Roland. *Mythologies.* New York: Hill & Wang, 1972.

Barton, Bruce. *The Man Nobody Knows: A Discovery of the Real Jesus.* Indianapolis: Bobbs-Merrill, 1926.

Benjou, Paul. "The Art of the Art of . . . " *Advertising Age*, March 12, 1990, p. 44.

Berger, John. *Ways of Seeing.* London: Penguin, 1972.

Bernstein, Sid. "Are Ads Less Important?" *Advertising Age*, September 21, 1992, p. 25.

Bird, Laura. "Loved the Ad—May (or May Not) Buy the Product." *Wall Street Journal*, April 7, 1994, p. B1.

——. "Study Questions the Value of Ad Dazzle." *Wall Street Journal*, May 19, 1992, p. B8.

Bloom, Harold. *The Anxiety of Influence: A Theory of Poetry.* New York: Oxford University Press, 1973.

Bogart, Leo. *Strategy in Advertising: Matching Media and Messages to Markets and Motivations.* Lincolnwood, Ill.: NTC Business Books, 1990.

Boorstin, Daniel J. "Advertising and American Civilization." In Yale Brozen, ed., *Advertising and Society*, pp. 11–23. New York: New York University Press, 1974.

——. *The Americans: The Democratic Experience.* New York: Random House, 1973.

——. *The Image: A Guide to Pseudo-Events in America.* New York: Atheneum, 1961.

Borden, Neil H. *The Economic Effects of Advertising.* Chicago: Richard D. Irwin, 1942.

Bronner, Simon J., ed. *Consuming Visions: Accumulation and Display of Goods in America, 1880–1920.* New York: W. W. Norton, 1989.

Brown, Les. *Television: The Business Behind the Box.* New York: Harcourt, Brace, 1971.

Brunvand, Jan Harold. *The Choking Doberman and Other "New" Urban Legends.* New York: W. W. Norton, 1984.

——. *The Vanishing Hitchhiker: American Urban Legends and Their Meanings.* New York: W. W. Norton, 1981.

Calkins, Earnest Elmo. *And Hearing Not.* New York: Scribner's, 1946.

——. "Beauty in the Machine Age: The New Concern with Esthetics." *Printers' Ink*, September 25, 1930, pp. 72–83.

Campbell, Joseph. *The Hero with a Thousand Faces.* Princeton, N.J.: Princeton University Press, 1968.

Carlson, Peter. "It's an Ad Ad Ad Ad World." *Washington Post*, November 3, 1991, p. W15.

Carlyle, Thomas. *Past and Present.* London: Dent, 1947.

Collins, Ronald. *Dictating Content: How Advertising Pressure Can Corrupt a Free Press.* Washington, D.C.: Center for the Study of Commercialism, 1992.

Cone, Fairfax. *Fairfax Cone's Blue Streaks: Some Observations, Mostly About Advertising.* Chicago: Crain Communications, 1973.

Coupland, Douglas. *Generation X: Tales for an Accelerated Culture.* New York: St. Martin's Press, 1991.

Crain, Rance. "Viewpoint: Power of Advertising More Like a Myth." *Advertising Age*, January 10, 1994, p. 21.

Csikszentmihalyi, Mihalay and Eugene Rochberg-Halton. *The Meaning of Things: Domestic Symbols and the Self.* New York: Cambridge University Press, 1981.

Degh, Linda and Andrew Vazsonyi. "Magic for Sale: Marchen and Legend in TV Advertising." *Fabula* 20 (1) (1979): 47–68.

Douglas, Ann. *The Feminization of American Culture*. New York: Alfred A. Knopf, 1977.

Douglas, Mary and Baron Isherwood. *The World of Goods*. New York: Basic Books, 1979.

Duff, Christina. "Secretaries Say This Is a Day to Hate." *Wall Street Journal*, April 23, 1993, p. B1.

Dunkel, Tom. "Big Bucks, Tough Tactics." *New York Times Magazine*, September 17, 1989, p. 56ff.

Dyer, Gillian. *Advertising as Communication*. London: Metheun, 1982.

Elliott, Stuart. "Advertisers Gather to Face Their Worst Fears." *New York Times*, October 18, 1994, p. D22.

———. "Agencies and Clients Look at Each Other." *New York Times*, June 28, 1994, p. D18.

———. "The Famous Brands on Death Row." *New York Times*, November 7, 1993, section 3, p. 1ff.

———. "Has Madison Avenue Gone Too Far?" *New York Times*, December 15, 1991, p. D17.

———. "Subaru's Problems Show That a Breakthrough Campaign . . . " *New York Times*, August 3, 1993, p. D19.

Esslin, Martin. "Aristotle and the Advertisers: The Television Commercial Considered as a Form of Drama." In Horace Newcomb, ed., *Television: The Critical View*, pp. 304–17. New York: Oxford University Press, 1987.

Ewen, Stuart. *Captains of Consciousness: Advertising and the Social Roots of Consumer Culture*. New York: McGraw-Hill, 1976.

Faludi, Susan. *Backlash: The Undeclared War Against American Women*. New York: Crown, 1991.

Fitz-Gibbon, Bernice. *Macy's, Gimbels, and Me: How to Earn $90,000 a Year in Retail Advertising*. New York: Simon & Schuster, 1967.

Fox, Stephen. *The Mirror Makers: A History of American Advertising and Its Creators*. New York: William Morrow, 1984.

Frazer, James. *The Golden Bough: A Study of Magic and Religion*. New York: Macmillan, 1922.

Friedman, Monroe. *A "Brand" New Language: Commercial Influences in Literature and Culture*. New York: Greenwood, 1991.

Galbraith, John Kenneth. *The Affluent Society*. New York: Houghton Mifflin, 1958.

Gardner, James. "High, Lows, and Furbelows." *National Review*, February 11, 1991, pp. 36–37.

Garfield, Bob. "Daytime Audience Does a Makeover." *Advertising Age*, October 4, 1993, p. S12.

Gerbner, George. "Television Violence: The Art of Asking the Wrong Question." *The World & I*, July 1994, pp. 385–97.

Glynn, Prudence. *Skin to Skin: Eroticism in Dress*. New York: Oxford University Press, 1982.

Goffmann, Erving. *Gender Advertisements*. Cambridge, Mass.: Harvard University Press, 1979.

Gold, Philip. *Advertising, Politics, and American Culture*. New York: Paragon House, 1987.

Goldenson, Leonard H. *Beating the Odds: The Untold Story Behind The Rise of ABC*. New York: Scribners, 1991.

Goldman, Kevin. "Scali Seeks to Control Mercedes Ad Space." *Wall Street Journal*, August 31, 1993, p. B4

Goldman, Robert. *Reading Ads Socially*. New York: Routledge, 1992.

Goldthwaite, Richard. *Wealth and the Demand for Art in Italy, 1300–1600*. Baltimore: Johns Hopkins University Press, 1993.

Goodman, Walter. "People Meter Tracks a Sitcom's Fall." *New York Times*, February 8, 1992, p. C18.

Goodrum, Charles and Helen Dalrymple. *Advertising in America: The First 200 Years.* New York: Abrams, 1990.

Gossage, Howard Luck. "The Gilded Bough: Magic and Advertising." In Floyd Matson, ed., *The Human Dialogue: Perspectives on Communication*, pp. 362–70. New York: Free Press, 1967.

Griff, Mason. "Advertising: The Central Institution of Mass Society." *Diogenes* vol. 68 (Winter 1969): 120–37.

Halberstam, David. "How Politicians Discovered TV." *Advertising Age*, June 26, 1993, p. 27.

Hambleton, Ronald. *The Branding of America: From Levi Strauss to Chrysler.* Camden, Maine: Yankee Books, 1987.

Hampel, Alvin. "Fear: the Ultimate Creative Motivator." *Advertising Age*, January 1, 1988, p. 25.

Hanlon, Rod. "'Guaranteed' Ad Results Won't Work." *Advertising Age*, August 30, 1993, p. 18.

Harmetz, Aljean. "'Amazing Stories' Tries New Tactics." *New York Times*, June 2, 1986, p. 21.

Harrington, Richard. "Message That Bears Repeating." *Washington Post*, July 15, 1992, p. F7.

Harris, Neil. "The Drama of Consumer Desire." In Otto Mayr and Robert C. Post, eds., *Yankee Enterprise: The Rise of the American System of Manufactures*, pp. 189–216. Washington, D.C.: Smithsonian Institution Press, 1981.

Hirsh, E. D. *Cultural Literacy: What Every American Needs to Know.* New York: Houghton Mifflin, 1987.

Hoving, Thomas. *Making the Mummies Dance: Inside the Metropolitan Museum of Art.* New York: Simon & Schuster, 1993.

Hovland, Roxanne and Gary Wilcox, eds. *Advertising in Society: Classic and Contemporary Readings.* Lincolnwood, Ill.: NTC Business Books, 1989.

Huxley, Aldous. "Advertisement." *Essays Old and New*, pp. 126–31. New York: Harper & Row, 1968.

James, Clive. *Fame in the Twentieth Century.* New York: Random House, 1993.

James, Susannah. *Love over Gold: The Untold Story of TV's Greatest Romance.* London: Corgi Books, 1993.

Jarvis, Jeff. "A Pat on Your Back." *People*, May 11, 1987, p. 9.

Jhally, Sut. *The Codes of Advertising: Fetishism and the Political Economy of Meaning in the Consumer Society.* New York: Routledge, 1990.

——. "Advertising as Religion: The Dialectic of Technology and Magic." In Ian Angus and Sut Jhally, eds., *Cultural Politics in Contemporary America*, pp. 217–29. New York: Routledge, 1978.

Jones, Kathleen W. "Mother's Day: The Creation, Promotion and Meaning of a New Holiday in the Progressive Era." *Texas Studies in Language and Literature* 22 (2) (Summer 1980): 175–96.

Key, Wilson Brian. *Media Sexploitation.* Englewood Cliffs, N.J.: Prentice-Hall, 1976.

——. *Subliminal Seduction.* New York: New American Library, 1973.

Kimball, Roger. "Pop Art Then and Now." *National Review*, March 2, 1992, pp. 24–25.

Kline, Stephen and William Leiss. "Advertising, Needs, and 'Commodity Fetishism.'" *Canadian Journal of Political and Social Theory* 2 (1) (1978): 5–27.

Lambert, Gerard B. "How I Sold Listerine." In Editors of *Fortune*, eds., *The Amazing Advertising Business*, pp. 49–59. New York: Simon & Schuster, 1957.

Laski, Marghanita. "Advertising: Sacred and Profane." *Twentieth Century* vol. 165 (1965): 118–29.

Lears, T. J. Jackson. *Fables of Abundance: A Cultural History of Advertising in America.* New York: Basic, 1994.

——. "Some Versions of Fantasy: Toward a Cultural History of American Advertising, 1880–1930." In Jack Salzman, ed., *Prospects: The Annual of American Cultural Studies*, pp. 349–405. New York: Cambridge University Press, 1984.

——. "From Salvation to Self-Realization: Advertising and the Therapeutic Roots of the Consumer Culture, 1880–1930." In Richard Fox and T. J. Jackson Lears, eds., *The Culture of Consumption: Critical Essays in American History*, pp. 3–38. New York: Pantheon, 1983.

Leffingwell, Edward, ed. *Modern Dreams: The Rise and Fall and Rise of Pop.* Boston: MIT Press, 1988.

Leiss, William, Stephen Kline and Sut Jhally. *Social Communication in Advertising: Persons, Products & Images of Well-Being.* New York: Routledge, 1990.

Lewis, Tom. *Empire of the Air: The Men Who Made Radio.* New York: HarperCollins, 1991.

Linder, Staffan. *The Harried Leisure Class.* New York: Columbia University Press, 1970.

Lipman, Joanne. "Media Content Is Linked to Cigarette Ads." *Wall Street Journal,* January 30, 1992, p. B5.

——. "Ads on TV: Out of Sight, Out of Mind?" *Wall Street Journal,* May 14, 1991, p. B1.

——. "Research Tactic Misses the Big Question: Why?" *Wall Street Journal,* November 4, 1991, p. B1.

Louis, George. *The Art of Advertising: George Louis on Mass Communication.* New York: Abrams, 1977.

Lubow, Arthur. "Annals of Advertising: This Vodka Has Legs." *New Yorker,* September 12, 1994, pp. 62–87.

Lupton, Ellen. *Mechanical Brides: Women and Machines from Home to Office.* New York: Cooper-Hewitt and Princeton Architectural Press, 1993.

Mamiya, Christin. *Pop Art and Consumer Culture.* Austin: University of Texas Press, 1992.

Marchand, Roland. *Advertising the American Dream: Making Way for Modernity, 1920–1940.* Berkeley: University of California Press, 1985.

Martorella, Rosanne. *Corporate Art.* New Brunswick, N.J.: Rutgers University Press, 1990.

Mayer, Martin. *Whatever Happened to Madison Avenue? Advertising in the '90's.* New York: Little, Brown, 1991.

——. *Madison Avenue, U.S.A..* New York: Harper & Row, 1958.

McLuhan, Marshall. *Understanding Media: The Extensions of Man.* New York: McGraw-Hill, 1964.

——. *The Mechanical Bride: Folklore of Industrial Man.* New York: Vanguard Press, 1951.

——. "American Advertising." *Horizon* vol. 93-94 (October 1947): 132–41.

Miller, Mark Crispin. "Hollywood: The Ad." *Atlantic Monthly,* April 1990, pp. 41–54.

Moog, Carol. *Are They Selling Her Lips? Advertising and Identity.* New York: William Morrow, 1990.

Muschamp, Herbert. "Women, Machines and Sexual Revolution." *New York Times,* August 20, 1993, p. C1.

Naremore, James and Patrick Brantlinger. "Six Artistic Cultures." Introduction to James Naremore and Patrick Brantlinger, eds., *Modernity and Mass Culture*, pp. 2–35. Bloomington: Indiana University Press, 1991.

Nast, Thomas. *Santa Claus and His Works.* New York: Dover, 1978.

Norris, James, D. *Advertising and the Transformation of American Society, 1865–1920.* Westport, Conn.: Greenwood, 1990.

O'Connor, John. "Birds Do It, Bees Do It, So Does TV." *New York Times,* October 13, 1991, p. C29ff.

——. "Today TV Outshines The Movies." *New York Times,* July 8, 1990, p. B1ff.

Ogilvy, David. *On Advertising.* New York: Vintage, 1985.

——. *Confessions of an Advertising Man.* New York: Antheneum, 1963.

Packard, Vance. *The Hidden Persuaders.* New York, D. K. McKay, 1957.

Paige, Douglas D. "Should Copy Writers be Cultured?" *Printers' Ink,* October 1, 1954, p. 25.

Paley, William. *As It Happened: A Memoir.* New York: Doubleday, 1979.

Peterson, Theodore. "Magazine Advertising: Its Growth and Effects." In John Wright, ed., *The Commercial Connection: Advertising and the American Mass Media,* pp. 38–57. New York: Dell, 1979.

Pope, Daniel. *The Making of Modern Advertising.* New York: Basic Books, 1983.

Potter, David. *People of Plenty: Economic Abundance and the American Character.* Chicago: University of Chicago Press, 1954.

Randazzo, Sal. *Mythmaking on Madison Avenue: How Advertisers Apply the Power to Myth & Symbolism to Create Leadership Brands.* Chicago: Probus, 1993.

Richards, Thomas. *The Commodity Culture of Victorian England: Advertising and Spectacle.* Palo Alto, Calif.: Stanford University Press, 1990.

Rogers, Stuart. "How a Publicity Blitz Created the Myth of Subliminal Advertising." *Public Relations Quarterly* 34 (4) (1992): 1–12.

Rorty, James. *Our Master's Voice: Advertising.* New York: John Day, 1934.

Rose, Barbara. *Readings in American Art, 1900–1975.* New York: Praeger, 1975.

Rothenberg, Randall. *Where the Suckers Moon: An Advertising Story.* New York: Alfred A. Knopf, 1994.

Rowe, Jonathan. "Modern Advertising—The Subtle Persuasion." *Christian Science Monitor,* January 28, 1987, part two, p. 14ff.

Rowsome, Frank. *They Laughed When I Sat Down: An Informal History of Advertising.* New York: Bonanza Books, 1959.

Rybczynski, Witold. *Waiting for the Weekend.* New York: Viking, 1991.

Savan, Leslie. *The Sponsored Life: Ads, TV and American Culture.* Philadelphia: Temple University Press, 1994.

——. "The Ad Mission." *Village Voice,* June 8, 1993, p. 50.

——. "Burying Messages." *Village Voice,* August 13, 1991, p. 51.

Schiller, Herbert I. *Culture Inc.: The Corporate Takeover of Public Expression.* New York: Oxford University Press, 1989.

Schudson, Michael. "Delectable Materialism: Were the Critics of Consumer Culture Wrong All Along?" *American Prospect* vol. 3 (Summer 1991): 26–35.

——. *Advertising, The Uneasy Profession: Its Dubious Impact on American Society.* New York: Basic Books, 1984.

Schwartz, Tony. *The Responsive Chord.* Garden City, N.Y.: Anchor Books, 1973.

Seldin, Joseph J. *The Golden Fleece: Selling the Good Life to Americans.* New York: Macmillan, 1963.

Shi, David E. "Advertising and the Literary Imagination During the Jazz Age." *Journal of American Culture* 2 (1) (1979): 167–75.

Simon, Richard. "Advertising as Literature: The Utopian Fiction of the American Marketplace." *Texas Studies in Language and Literature* 22 (2) (Summer 1980): 154–74.

Simpson, James B. *Contemporary Quotations.* New York: Crowell, 1964.

Sinclair, John. *Images Incorporated: Advertising as Industry and Ideology*. Kent, England: Croom Helm, 1987.

Smith, Sally Bedell. *In His Glory: The Life and Times of William S. Paley*. New York: Simon & Schuster, 1990.

Sommers, Christina Hoff. *Who Stole Feminism? How Women Have Betrayed Women*. New York: Simon & Schuster, 1994.

Specter, Michael. "Define 'Recycled'? A Drive to Clarify Environmental Labels." *New York Times*, December 16, 1991, p. B1.

Spitzer, Leo. "American Advertising Explained as American Art." In *Essays on English and American Literature*, pp. 248–77. Princeton, N.J.: Princeton University Press, 1962.

Squires, James D. *Read All About It! The Corporate Takeover of America's Newspapers*. New York: Times Books, 1993.

Stabiner, Karen. *Inventing Desire: Inside Chiat/Day*. New York: Simon & Schuster, 1993.

Stein, Duce. *Don't Blame Me for Those Ads, I Only Worked There: Confessions of a CEO*. Palo Alto, Calif.: Waverly House, 1993.

Stern, Barbara B. "Literary Criticism and Consumer Research: Overview and Illustrative Analysis." *Journal of Consumer Research* 16 (December 1989): 322–34.

Strasser, Susan. *Satisfaction Guaranteed: The Making of the American Mass Market*. New York: Pantheon, 1989.

Strnad, Patricia. "Nothing Tops the Woman's Touch." *Advertising Age*, October 4, 1993, p. S6.

Tankard, James, W. "The Effects of Advertising on Language: Making the Sacred Profane." *Journal of Popular Culture* 9 (2) (1975): 325–30.

Tedlow, Richard. *New and Improved: The Story of Mass Marketing in America*. New York: Basic Books, 1990.

Turner, E. S. *The Shocking History of Advertising*. New York: E. P. Dutton, 1953.

Updike, John. "The Golden Age of the Thirty-Second Spot." *Harper's*, June 1984, p. 17.

Vadehra, David. "My, How TV Spots Have Changed." *Advertising Age*, August 16, 1993, p. 16

Varnedoe, Kirk and Adam Gopnik. *High & Low: Modern Culture and Popular Art*. New York: Museum of Modern Art, 1991.

Vinikas, Vincent. *Soft Soap, Hard Sell: American Hygiene in an Age of Advertisement*. Aimes: Iowa State University Press, 1992.

Vogel, Carol. "The Art Market: The Guggenheim Rearranges Its Exhibitions While Searching for Money." *New York Times*, January 1, 1993, p. B4.

Wakeman, Frederic. *The Hucksters*. New York: Rinehard, 1946.

Waldfogel, Joel. "The Deadweight Loss of Christmas." *American Economic Review* 8 (5) (1993): 1328–37.

Walker, John A. *Art in the Age of Mass Media*. London: Pluto Press, 1983.

Watkins, Julian. *The One Hundred Greatest Advertisements: Who Wrote Them and What They Did*. New York: Moore, 1949.

Wernick, Andrew. *Promotional Culture: Advertising, Ideology and Symbolic Expression*. London: Sage, 1991.

White, Larry. *Merchants of Death: The American Tobacco Industry*. New York: William Morrow, 1988.

Whitney, Craig R. "British TV on the Edge of Competitive Era." *New York Times*, October 24, 1989, p. C24.

Wicke, Jennifer. *Advertising Fictions: Literature, Advertisement, and Social Reading*. New York: Columbia University Press, 1988.

Williams, Lena. "For Advice, the Media as Mom." *New York Times*, August 2, 1989, p. C1.

Williams, Raymond. "The Magic System." *New Left Review* 4 (1960): 27–32.

Williams, Rosalind H. *Dream Worlds: Mass Consumption in Late Nineteenth Century France.* Berkeley: University of California Press, 1982.

Williamson, Judith. *Decoding Advertisements: Ideology and Meaning in Advertising.* London: Marion Boyars, 1978.

Wilson, Sloan. *The Man in the Grey Flannel Suit.* New York: Simon & Schuster, 1955.

Wolf, John. "First Person: A. M. Rosenthal." *Advertising Age*, March 3, 1993, p. 25.

Wolf, Naomi. *The Beauty Myth: How Images of Beauty Are Used Against Women.* New York: William Morrow, 1991.

Wood, James Playsted. *The Story of Advertising.* New York: Roland Press, 1958.

Wright, David E. and Robert E. Snow. "Consumption as Ritual in the High Technology Society." In Ray Browne, ed., *Rituals and Ceremonies in Popular Culture*, pp. 326–7. Bowling Green, Ohio: Bowling Green State University Press, 1980.

Wright, John W., ed. *The Commercial Connection: Advertising and the American Mass Media.* New York: Dell, 1979.

INDEX

as entertainment medium, 105; future of, 104–6; as gatekeeper, 92; history of, 95; history of advertising on, 103; how it works, 93; and "information superhighway," 105; legal restrictions on, 104–5; losing viewers, 96; and networks, 97; problems as advertising medium, 97, 100; and product placement on, 93; and programming of, 95, 97, 100–101; purpose of, 100; and religion, 92; and remote control, 100, 101; rise of, 90–91; as selling tool, 105; and shop-at-home channels, 106–7; and "smart" sets, 98; and soft sell, 98; and syndication, 103–4; *see also* Infomercial, Remote control, Music Television, Public Broadcasting System

Terrey, Tom, 234

Tertullian, 154

Theurgy (magic), 30

thirtysomething (television show), 238

Thundercats (toy-based cartoon), 104

Tide (soap), 251

Tiegs, Cheryl, 134

Timberland Corp., 27, 123

Time, 118

Time Warner Inc., 42, 49, 61, 74, 75, 107, 117, 167, 181

Toll broadcasting, 82

Tony the Tiger, 18, 39

Toscani, Oliviero, 227

Toulouse-Lautrec, Henri de, 186, 208

Toynbee, Arnold, 12, 229

Toyota Motor Corp., 22, 23, 41, 116, 117

Trading cards, 78–81; as art, 79; and branding, 79; and Christmas cards, 79; cost efficiencies of, 78; demise of, 80; descendants of, 80; and girlie calendars, 79; history of, 78–79; illustrated, 79; and lithography, 78–79; and patent medicine, 78–80; why collected, 78

Trashvertising, 61

Tribune Company, 75

Trollope, Anthony, 13

Trudeau, Gary, 71, 238

Truman, Harry, 90

Trump, Donald, 182

Turner, Tina, 132

Turner Broadcasting Corp., 61, 107

Turner, Ted, 58

TV Guide, 102

Twiggy (model), 153

Tyson, Mike, 136

Unilever Corp., 123

Union Carbide Co., 56

United Airlines, 102

United Independent Broadcasters, 86

Unique Selling Proposition (USP), 129

United States Postal Service, 171

United Postal Service (UPS), 65, 169

Universal product code, 58, 252

Uptown cigarettes, 248

U.S. Rubber Co., 90

US Steel Hour (television show), 91

USA Network, 105

USA Today, 7, 8, 61, 70, 137, 139

Vacarro, Brenda, 106

Van Gogh, Vincent, 200, 216, 217, 219

Vanity Fair magazine, 74, 75; and "poly-bagged outsert," 75

Varnedoe, Kirk, 207

Vasari, Giorgio, 183, 201

Veblen, Thorstein, 12

Vermeer, Jan, 219

Viacom Corp., 42, 107, 162, 181

Vicary, James M., 111–13, 115; debunked, 113–14; N.J. experiment of, 113

Victoria and Albert Museum, 215

VideOcart, 58

Videocassete recorder, 98

Video grazing/surfing, 98

Video Storyboard Tests, 3, 135

Village Voice (newspaper), 8

Vinikas, Vincent, 149

Virginia Slims cigarette, 60, 157

Visa Corp., 18, 22, 140

"Visit from St. Nicholas, A," 174–75

Volkswagen automobile, 21, 50

Volvo automobile, 106

Von Furstenberg, Diane, 107

Wagner, Robert, 88

Wakeman, Frederic: *The Hucksters* (book and movie), 86, 235–37

Waldenbooks, 252

Wall Street Week with Louis Rukeyser, 102

Wall Street Journal, 7, 70, 117, 139, 169, 251; and advertising campaign, 29

Wal-Mart, 81, 128, 252

Walton, Sam, 81

Wanamaker, John, 33, 50, 97, 170, 242

War Advertising Council, 90, 91

Ward, Artemas, 33

Ward, John, 126

Designer:	Teresa Bonner
Text:	Minion
Compositor:	Impressions
Printer:	Edwards Brothers
Binder:	Edwards Brothers